THE
WISDEN
BOOK OF
CAPTAINS ON
TOUR

By the same author:

The Best Job in the World
We Don't Play it for Fun
Fred Trueman's Yorkshire
(jointly with F. S. Trueman)
Cricket Statistics year by year, 1946–87
(jointly with F. S. Trueman)
Boycott
Botham
Laker
On the Golf Tour
(jointly with his son, Ian Mosey)

THE
WISDEN
BOOK OF
CAPTAINS ON TOUR

Test Cricket 1946–89

Don Mosey

STANLEY PAUL
London Sydney Auckland Johannesburg

Stanley Paul & Co. Ltd

An imprint of Random Century Group Ltd
20 Vauxhall Bridge Road, London SW1V 2SA

Random Century Australia (Pty) Ltd
20 Alfred Street, Milsons Point, Sydney 2061

Random Century New Zealand Limited
PO Box 40–086, Glenfield, Auckland 10

Century Hutchinson South Africa (Pty) Ltd
PO Box 337, Bergvlei 2012, South Africa

First published 1990
© Don Mosey 1990

Set in Sabon

Phototypeset by Input Typesetting Ltd, London
Printed and bound in Great Britain by Richard Clay

British Library Cataloguing in Publication Data

Mosey, Don, *1924–*
   Wisden book of captains on tour.
   1. Cricket. English teams. Captains, history
   I. Title
   796.35865

ISBN 0 09 174366 4

Contents

Acknowledgements

I am grateful to all the captains who talked to me during the preparation of this book and to the contemporary players who gave me the benefit of their experience under other captains. My thanks for help are due, too, to David Edmundson, of BBC Radio Lancashire, and to Edgar Appleby, of Keswick.

Invaluable reference books (in addition to those mentioned in the text) have been, as ever, *Wisden Cricketers' Almanack*, the *Wisden Book of Test Cricket* and the *Playfair Cricket Annual*.

The publishers would like to thank the following photographers and agencies for the use of their copyright photographs: Hulton-Deutsch, Sport & General, Patrick Eagar and AllSport.

The Captains on Tour since 1945–6

Details by Robert Brooke

Name & Country	1st Tour as Captain		P	W	L	D	T
W. A. Brown (A)	1945–6	Tests on Tour	1	1	–	–	–
		All Tests	1	1	–	–	–
Nawab of Pataudi (snr) (I)	1946	Tests on Tour	3	–	2	1	–
		All Tests	3	–	2	1	–
W. R. Hammond (E)	1946–7	Tests on Tour	5	–	3	2	–
		All Tests	8	1	2	5	–
N. W. D. Yardley (E)	1946–7	Tests on Tour	1	–	1	–	–
		All Tests	14	4	7	3	–
A. Melville (SA)	1947	Tests on Tour	5	–	3	2	–
		All Tests	10	–	4	6	–
Lala Amarnath (I)	1947–8	Tests on Tour	5	–	4	1	–
		All Tests	15	2	6	7	–
K. Cranston (E)	1947–8	Tests on Tour	1	–	–	1	–
		All Tests	1	–	–	1	–
G. O. Allen (E)	1947–8	Tests on Tour	3	–	2	1	–
		All Tests	3	–	2	1	–
D. G. Bradman (A)	1948	Tests on Tour	5	4	–	1	–
		All Tests	15	11	–	4	–
J. D. C. Goddard (WI)	1948–9	Tests on Tour	20	6	7	7	–
		All Tests	22	8	7	7	–
F. G. Mann (E)	1948–9	Tests on Tour	5	2	–	3	–
		All Tests	7	2	–	5	–
W. A. Hadlee (NZ)	1949	Tests on Tour	4	–	–	4	–
		All Tests	8	–	2	6	–
A. L. Hassett (A)	1949–50	Tests on Tour	10	4	1	5	–
		All Tests	24	14	4	6	–

Name & Country	1st Tour as Captain		P	W	L	D	T
F. R. Brown (E)	1950–1	Tests on Tour	7	2	4	1	–
		All Tests	15	5	6	4	–
A. D. Nourse (jnr) (SA)	1951	Tests on Tour	5	1	3	1	–
		All Tests	15	1	9	5	–
N. D. Howard (E)	1951–2	Tests on Tour	4	1	–	3	–
		All Tests	4	1	–	3	–
D. B. Carr (E)	1951–2	Tests on Tour	1	–	1	–	–
		All Tests	1	–	1	–	–
J. B. Stollmeyer (WI)	1951–2	Tests on Tour	1	–	1	–	–
		All Tests	13	3	4	6	–
V. S. Hazare (I)	1952	Tests on Tour	9	–	4	5	–
		All Tests	14	1	5	8	–
A. H. Kardar (P)	1952–3	Tests on Tour	14	3	6	5	–
		All Tests	23	6	6	11	–
J. E. Cheetham (SA)	1952–3	Tests on Tour	10	3	5	2	–
		All Tests	15	7	5	3	–
G. O. Rabone (NW)	1953–4	Tests on Tour	3	–	2	1	–
		All Tests	5	–	4	1	–
B. Sutcliffe (NZ)	1953–4	Tests on Tour	2	–	2	–	–
		All Tests	4	–	3	1	–
L. Hutton (E)	1953–4	Tests on Tour	12	7	3	2	–
		All Tests	23	11	4	8	–
Vinoo Mankad (I)	1954–5	Tests on Tour	5	–	–	5	–
		All Tests	6	–	1	5	–
I. W. Johnson (A)	1954–5	Tests on Tour	12	6	2	4	–
		All Tests	17	7	5	5	–
D. J. McGlew (SA)	1955	Tests on Tour	7	2	3	2	–
		All Tests	14	4	6	4	–
H. B. Cave (NZ)	1955–6	Tests on Tour	8	–	4	4	–
		All Tests	9	–	5	4	–
D. St E. Atkinson (WI)	1955–6	Tests on Tour	4	3	1	–	–
		All Tests	7	3	3	1	–
R. R. Lindwall (A)	1956–7	Tests on Tour	1	–	–	1	–
		All Tests	1	–	–	1	–
P. B. H. May (E)	1956–7	Tests on Tour	15	4	6	5	–
		All Tests	41	20	10	11	–
I. D. Craig (A)	1957–8	Tests on Tour	5	3	–	2	–
		All Tests	5	3	–	2	–
J. R. Reid (NZ)	1958	Tests on Tour	20	2	12	6	–
		All Tests	34	3	18	13	–

Name & Country	1st Tour as Captain		P	W	L	D	T
F. C. M. Alexander (WI)	1958–9	Tests on Tour	8	4	2	2	–
		All Tests	18	7	4	7	–
D. K. Gaekwad (I)	1959	Tests on Tour	4	–	4	–	–
		All Tests	4	–	4	–	–
Pankaj Roy (I)	1959	Tests on Tour	1	–	1	–	–
		All Tests	1	–	1	–	–
R. Benaud (A)	1959–60	Tests on Tour	12	5	2	5	–
		All Tests	28	12	4	11	1
M. C. Cowdrey (E)	1959–60	Tests on Tour	10	1	–	9	–
		All Tests	27	8	4	15	–
Fazal Mahmood (P)	1960–1	Tests on Tour	5	–	–	5	–
		All Tests	10	2	2	6	–
F. M. M. Worrell (WI)	1960–1	Tests on Tour	10	4	3	2	1
		All Tests	15	9	3	2	1
R. N. Harvey (A)	1961	Tests on Tour	1	1	–	–	–
		All Tests	1	1	–	–	–
E. R. Dexter (E)	1961–2	Tests on Tour	16	5	3	8	–
		All Tests	30	9	7	14	–
N. J. Contractor (I)	1961–2	Tests on Tour	2	–	2	–	–
		All Tests	12	2	2	8	–
Nawab of Pataudi (jnr) (I)	1961–2	Tests on Tour	13	3	10	–	–
		All Tests	40	9	19	12	–
Javed Burki (P)	1962	Tests on Tour	5	–	4	1	–
		All Tests	5	–	4	1	–
T. L. Goddard (SA)	1963–4	Tests on Tour	8	1	1	6	–
		All Tests	13	1	2	10	–
M. J. K. Smith (E)	1963–4	Tests on Tour	18	2	1	15	–
		All Tests	25	5	3	17	–
R. B. Simpson (A)	1964	Tests on Tour	24	5	9	10	–
		All Tests	39	12	12	15	–
Hanif Mohammad (P)	1964–5	Tests on Tour	7	–	2	5	–
		All Tests	11	2	2	7	–
P. L. van der Merwe (SA)	1965	Tests on Tour	3	1	–	2	–
		All Tests	8	4	1	2	–
G. S. Sobers (WI)	1966	Tests on Tour	19	7	7	5	–
		All Tests	39	9	10	20	–
C. G. Borde (I)	1967–8	Tests on Tour	1	–	1	–	–
		All Tests	1	–	1	–	–
W. M. Lawry (A)	1968	Tests on Tour	13	4	6	3	–
		All Tests	25	9	8	8	–

Name & Country	1st Tour as Captain		P	W	L	D	T
B. N. Jarman (A)	1968	Tests on Tour	1	–	–	1	–
		All Tests	1	–	–	1	–
G. T. Dowling (NZ)	1969	Tests on Tour	11	2	3	6	–
		All Tests	19	4	7	8	–
R. Illingworth (E)	1970–1	Tests on Tour	8	3	–	5	–
		All Tests	31	12	5	14	–
Intikhab Alam (P)	1971	Tests on Tour	12	1	4	7	–
		All Tests	17	1	5	11	–
A. L. Wadekar (I)	1971	Tests on Tour	11	2	3	6	–
		All Tests	16	4	4	8	–
B. E. Congdon (NZ)	1971–2	Tests on Tour	9	–	4	5	–
		All Tests	17	1	7	9	–
I. M. Chappell (A)	1972	Tests on Tour	17	6	3	8	–
		All Tests	30	15	5	10	–
A. R. Lewis (E)	1972–3	Tests on Tour	8	1	2	5	–
		All Tests	8	1	2	5	–
R. Kanhai (WI)	1973	Tests on Tour	3	2	–	1	–
		All Tests	13	3	3	7	–
M. H. Denness (E)	1973–4	Tests on Tour	12	3	4	5	–
		All Tests	19	6	5	8	–
C. H. Lloyd (WI)	1974–5	Tests on Tour	50	23	10	17	–
		All Tests	74	36	12	26	–
J. H. Edrich (E)	1974–5	Tests on Tour	1	–	1	–	–
		All Tests	1	–	1	–	–
S. M. Gavaskar (I)	1975–6	Tests on Tour	18	2	6	10	–
		All Tests	47	9	8	30	–
B. S. Bedi (I)	1975–6	Tests on Tour	14	3	8	3	–
		All Tests	22	6	11	5	–
G. M. Turner (NZ)	1976–7	Tests on Tour	5	–	4	1	–
		All Tests	10	1	6	3	–
J. M. Parker (NZ)	1976–7	Tests on Tour	1	–	–	1	–
		All Tests	1	–	–	1	–
A. W. Greig (E)	1976–7	Tests on Tour	6	3	2	1	–
		All Tests	14	3	5	6	–
Mushtaq Mohammad (P)	1976–7	Tests on Tour	13	4	4	5	–
		All Tests	19	8	4	7	–
G. S. Chappell (A)	1976–7	Tests on Tour	15	3	5	7	–
		All Tests	48	21	13	14	–
J. M. Brearley (E)	1977–8	Tests on Tour	12	6	4	2	–
		All Tests	31	18	4	9	–

Name & Country	1st Tour as Captain		P	W	L	D	T
G. Boycott (E)	1977–8	Tests on Tour	4	1	1	2	–
		All Tests	4	1	1	2	–
Wasim Bari (P)	1978	Tests on Tour	3	–	2	1	–
		All Tests	6	–	2	4	–
M. G. Burgess (NZ)	1978	Tests on Tour	4	–	3	1	–
		All Tests	10	1	6	3	–
A. I. Kallicharran (WI)	1978–9	Tests on Tour	6	–	1	5	–
		All Tests	9	1	2	6	–
S. Venkataraghavan (I)	1979	Tests on Tour	4	–	1	3	–
		All Tests	5	–	2	3	–
K. J. Hughes (A)	1979–80	Tests on Tour	20	1	11	8	–
		All Tests	28	4	13	11	–
Asif Iqbal (P)	1979–80	Tests on Tour	6	–	2	4	–
		All Tests	6	–	2	4	–
D. L. Murray (WI)	1979–80	Tests on Tour	1	–	–	1	–
		All Tests	1	–	–	1	–
G. P. Howarth (NZ)	1980–1	Tests on Tour	13	3	6	4	–
		All Tests	30	11	7	12	–
I. T. Botham (E)	1980–1	Tests on Tour	4	–	2	2	–
		All Tests	10	–	3	7	–
Javed Miandad (P)	1981–2	Tests on Tour	6	1	4	1	–
		All Tests	25	8	5	12	–
I. V. A. Richards (WI)	1980	Tests on Tour	21	10	4	7	–
		All Tests	36	21	4	11	–
K. W. R. Fletcher (E)	1981–2	Tests on Tour	7	1	1	5	–
		All Tests	7	1	1	5	–
B. Warnapura (SL)	1981–2	Tests on Tour	3	–	2	1	–
		All Tests	4	–	3	1	–
L. R. D. Mendis (SL)	1981–2	Tests on Tour	8	–	4	4	–
		All Tests	19	2	8	9	–
Imran Khan (P)	1982	Tests on Tour	23	5	4	13	–
		All Tests	35	12	6	17	–
R. G. D. Willis (E)	1982–3	Tests on Tour	9	1	4	4	–
		All Tests	18	7	5	6	–
Kapil Dev (I)	1982–3	Tests on Tour	14	2	3	9	–
		All Tests	34	4	7	22	1
D. S. de Silva (SL)	1982–3	Tests on Tour	2	–	2	–	–
		All Tests	2	–	2	–	–
Zaheer Abbas (P)	1983–4	Tests on Tour	6	–	1	5	–
		All Tests	14	3	1	10	–

Name & Country	1st Tour as Captain		P	W	L	D	T
D. I. Gower (E)	1983–4	Tests on Tour	12	2	6	4	–
		All Tests	32	5	18	9	–
J. V. Coney (NZ)	1984–5	Tests on Tour	9	3	3	3	–
		All Tests	18	5	4	9	–
A. R. Border (A)	1985	Tests on Tour	24	5	5	13	1
		All Tests	48	11	13	23	1
M. W. Gatting (E)	1986–7	Tests on Tour	12	2	2	8	–
		All Tests	23	2	5	16	–
J. J. Crowe (NZ)	1986–7	Tests on Tour	4	–	1	3	–
		All Tests	6	–	1	5	–
R. S. Madugalle (SL)	1987–8	Tests on Tour	2	–	2	–	–
		All Tests	2	–	2	–	–
J. G. Wright (NZ)	1988–9	Tests on Tour	3	1	2	–	–
		All Tests	6	1	2	3	–
D. B. Vengsarkar (I)	1988–9	Tests on Tour	4	–	3	1	–
		All Tests	10	2	5	3	–

Introduction

In 113 years of Test cricket, international captains have come in all shapes and sizes, colours and creeds, characters and personalities. They have experienced approbation and abuse, found themselves at the centre of bitter controversy which has reached Governmental level, returned home to ticker-tape welcomes or deathly silence. Populations have danced in the streets at their achievements, or nominated them as national disasters. Captains have led their men through hurricanes and earthquakes, collisions at sea, tropical disease, wars and assassinations; one had to help his men manoeuvre their stage coach transport through a flooded river.

In recent years the spotlight of critical scrutiny has been focused more fiercely than before upon England captains in particular. They have been reviled and despised not simply for their leadership on the field but for the more intimate aspects of their personal lives, for political reasons and for their choice of a way of earning a living when rejected by their country's selectors. On the other hand, the rewards for leading one's side have become infinitely and incomparably greater than at any time in history with fringe benefits far out-stripping basic salaries.

Things, it may seem, used to be so much simpler, but is this strictly true? There is a school of thought which believes that captains before Len Hutton became England's first professional skipper were automatically chosen as paternal guardians of the team, their upper-middle-class birth and breeding sufficient to induce the respect and obedience of their forces. It is a generalisation which is not supported by the facts. Walter Hammond, for example, was the best *player* in England in his day and he had to switch from the paid ranks to become an amateur before he was made captain. Douglas Jardine was most certainly an amateur but as ruthless and single-minded in his quest for the Ashes as any professional who followed.

Is it, perhaps, the way the game has changed which has required a new style of leadership and given rise to a sharper appraisal of the men selected as leaders? Contrast, if you will, the description in a Melbourne newspaper of Lord Harris's 1878–79 tourists as 'all young men with a decidedly military bearing and certainly not difficient in good looks' with the descent into gutter-snipe terminology of an English tabloid in the 1980s in dismissing a captain of his country as 'Gatt the Prat'. With that sort of media coverage is it any wonder that a decline in respect for standards of all sorts is now horribly apparent?

Peter May, a magnificent player and highly regarded captain of England, was driven out of office as chairman of selectors after the 1988 season – in which no fewer than four different captains led England in six Tests – sickened by criticism of his Committee which, however much some of it might have been justified, was couched in terms of tasteless vulgarity. His brief from the Test and County Cricket Board to restore standards of conduct by England players had forced upon him the expulsion of Mike Gatting from the captaincy when he was 'exposed' by the seediest organ of the British press for socialising with a waitress during the course of a Test match. The England side was therefore deprived of its best available captain. There was a huge swell of sympathy for Gatting, and for Mr May.

An earlier selector, Douglas Insole, once said that according to the press and the public, the chief qualifications for becoming a selector were an impenetrable skin, a deep longing for power and a profound ignorance of all aspects of cricket. That is, of course, a deeply cynical view based on a misconception that *all* the press and *all* the public are stupid while all men who become selectors are immediately invested with a form of omniscience. Manifestly, selectorial mistakes have been made in recent years just as they were in far-off days. But they did not have quite the same impact fifty years ago as during the past decade because they were not subject to the same detailed examination by the media and, in consequence, the public.

Since the Second World War and up to the end of 1989 more than a hundred cricketers have led the national sides of England, Australia, West Indies, India, Pakistan, New Zealand and Sri Lanka on tours abroad and they have done so in increasingly difficult circumstances. They have had to contend with allegations of illegal bowling and intimidatory bowling; with pitch invasions by inflamed crowds and exhibitionist drunks; with a lack of discipline within the ranks and unfair pressure imposed on umpires by massed choruses of appeals, irrespective of the circumstances; with sometimes incompetent umpiring; with accompanying hordes of media representatives, some involved with cricket-reporting, some solely concerned with players' off-duty moments; with ever-more obtrusive television coverage, revealing elements of the game in a detail no spectator ever expected to see and, moreover, detail which an umpire cannot be expected to follow with the naked eye; with microphones developed to such a high standard of snooping efficiency that they can bring home to televiewers those personal exchanges by players on the field which should, surely, be entirely their own business. And with political interference.

A modern Test captain has, therefore, to be not only an outstanding player, a tactician, a leader of men, and an ambassador abroad. He must also be a pragmatist, a public relations expert and a spokesman so lucid that his words are not open to misrepresentation and distortion. He must wear armour-plating on his back because defence against critical knives off the field is just as necessary as protection of other parts of the body is vital on it.

Amateur status in England ended in 1962 when all players became simply *cricketers*, a move largely forced upon MCC by the severe shortage of men who were able to play at their own expense, simply for the love of the game. Shamateurism was rife, making a mockery of the lofty Corinthian concept and clearly the time had come to end it. But have we not seen in recent years a yearning (by the press and the public, as well as at Lord's) for a return to the *ideal* of the amateur captain, patrician by birth and/or public school educated, a man who could distance himself from his mercenaries when necessary and maintain standards of discipline and sportsmanship as in those benevolent dictatorships which were the norm in England teams of fifty and more years ago? Captains now have to be better players than they were in the first half of the century; an England captain cannot be carried as a passenger. So is it not possible to glimpse that yearning in the selectors' recent flirtations with men like Chris Cowdrey, of Tonbridge School and Kent, and Mark Nicholas, of Bradfield College and Hampshire, as captaincy material? One could almost hear the wistful sighs at Lord's: if only they were *just a little bit* better as players.

Other countries have experienced different problems in appointing their leaders. West Indies Test cricket only *really* started to make genuine progress when they reluctantly abandoned the principle – to which their Board clung for so long – of a white officer to command the black troops. Appointments in India are still bedevilled by the age-old power struggle between different factions of cricketing politics within the country. Pakistan's cricket history, according to Imran Khan, their greatest captain, has been one of 'nepotism, corruption, inefficiency and constant bickering', and that country's 38-year-old Test career has seen only two really strong men in charge, able to command their forces on the field and keep administrative interference at bay: Imran himself and Abdul Hafeez Kardar. New Zealand cricket had bumbled along quietly on a completely amateur basis for half a century with occasional and isolated success, forced to accept the role of 'good losers and nice chaps' until captains like Glenn Turner and Geoff Howarth, from their years in English county cricket, provided a steely core of professionalism.

History goes a long way towards establishing the Australians as the people with the best method: choosing a Test squad and appointing from that party the best leaders. This is, of course, the reverse of the English system of picking the captain first and co-opting him to help with team selection. Both methods have their supporters and it is a matter of debate which of them is better, but let us try looking at it from a negative point of view and asking ourselves: have the Aussies found as many *unsuccessful* captains as England?

Bradman was the best batsman in the world but he was also a thoughtful, shrewd, calculating and brilliantly successful captain; Benaud had charm, a nice touch of humour, was a superb communicator, a gifted all-rounder and a magnificent captain; Ian Chappell was one of the leading batsmen of his day, an outstanding close fielder, a useful bowler, splendid tactician and ruthless opponent. And very close behind that trio of excellent skippers come Bobby Simpson, Lindsay Hassett and, more recently, Allan Border. So what of Bill Lawry, Greg Chappell and Ian Johnson who may have lacked some of the most valuable attributes of Bradman, Benaud and Ian Chappell but who most certainly left their mark on international cricket in one way or another? Can England point to the same measure of success in their choice of captain?

Different countries, different problems, different selection methods, different criteria, different results ... probably no one will ever get it completely right and who would want that, with the outcome of games more or less predictable? If the West Indies, on recent results, have come as close to it as anyone we are still left with the question of whether their methods have been the most desirable in the long-term interests of cricket.

The author does not claim to have all the answers; this book seeks only to identify one or two thought-provoking questions – and, it is hoped, to provide a little pleasurable reminiscence along the way.

1
IMMEDIATE POSTWAR YEARS

The Victory Tests
1945

England v. Australia:
  Lord's: *Australia won by 6 wickets*
  Bramall Lane, Sheffield: *England won by 41 runs*
  Lord's: *Australia won by 4 wickets*
  Lord's: *Match drawn*
  Old Trafford: *England won by 6 wickets*

Australia v. India:
  Bombay: *Match drawn*
  Calcutta: *Match drawn*
  Madras: *India won by 6 wickets*

To describe Lindsay Hassett as the first postwar tour captain will satisfy neither the purists nor the historians since the 'Victory Tests', played in England during the summer of 1945, have not been recognised as official. MCC sought the Australian Board of Control's sanction for the series to be given Test status but it was refused on the grounds that three players – Arthur Morris, Ray Lindwall and Ian Johnson – who would most certainly have been in a full-strength Australian team were still on active service in the unfinished war against Japan. (In point of fact, the first 'Victory Test' was played at Lord's less than a fortnight after the War in Europe had ended.) England, on the other hand, were able to field almost a full-strength side because only Denis Compton, still serving in India, was unavailable.

The opposition of 1945, therefore, are referred to as an Australian Services XI and that is correct since all were currently serving members of either Army or Royal Australian Air Force. England's ranks, too, bristled with crowns and pips and stripes and the pegs in the dressing-rooms of both teams were festooned with the ribbons of DSOs and DFCs. History may have no place for that series of five 'Tests' but sentiment most assuredly has. R. S. Whitington – opening batsman, artillery officer, journalist and author – has called it 'the Happy Series' and no more felicitous phrase could have been contrived.

It was cricket played with the serious resolve demanded of any England-Australia encounter and yet enjoyed in the spirit of a meeting of comrades-in-arms – a camaraderie which it is virtually impossible to communicate to those who have not experienced it personally. These were men who for five and a half years had been battling in earnest against Wehrmacht and Luftwaffe now pitting their sporting skills against each other. Off the field they were united in the common cause; on it, they were the descendants of Trumper and Gregory, Rhodes and Larwood, of Woodfull and Ponsford, Hobbs and Sutcliffe. Cricket had returned to Lord's on that May morning of 1945 where so recently bright-eyed, beardless boys had queued for their first pay-parade, been tested for aircraft recognition and Morse Code aptitude, as the world headquarters of cricket was transformed into the Aircrew Receiving Centre. The public, starved of properly competitive cricket for so long (despite a multitude of contrived combats), flocked to Lord's and to the bomb-scarred Bramall Lane and Old Trafford. The rumble of gunfire had faded across the Channel and over the Rhine. God was in his heaven and Australia were playing England once more in NW8.

Lindsay Hassett captained Australia in the series while England were led by their immediate prewar skipper, Walter Hammond. We shall look at them in more detail as tour captains but the 31-year-old artillery-man and the 42-year-old RAF officer, in addition to all their other claims, deserve a special place in the annals of the game as the two who led out their sides at Lord's, 19–22 May 1945. Those who had danced in Trafalgar Square to celebrate VE Day were still nursing hangovers; the last echoes of the joy-bells had scarcely died away; what better way to mark the fact that the world had returned to sanity?

The men who took part deserve no less recognition in this opening chapter of the story of post-war touring:

ENGLAND v. AUSTRALIAN SERVICES XI
Lord's, 1945

ENGLAND

First Innings		Second Innings	
L. Hutton c Sismey b Williams	1	b Pepper	21
C. Washbrook st Sismey b Ellis	28	lbw b Pepper	32
J. D. Robertson lbw b Ellis	53	c Sismey b Cheetham	84
W. R. Hammond b Williams	29	lbw b Ellis	33
L. E. G. Ames c Price b Cheetham	57	b Ellis	7
W. J. Edrich b Miller	45	c Workman b Price	50
R. W. V. Robins b Cheetham	5	c Hassett b Pepper	33
J. W. A. Stephenson c Sismey b Price	31	b Price	1
S. C. Griffith c Sismey b Cheetham			
D. V. P. Wright b Price	9	not out	4
A. R. Gover not out	0	run out	1
Extras	0	st Sismey b Pepper	1
	9	Extras	27
Total	267	Total	294

Bowling: Cheetham 13.1–1–49–3; Williams 19–2–56–2; Pepper 19–2–59–0; Ellis 31–8–59–2; Miller 9–2–11–1; Price 9–1–24–2

Bowling: Cheetham 17–2–44–1; Williams 21–7–47–0; Pepper 32.4–7–80–4; Ellis 17–3–33–2; Miller 9–1–23–0; Price 19–3–40–2

AUSTRALIA

First Innings		*Second Innings*	
J. A. Workman b Gover	1		
R. S. Whitington c Griffith b Wright	36	(1) lbw b Stephenson	0
A. L. Hassett b Stephenson	77	(2) c Hammond b Gover	37
S. G. Sismey c Wright b Edrich	37		
K. R. Miller c Ames b Stephenson	105	(3) run out	1
R. M. Sandford st Griffith b Stephenson	49		
C. G. Pepper c Griffith b Stephenson	40		
A. G. Cheetham s Hammond b Wright	0	(4) not out	54
R. G. Williams c Griffith b Wright	53	(5) run out	0
C. F. Price c Robertson b Stephenson	35		
R. S. Ellis not out	1	(6) not out	10
Extras	21	Extras	5
Total	455	Total (for 4 wkts)	107

Bowling: Gover 25–3–90–1; Stephenson 36–4–116–5; Edrich 17–2–61–1; Wright 37.3–9–122–3; Robins 10–0–45–0

Bowling: Gover 11.4–1–51–1; Stephenson 11–0–51–1

Keith Miller, therefore, has the distinction of scoring the first first-class century in a postwar match at Lord's and if Denis Compton couldn't be around to score it for England, then it was probably appropriate that the honour should go to the popular and heroic figure of Keith Ross Miller who was destined to become one of Compton's closest and most enduring friends. Receipts for the match were £1,935 and the money was divided between British and Australian charities. At Bramall Lane, Hammond made exactly 100 on a rain-affected wicket in one of the finest innings he ever played; George Pope and Dick Pollard had five-wicket hauls.

It is fascinating to note that even in these first few weeks of peace, controversy was rearing its ugly head in two guises: selectors' alleged mistakes and the Australians' allegedly slow batting rate.

For the third 'Victory Test' at Lord's, England included Donald Carr, the 18-year-old captain of Repton School; naval cadet John Dewes, who was barely two months older than Carr, and the Hon. Luke White who was younger than both of them. White, the future Baron Annaly, must surely have enjoyed one of the strangest first-class careers of all time. He had played merely for Eton and as a Cambridge freshman when he was called up to meet Australia at Lord's. He played three matches for Middlesex in the following two seasons and his final first-class appearance was for MCC in 1950. The dashing nature of these selectorial changes perhaps deserved a better fate: Cadet Dewes managed 27 runs in his two innings, the Hon. Luke totalled 15 in his two and the future captain of Derbyshire and secretary of the Test and County Cricket Board managed just five.

With only a few exceptions, the cricket-writers of 1945 launched an attack on the Australian scoring rate after the third Test which gave them a two-one lead in the series. Unfortunately, they had not checked their facts carefully enough and 'Dick' Whitington, in a letter to the *Daily Telegraph*, was able to point out that England's scoring rate in the first three Tests was slower than Australia's. There is too much statistical help around today for that mistake to be repeated. But just look at the scoring rates achieved by the two sides and detailed by Whitington: England 54.2 an hour, Australia 60 – and the critics complained!

Australia to New Zealand
1946
Tour captain: W. A. Brown

Wellington: *Australia won by an innings and 103 runs*

Bill Brown led Australia in their single Test at Wellington which thus became the first official Test to be played after the war, although that status was not accorded the match by the ICC until two years later. Although Brown made three tours to England, two to New Zealand and one to South Africa, this was his only appointment to the captaincy of his country and was seen by many as a deliberate affront to Hassett (Bradman not being available at the time) who had led the Services team with such great popularity. Politics and prejudice in selectorial circles had not taken long to reappear. The two-day Test was something of a farce since New Zealand introduced six new faces and were bowled out for 42 and 54 by O'Reilly, Toshack, Lindwall and Miller. Australia's 199 for eight declared (with the captain making 67 on a difficult, rain-affected pitch) was more than enough to give them a huge win. Brown had a Jekyll and Hyde approach to batting; he could be an elegant and graceful stroke-maker or a most obdurate stone-waller, a role he seemed to reserve for performances in England, notably in 1938. At Lord's in that year he carried his bat through the first innings of the second Test for 206 not out which was, by happy coincidence, Australia's 100th hundred against England.

It was a strong Australian side, carrying far too many guns in terms of experience and ability for the Kiwis. The 13 players with a manager travelled across the Tasman Sea in a Catalina fly-boat, not long released by the Royal New Zealand Air Force from anti-submarine and reconaissance patrol duties in the South Pacific and still in working, operational order. The flight, therefore, was not one of luxurious comfort but as the party, almost to a man, had recently been Servicemen it presented no great problem to them. This was another tour imbued with a wartime spirit of togetherness and there was only one cloud on the horizon. To many of the team, Test status had been simply a prewar dream and now it had arrived there was a sense of crushing disappointment when blazers were issued bearing not the official crest on the breast pocket but a monogram made up of the letters 'ABC'. While these were undeniably the initials of the Australian Board of Control they were, of course, translatable as many other things and there was a great deal of resentment at the Board's failure to provide proper badges, especially amongst the men who had actually represented Australia before the war – Brown, Hassett, O'Reilly and Barnes. At long range, it is possible to get a good deal of amusement when one thinks of O'Reilly and Barnes in particular getting into a corner, contemplating their monogrammed badges with distaste, and offering their considered views on the character and antecedents of the Board of Control.

Nevertheless, in true wartime spirit, a shared cause of complaint was something which could be thoroughly enjoyed and the party, crammed into areas of the Catalina which had certainly not been designed for passenger transport, winged its way happily across the Tasman. Ian Johnson, not the most joyous of Australians, doubted if 'first-class cricket, before or since, had been played in the same light-hearted atmosphere'.

India to England
1946

Tour captain: The Nawab of Pataudi (sen.)

Lord's: *England won by 10 wickets*
Old Trafford: *Match drawn*
The Oval: *Match drawn*

India in England in the first postwar official Test series were led by Iftikar Ali Khan, Nawab of Pataudi, who ruled one of the 350 princely states established by the British. His life followed a fairly typical pattern with three years at Balliol College, Oxford, after attending the very-British-indeed Aitchison College in Lahore. He won three Blues at Oxford and scored 238 not out in the 1931 Varsity match at Lord's. He then 'stayed on' in England to play for Worcestershire where he made three more double hundreds.

On 2 December, 1932, Pataudi became the third Indian prince to play cricket for England (Ranjitsinhji and Duleepsinhji being the others) and scored 102 in his first innings for England against Australia. This was, however, Jardine's 'bodyline' tour and Pataudi, soured by the atmosphere of the series, returned home before the end of the tour. With splendid dignity, he never openly discussed his views on Jardine's policy but his wife and son were convinced that it was disapproval of 'bodyline' which caused him to abandon the trip early. Others believed he resented being dropped after the first Test.

In 1946 he brought to England a team in which his opening batsmen were the brilliant and prolific Vijay Merchant (who was reputed to be, outside cricket, a millionaire) and the magnificent all-rounder Vinoo Mankad, a man destined to play much very successful professional cricket in the leagues of northern England in later years. As ever with Indian teams, until the appearance of Kapil Dev 30 years afterwards, the party was short of quick bowling and the attack was led by 'Lol' Amarnath, who despite his undoubted ability as an all-round cricketer, would be classed as a very gentle opener indeed by modern standards.

Pataudi, therefore, was always going to struggle to bowl out an England side with batsmen like Hutton, Washbrook, Compton, Hammond and Hardstaff, who took 205 off the Indian bowling at Lord's. Alec Bedser, who made his first appearance in that match, is usually described in 1990 terms as a medium-paced bowler but was quicker than anything most of the tourists had seen and was already an accomplished swing bowler. Throughout the series, Pataudi juggled with his batting order without ever finding an answer to Bedser who, in five innings, took 24 wickets for 298 runs. It had been a depressing summer for the tourists who experienced a great deal of rain but Pataudi remained a courteous and dignified captain in adversity. He was a man who passionately believed in cricket's best traditions of gentlemanly conduct and was distressed by any departure from it. Like his son, he loved the game as a sporting exercise enjoyed by opponents with proper respect for each other – but most of all, for the game itself. He would have been anguished by much of what was to follow, in particular the internal feuds which beset Indian Test cricket in the 1980s.

England to Australia and New Zealand
1946–7

Tour captain: W. R. Hammond (N. W. D. Yardley)

Brisbane: *Australia won by an innings and 332 runs*
Sydney: *Australia won by an innings and 33 runs*
Melbourne: *Match drawn*
Adelaide: *Match drawn*
Sydney: *Australia won by five wickets*

Christchurch (New Zealand): *Match drawn*

Walter Reginald Hammond was 43 when he sailed to Australia with what we might describe as an experienced and mature party in August 1946, in an attempt to win back the Ashes which had been held by the Aussies since 1934 (notwithstanding the huge defeat at The Oval in 1938, they had still drawn the series in which Hammond had skippered England for the first time). For a decade before the war Hammond had been by far England's outstanding cricketer – a brilliant batsman, better-than-average medium-fast bowler and outstanding slip catcher. Indeed, in the seven immediate prewar seasons he had led the first-class batting averages in England and in 1946 he made it eight in a row. As his captaincy took in the 1938 home series, the 1938–9 tour to South Africa, the 1939 series against West Indies and the 'Victory Tests', plus those at home to India in 1946, he was the only possible choice, despite his age.

Hammond had started his life as a struggling professional, tormented like so many of his contemporaries by the problem of making a living in winter when there was no tour abroad. He had tried professional football and quickly realised that the jump from amateur standards at that game was a huge one. In 1937, he was given the opportunity to jump the other way, and switch to the amateur ranks as a cricketer which, with his background, experience and ability, would mean the captaincy of his country. He joined a business which gave him time to play cricket throughout the summer and so led England against Australia in 1938. In essence, Hammond was a prewar player; he *thought* the game very much like those who had been his captains at home and abroad – Gubby Allen, Bob Wyatt, Walter Robins – if not perhaps quite like Douglas Jardine. In 1946–7 the game had not had time to change radically from the prewar years he had known; it had not yet developed the hard edge of 'professionalism' – the 'bodyline' tour excepted.

Hammond was extremely conscious of the pitfalls of captaincy in ways which might not have occurred to him but for his years in the professional ranks. He had seen amateur captains come and go in a way which caused them no great concern, but to his essentially professional mind it would be a black mark on his record to lose the leadership because of poor results and performances or for something as dramatically controversial as the 'bodyline' tour. He was acutely aware that as a co-opted member of the selection committee, his insistence upon a player who failed to come up to expectations would be seen as a shortfall on his part, too. Yet there is no doubt that Hammond wanted the captaincy badly and was happy to retain it in those first two postwar years.

He had ambivalent views about cricket in Australia. On the one hand, it represented the ultimate challenge and thus had to be faced with confidence and enthusiasm. On the other, he found it harder work than in England. The light was brighter, the sun hotter, the wickets faster; he found the constant noise of the crowds 'disturbing and wear-ing' and he found the constant travel between fixtures a great strain and some of the cold lunchtime snacks provided during games 'repul-sive'. These were mostly quibbles which are more easily understood in a man of 43 than in younger, more resilient tourists and it was easier to draw from Hammond in his retirement years a kinder reminiscence of touring than when he recalled the 1946–7 trip shortly afterwards. It has to be remembered, too, that although he felt he had retained his personal friendships with those who had been his fellow-professionals, a certain degree of aloofness was regarded as essential once he had become an amateur captain.

He had enjoyed the companionship of the lower orders, notably the clowning of Patsy Hendren which was so vital in cheering those two-day journeys undertaken by train across Australia, and he had delighted in a visit to Hollywood on one of the return trips from 'down under' to meet (Sir) Charles Aubrey Smith, Sussex and England captain-turned-filmstar. On one such trip the party visited Chicago, 'happily now cleared of gangsters,' reported Hammond and this prompted a recollec-tion that the first time I saw Hammond leaving a ground in 'mufti' he reminded me irresistibly of a gangster himself – with coat collar upturned and trilby hat pulled almost menacingly over the right eye. Facially, he bore a marked resemblance to John Arlott who, in fact, hero-worshipped Hammond as a young spectator.

In Australia in that antipodean summer of 1946–7, Hammond was some way past his best as a batsman and he no longer bowled, although the eyesight was still sharp enough to take more catches in that supremely competent but unspectacular way of his. Perhaps he attempted one tour too many, even though, as we have seen, there was no logical alternative to him as captain. But his attack had lost its cutting-edge with the deaths during the war of Ken Farnes and Hedley Verity and there was a certain amount of Press criticism that the party as a whole had too many 'old men'.

Bradman had not played in Test cricket since before the war and he had experienced a lot of ill-health; there was a big question mark against his returning to the game. He himself agonised over whether he should come back into Test cricket. But return he did, as captain, for the opening Test at The Gabba on 29 November 1946. Hammond, reared on years of bitter experience of The Don's greatness, stood at slip (where he had caught Arthur Morris in his first Test innings, for 2) muttering to himself, 'We have *got* to get Don out.' He probably added a prayer or two as well. Bradman, uncharacteristically, but understandably after a seven-year absence, started uneasily. He was,

Hammond recalled later, 'full of nervous little gestures. He did not start with his old divine right, flashing at the ball like one who drives beasts with a whip.' Barnes went for 32 (Australia 46 for 2) and Hassett joined his captain. When he reached 28, Bradman slashed at a ball from Bill Voce which was leaving him; it flew high to second slip and Jack Ikin held a shoulder-high catch. Bradman, convinced that the ball had touched the bottom of the bat, then *bounced* to slip, did not move and in answer to the appeal which England's fielders had regarded as unnecessary, the umpire slowly shook his head. The Don went on to score 187, Hassett 128; together they made a record 276 for the third wicket, Australia totalled 645, won by an innings and the first great postwar controversy between the oldest Test opponents had been born.

Now in those days cricket correspondents did not rush to dressing-rooms in search of a controversial 'quote' and captains did not hold regular Press conferences to deal with such inquiries.

Nor did players produce ghost-written books at the season's (or tour's) end in the hope of the more sensational chapters being serialised in the Sunday papers. Hammond, in a book *Cricket my World*, merely commented, 'If he had gone out then, history might have been written differently. But cricket is a game of such "ifs" and our job was to get on with the game.' Len Hutton in *Cricket is My Life* does not mention the incident at all, though he does refer to Bradman's innings. A few years after those two books, R. S. Whitington, in his Hassett biography, *The Quiet Australian*, quoted Lindsay as being firmly of the opinion that Bradman did not get a touch to the ball. It is difficult, more than 40 years later, when the game is publicised in an entirely different fashion, to credit an incident of that nature being viewed with relative equanimity. Bradman, tough and uncompromising though he was as an opponent and opposition captain, was known as a good 'walker' but even that is a relative term since in his incredible career he was not called upon to walk very often! But in these modern times of television replays in slow motion we are bound to ask ourselves how a batsman can give a high catch to *second* slip without getting a touch. Today it would have been a cause célèbre and, involving a man like Bradman, it would have been page 1 news.

In 1946 it passed off without further comment, though it has remained in the minds of those who played in the game. Maybe it would have changed the course of the game, and thus the series, if Bradman had been given out and then, perhaps, *he* would have been left to reflect that a wrong decision had cost him dearly. Whether history was altered or not, one cannot help reflecting that Test cricket emerged with greater dignity from that day at The Gabba than it has done from so many later occasions.

It was sad for Hammond that he lost his last series as captain, two-nil with two drawn (Norman Yardley skippered England because of Hammond's illness in the final Test which was lost). He had led his country to victory in South Africa and in a home series against the West Indies, together with a drawn rubber against Australia in 1938. Most of all, he had been England's outstanding cricketer for something like 20 years. I like to think of him on that final tour sitting amongst blind ex-Servicemen in Perth and giving them a ball-by-ball description of the play.

Or perhaps, after his retirement to live in South Africa and to coach at Natal University, hospitably greeting old friends on later tours and recalling the days when he scored 7,249 Test runs, took 83 wickets and held 110 catches. He had started his career barely two years after the First World War and had graced the game until after the Second. His style of captaincy was to lead by example and to expect all his men to give everything they had got to justify the honour of representing their country. There was nothing theatrical or jingoistic about this; it was simply what was expected and everyone was aware of it.

South Africa to England
1947
Tour captain: A. Melville

Trent Bridge: *Match drawn*
Lord's: *England won by 10 wickets*
Old Trafford: *England won by 7 wickets*
Headingley: *England won by 10 wickets*
The Oval: *Match drawn*

One of the most distinguished Anglo-Springboks, Alan Melville, led South Africa in the golden summer of 1947 when life (as well as cricket) was beginning to settle down at last after the war and Edrich and Compton dominated domestic cricket, scoring more than 7,300 runs and a total of 30 centuries between them. Both made their significant mark against the tourists. After starting his career with Natal, Melville came to England to win four Blues at Oxford University (captain in 1931 and 1932), then skippered Sussex in 1934 and 1935 before returning home to play for Transvaal. He was a fluent and cultured opening batsman who averaged 52.5 in his Test innings and although the high hopes of the tourists were shattered by three substantial defeats in five

Tests it was a summer which rivalled the 'Happy Series' of 'Victory Tests' in its spirit and atmosphere for much the same reason. A whole generation of servicemen, on their way to the Middle and Far East from austerity-ravaged Britain, had experienced the warmth and generosity of South African hospitality when their transports put in at Durban or Cape Town.

Royal Navy crews had enjoyed similar experiences when their ships refuelled or re-victualled at the Cape; thousands of RAF aircrews had trained there; South African soldiers and aircrews had served alongside British Forces with great distinction, notably in the Western Desert. Politics had not yet thrust itself, unwanted, into cricket and there was an enormous goodwill between the sides which was strengthened further by South African donations which helped to restore the bomb-damaged headquarters of Lancashire and Surrey. Also, this was the ninth South African party to tour England since 1894; the Springboks were the second oldest adversary.

A wet May gave way to sunny June, July and August and the tourists, weak in fast bowling, always struggled to dismiss an extremely strong England batting line-up with Edrich at number 3 and Compton number 4 behind the reliable opening partnership of Hutton and Washbrook. Melville led brilliantly from the front with 189 and 104 not out in the first Test — the first Springbok to make two centuries in a Test — and followed this with another hundred at Lord's. With his 103 in the second innings of the 'timeless' Test in Durban (which spread over 10 days of March 1939) he had then hit four centuries in consecutive Test innings spread over eight years! Melville had to struggle through that series not only with an attack which relied too heavily on the spin of Athol Rowan and 'Tufty' Mann but with batting which was brittle apart from that of the captain himself, Bruce Mitchell and Dudley Nourse. Yet he was a prewar cricketer in mind and heart with much of the adventurous spirit he had absorbed in happy days at The Parks and in Sussex. His approach to his final Test match in England shall be his epitaph in these pages, not least of all because it excited the admiration of Wally Hammond (merely an observer on that occasion) as well as providing a lasting memory for all who watched the game on 16, 18, 19 and 20 August 1947, at The Oval. Faced with a target of 451 to win in one day plus that dreaded half hour on the previous evening, Melville instructed his men to attack the target. His own contribution to the match (batting at number 5 at that stage of the tour) was a mere 45 runs but the delight that final day provided for the spectators is incalculable.

Immediate Postwar Years

ENGLAND v. SOUTH AFRICA

The Oval, 1947

ENGLAND

First Innings

Hutton b Mann	83
Washbrook lbw b Mann	32
Robertson c Melville b Smith	4
Compton c Tuckett b Rowan	53
Yardley b Mann	59
Cranston st Fullerton b Rowan	45
Howorth c Fullerton b Rowan	23
Evans run out	45
Gladwin not out	51
Wright b Mann	14
Copson b Dawson	6
Extras (b4 lb7 nb 1)	12
Total	427

Bowling: Tuckett 32–6–82–0; Dawson 35–5–80–1; Mann 64–28–93–4; Rowan 38–9–92–3; Smith 21–0–68–1

Second Innings

c Tuckett b Mann	36
c Fullerton b Rowan	43
b Rowan	30
c Nourse b Dawson	113
c sub b Mann	11
c Mitchell b Rowan	0
not out	45
not out	39
Extras (b6 w2)	8
Total (6 wkts declared)	325

Bowling: Tuckett 7–0–34–0; Dawson 15–1–59–1; Mann 27–7–102–2; Rowan 25–1–95–3; Smith 3–0–27–0

SOUTH AFRICA

First Innings

Mitchell c Evans b Copson	120
Dyer c Gladwin b Howorth	18
Viljoen c Evans b Wright	10
Nourse c Yardley b Howorth	10
Melville lbw b Cranston	39
Dawson lbw b Wright	55
Fullerton c Howorth b Cranston	6
Rowan b Howorth	0
Mann b Copson	36
Tuckett not out	0
Smith lbw b Copson	0
Extras (b3 lb2 w1 nb2)	8
Total	302

Bowling: Copson 27–13–46–3; Gladwin 16–2–39–0; Wright 29–7–89–2; Howorth 39–16–64–3; Compton 11–4–31–0; Cranston 9–2–25–2

Second Innings

not out	189
lbw b Wright	4
st Evans b Howorth	33
b Howorth	97
c Evans b Cranston	6
c Howorth b Cranston	0
c Evans b Howorth	14
......	
c Hutton b Wright	10
not out	40
Extras (b 12 lb14 w4)	30
Total (for 7 wkts)	423

Bowling: Copson 30–11–66–0; Gladwin 16–5–33–0; Wright 30–8–103–2; Howorth 37–12–85–3; Compton 4–0–30–0; Cranston 21–3–61–2; Hutton 2–0–14–0; Yardley 1–0–1–0

South Africa finished just 28 runs short of what would have been an astounding win, given the number of runs required in the fourth innings. It was a first Test Match for Jack Robertson, the Middlesex batsman, and Dick Howorth, the Worcs slow left-armer. Mitchell, who equalled Melville's first Test feat of a hundred in each innings with one not out, was on the field for all but eight minutes of the four days of play.

As Walter Hammond said, 'They had come to England to play the best cricket they had in them and not just to hide behind a pair of pads.' It had been a wonderful summer for cricket and Melville's captaincy had been a most notable aspect. To the author (a schoolboy before the war) returning after service abroad and now looking at cricket with adult eyes, it opened up a world I had never dreamed existed. Happily, it was to continue through many more years.

One last thought on Alan Melville. He used for the toss a threepenny bit which had been given to him before the war by Walter Hammond. To those mature enough to remember the tiny, silver, threepenny diddler I ask: how on earth could anyone toss with a coin that size without its blowing away on the breeze or being lost behind a couple of blades of grass?

India to Australia
1947–8
Tour captain: N. B. Amarnath

Brisbane: *Australia won by an innings and 226 runs*
Sydney: *Match drawn*
Melbourne: *Australia won by 233 runs*
Adelaide: *Australia won by an innings and 16 runs*
Melbourne: *Australia won by an innings and 177 runs*

India, once again without any bowling above medium pace, were hopelessly outclassed by Bradman's Australians yet in an utterly disastrous tour they still contrived to get themselves into the pages of cricket history. The captain, Nanik Bhardwaj ('Lol') Amarnath, is the only man to lead his country abroad after being sent home for disciplinary reasons from a previous tour (England, 1936). He had to endure the taunts of spectators when one of his bowlers, Vinoo Mankad, ran out Bill Brown – backing up as the non-striker – but he had some compensation in seeing Vijay Hazare, in Adelaide, become the first Indian batsman to score a century in each innings of a Test.

Amarnath started cricketing life as a wicket-keeper, developed into a hard-hitting batsman and his bowling talents (medium pace off a very short run) were discovered by accident during a pre-Test net practice. Perhaps his greatest claim to fame is as the father of three first-class cricketing sons (like Walter Hadlee of New Zealand), of whom the best known is Mohinder, man of the match at Lord's when India won the World Cup in 1983.

England to West Indies
1948

Tour captain: G. O. Allen (K. Cranston)

Barbados: *Match drawn*
Trinidad: *Match drawn*
British Guiana: *West Indies won by 7 wickets*
Jamaica: *West Indies won by 10 wickets*

In prewar years, MCC had regularly indulged themselves in sending teams to play in the West Indies which were far from Test standard and in January–April 1948, the policy came to grief in salutary fashion with a two-nil defeat and the other two Tests drawn. England's four leading batsmen of the previous summer – Compton, Edrich, Hutton and Washbrook – declined the invitation to tour as did the captain, Yardley, and two leading bowlers, Bedser and Wright. To skipper the side (Sir) George 'Gubby' Allen was called out of virtual retirement at the age of 45 and before a stormy crossing of the Atlantic had been completed he had pulled a calf muscle while exercising on the decks of the banana boat, *SS Tettela*. No fewer than five Test debutants appeared for England in Barbados – Dennis Brookes, Jim Laker, Winston Place, Gerry Smithson and Maurice Tremlett – where they were rescued from a perilous position on the last day by a tropical storm; Ken Cranston, the Liverpool dentist, skippered the side in the absence of the injured Allen. After two drawn Tests, Hutton was flown out to strengthen the party but he could not save them from defeat in the two final matches.

After a distinguished, though intermittent, playing career which began when he was the outstanding public school (Eton) bowler in the country in 1921, and continued with two Blues at Cambridge and 146 matches for Middlesex spread over 29 years, George Oswald Allen became one of the outstanding administrators in the history of the game.

He was chairman of the selectors from 1955 to 1961, Treasurer of MCC from 1964 to 1976 and President in 1963–4. No one in the twentieth century has wielded greater behind-the-scenes influence on MCC policy. His bowling, by modern standards, would probably be described as lively medium-fast and he was a forceful middle-order batsman. He was one of Jardine's back-up bowlers on the 1932–3 tour to Australia but disapproved of leg-theory and declined to apply it himself. He led England on the following tour to Australia (1936–7) which has been called the 'Reconciliation' tour and there can be no doubt that his tact and his personal stature did much to heal the wounds of the previous visit. It was obviously a mistake to ask him to lead a side in the West Indies in 1948 – he had played only two first-class innings for Middlesex during the previous summer – and on his Test record he earned the right to go out on a higher note. He was, however, to leave his mark on the game to a more pronounced degree with his work at Lord's over the next 40 years, a period which saw the most immense changes in the game, not all of which can have given him unqualified pleasure.

Australia to England
1948
Tour captain: D. G. Bradman

Trent Bridge: *Australia won by 8 wickets*
Lord's: *Australia won by 409 runs*
Old Trafford: *Match drawn*
Headingley: *Australia won by 7 wickets*
The Oval: *Australia won by an innings and 149 runs*

If cricket was purely a game of statistics, then one might possibly look no further than West Indian teams of the 1980s for the greatest touring parties of all time. Mercifully, the game is about much more than that and so to many followers (the author included) that title rests firmly with Don Bradman's 1948 players, the 20th Australians to tour England. The team, whatever its composition from game to game, was magnificently, if ruthlessly, efficient and went through all first-class matches unbeaten – the first time this had been done.

The tour provided wonderful cricket but always, in every day's play, there was a tinge of curious sentiment because it was known from the first that this was The Don's farewell tour and for 18 years there had been a special relationship between the British cricketing public and the greatest of all batsmen. I use the term 'curious' because those who watched Bradman in 1930, 1934 and 1948 at close quarters (and at long range during England's visits to Australia) did so with a kind of schizophrenic fascination: as supporters of our national side we longed to see the back of him, yet as cricket-lovers we wondered what new records we might see established. It was ever a love-hate relationship with the man and in the last analysis love conquered all in that huge surge of emotion which swept over The Oval on Saturday 14 August 1948, when he walked out to bat in a Test for the last time.

The occasion really established the British as the most sentimental of all sporting nations since Bradman's clear policy throughout the tour had been to crush England totally, to demoralise and humiliate in revenge for the indignities heaped upon his, and Australia's collective head, at The Oval 10 years previously. It had been Bradman at his most ruthless and inexorable. As a captain he was tough – very tough indeed. He bore in mind the advice of a friend from his very earliest days in cricket: 'You cannot make people love you, but you can make them respect you.' And while it is true that he had not – to use the overworked word – the 'charisma' to inspire love, either personally or through his batting style, he most assuredly made the world respect him, my word he did. 'Test cricket is not a light-hearted business,' he once said, 'especially that between England and Australia.' And he followed that precept throughout his career.

He was not a great lover of the cricket critic, though he did respect some, and he had no time whatsoever for those who specialised in being wise after the event. Captains, Bradman insisted with perfect truth, must make decisions *before* they knew what the results would be and must carry the responsibility for those decisions, so criticism when things went wrong must be tempered with that in mind. It goes without saying if one looks at his record of captaincy in four series against England and one against India (not one was lost): he did not make many obvious mistakes. Bradman believed strongly in balanced attacks of varying types of bowling and was almost fanatical in his attention to detail in his field-placing. So had Wilfred Rhodes been in an earlier era but he was a bowler supreme in an age when many captains were superfluous. Bradman took it as simple commonsense to work in concert with his bowlers but to assume the final responsibility himself. He did not accept that there was any place in a side for a man who simply showed qualities of leadership; he must *indisputably* earn his place as a player. Bradman was firm but, he believed, fair and certainly there could be no doubt in the minds of any of his men about who was in charge. Possibly he found it a little more difficult to read the minds and attitudes of *postwar* players – men who had gone through years of action and risked their lives a hundred times in pursuit of objectives somewhat more important than a successful outcome to a cricket match. On the other hand, it is almost possible to believe that Bradman thought there was *nothing* more important than winning a Test.

That is not to criticise in any way a man I have always regarded with something approaching idolatry. Indeed, Bradman had a fine mind which was consulted by Prime Minister Robert Menzies on matters of great importance. One merely seeks to illustrate the intensity of the concentration he brought to bear on his responsibilities as captain of Australia. Over the years I have enjoyed an occasional correspondence with the great man which has always been courteous and helpful on his part. His response to a request for an appreciation of Len Hutton's 364 at The Oval, for instance, when the 50th anniversary of that monumental innings came round, was immediate, gracious and generous. Those are not qualities which would always have been easily recognisable by those who battled against him; on the other hand, none would regard him as capable of a mean or petty action or attitude on the field. Bradman was a great batsman, a great opponent and a great captain; that is why it almost hurts to point to a previously unsuspected Achilles heel of sentiment when he walked out to bat for the last time at The Oval in 1948. Nothing – absolutely nothing – will ever convince me that Eric Hollies could ever have bowled Don Bradman second ball for a duck in any other circumstances.

England had been destroyed by Lindwall for just 52 runs of which Hutton had made 30 before being last out. Barnes and Morris put on 117 for Australia's first wicket and Bradman walked out slowly on the evening of the first day as a huge crowd stood to salute him. He progressed to the wicket through an avenue of Yardley's applauding Englishmen, took guard, played the first ball and was bowled by the second. A four, just one boundary, would have given him a Test aggregate of 7,000 runs in only 52 Tests – and an average of 100.

It was not his last innings in England; he went to the Scarborough Festival and made 153 against Leveson-Gower's XI. Nor was that his last century on British soil; he then took his marvellous tour party to Scotland and on 18 September made 123 not out in Aberdeen. Only then could bowlers and fieldsmen the world over take a rest. There is a great temptation to turn back to that final Test at The Oval, because of the occasion, as our favourite memory of Sir Donald Bradman, but it must be resisted. The Don himself cites Headingley 1938 as his favourite memory. In 1930 on that ground he made 334; in 1934 he made 304; in 1938 he hit a mere 103 and 16 but, typically, he approved the performance of his team and the excitement of the cricket:

Every phase of cricket was demonstrated at its highest peak. Who could ever forget the bowling of O'Reilly? He bowled Hardstaff with a ball which left that fine batsman simply dumbfounded. Hassett's daring and brilliant 33 in our second innings. At a critical stage Merv Waite took a catch at second slip which, to the spectators may have appeared simple, yet it was made possible only by brilliant anticipation. The closing stages were breathtaking in their excitement.

He does not say that on a rain-affected (uncovered) pitch he farmed the bowling in bad light to score 103 out of 242 and continue a sequence of Test innings which read 270, 26, 212, 169, 51, 144 not out, 18, 102 not out, 103. His next two Test innings came more than eight years later; they were 187 and 234!

This was, incidentally, the only Test in which Frank Price, the Middlesex wicket-keeper, played.

ENGLAND v. AUSTRALIA

Headingley, 1938

ENGLAND

First Innings		Second Innings	
Edrich b O'Reilly	12	st Barnett b Fleetwood-Smith	28
C. J. Barnett c B. A. Barnett b McCormick	30	c Barnett b McCormick	29
Hardstaff run out	4	b O'Reilly	11
Hammond b O'Reilly	76	c Brown b O'Reilly	0
Paynter st Barnett b Fleetwood-Smith	28	not out	21
Compton b O'Reilly	14	c Barnett b O'Reilly	15
Price c McCabe b O'Reilly	0	lbw b Fleetwood-Smith	6
Verity not out	25	b Fleetwood-Smith	0
Wright c Fingleton b Fleetwood-Smith	22	c Waite b Fleetwood-Smith	0
Farnes c Fingleton b Fleetwood-Smith	2	b O'Reilly	7
Bowes b O'Reilly	3	lbw b O'Reilly	0
Extras (lb4 nb3)	7	Extras (lb4 w1 nb1)	6
Total	223	Total	123

Bowling: McCormick 20–6–46–1; Waite 18–7–31–0; O'Reilly 34.1–17–66–5; Fleetwood-Smith 25–7–73–3; Waite 1–1–0–0

Bowling: McCormick 11–4–18–1; Waite 2–0–9–0; O'Reilly 21.5–8–56–5; Fleetwood-Smith 16–4–34–4

AUSTRALIA

First Innings		Second Innings	
Fingleton b Verity	30	lbw b Verity	9
Brown b Wright	22	lbw b Farnes	9
Barnett c Price b Farnes	57	(7) not out	15
Bradman b Bowes	103	(3) c Verity b Wright	16
McCabe b Farnes	1	(4) c Barnett b Wright	15
Badcock b Bowes	4	not out	5
Hassett c Hammond b Wright	13	(5) c Edrich b Wright	33
Waite c Price b Farnes	3		
O'Reilly c Hammond b Farnes	2		
McCormick b Bowes	0		
Fleetwood-Smith not out	2		
Extras (b2 lb3)	5	Extras (b4 nb 1)	5
Total	242	Total (for 5 wkts)	107

Bowling: Farnes 26–3–77–4; Bowes 35.4–6–79–3; Wright 15–4–38–2; Verity 19–6–30–1; Edrich 3–0–13–0

Bowling: Farnes 11.3–4–17–1; Bowes 11–0–35–0; Wright 5–0–26–3; Verity 5–2–24–1

West Indies to India
1948–9
Tour captain: J. D. C. Goddard

Delhi: *Match drawn*
Bombay: *Match drawn*
Calcutta: *Match drawn*
Madras: *West Indies won by an innings and 193 runs*
Bombay: *Match drawn*

West Indies' first tour to India was marked by some very heavy scoring indeed, the emergence of Jeff Stollmeyer and Allan Rae (right- and left-hand respectively) as the best opening partnership the islands were to produce until Haynes and Greenidge 30 years later, and a winning series under the leadership of John Goddard, the experienced Barbadian. He had taken over in 1948 in succession to, first, George Headley and then Gerry Gomez and while he was not an outstanding player in his own right – certainly not by later West Indian standards – Goddard established a reputation as a leader of men. He was a useful bits-and-pieces player, bowling his off-breaks at around medium pace and averaging over 30 with his left-handed batting in his 27 Tests. He was captain in 22 of them and that is undoubtedly where his greatest value lay. On low-bounce Indian wickets his side lacked the necessary firepower to disturb most of India's batsmen (only Prior Jones was more than medium pace) and a definite result was achieved in Madras, probably the fastest of Indian wickets though the term is relative, after Stollmeyer and Rae (239 for the first wicket) had laid the foundations of a total of 582. It was the first innings of the tour in which Everton Weekes failed to score a century; his previous knocks had been 128 in Delhi, 194 in Bombay, 162 and 101 in Calcutta, following on his 141 in the win over England at Sabina Park in April 1948. His 'failure' ultimately came in Madras – where he was run out on 90! Goddard won the toss and West Indies batted first in all five Tests.

England to South Africa
1948–9

Tour captain: F. G. Mann

Durban: *England won by 2 wickets*
Johannesburg (first Test at Ellis Park): *Match drawn*
Cape Town: *Match drawn*
Johannesburg: *Match drawn*
Port Elizabeth: *England won by 3 wickets*

The retirement of Hammond and the unavailability of Yardley meant that a new captain had to be found for the first postwar tour to South Africa. Edrich, who had switched from professional to amateur status in 1947, was an obvious candidate but he, too, declined the invitation to tour. MCC's choice – and they had recently established the firmest possible grip on all major touring matters – therefore fell on a man with a decidedly 'establishment' background: F. G. Mann, Eton, Cambridge and currently captain of Middlesex. A mild-mannered and quietly-spoken leader, George Mann was a popular skipper with his men, not least of all because he did not hesitate to seek advice from seasoned professionals like Hutton, Compton, Washbrook and Wright. Although he retained the captaincy in the first two Tests of the following summer at home, Mann, with a realistic appraisal of his own ability, probably saw himself as a stop-gap captain, but it gave him enormous personal satisfaction to score 136 not out in the final Test in Port Elizabeth and to see England win the game with one minute of play remaining. It is a reflection of the spirit in which the series was played and of the rapport between the two captains that Dudley Nourse opened the door for England in that last game by setting them 172 to win in 95 minutes. Hutton hit his first ball for four and Washbrook scored six off *his* first delivery.

New Zealand to England
1949
Tour captain: W. A. Hadlee

Headingley: *Match drawn*
Lord's: *Match drawn*
Old Trafford: *Match drawn*
The Oval: *Match drawn*

Walter Hadlee kept a diary of the tour he led to England in 1949, a meticulous and detailed record of every moment of play, every day of off-duty activity. I have been privileged to read that diary; it is the story of a very happy man on a very happy tour. Indeed, there is every reason for 'Wally' Hadlee to look back on his lifetime of service to cricket with the greatest delight. His son Richard, in the second half of a Test career that began in 1972 and may not yet be over, was arguably the best fast bowler in the world. Another son, Dayle, played 26 Tests for New Zealand at home, in England (three times), Australia, India and Pakistan. Yet another, Barrie, was a first-class cricketer with Canterbury and is now, like his father, an administrator.

Walter, one of the outstanding figures in world cricket, played for his country from 1937 to 1951, was captain from 1945 to 1951, a member of the NZ Cricket Council management committee from 1949 to 1981, has been chairman and president of the council, chairman of selectors and has managed tours to England, India and Pakistan. For many years he has been a leading campaigner against political intervention in purely sporting matters.

Hadlee brought his party to England in 1949 knowing that chances of victory were slim with an attack led by the 37-year-old Jack Cowie and relying heavily on the slow left-arm bowling of Tom Burtt. He hoped for not very much more than that New Zealand would bat well and that at all times the party would perform in the best traditions of the game. He regarded his first task as captain as being to build up the confidence of players who were largely unknown in England and he was delighted when Burtt 'started to get write-ups' in newspapers for his marathon spells of economical bowling: 20–12–16–1, 37–22–34–2, 55–26–78–4, 39.3–16–97–5. In all, Burtt bowled 1,231 overs during the 35-match tour in which the two fine left-handers, Bert Sutcliffe and Martin Donnelly, both scored more than 2,000 runs. What pleased Hadlee as much as anything was that the British public turned out in sufficient numbers to watch tourists who went through their programme with only one defeat and took home a profit of £10,000.

The captain's diary describes a television interview with Leslie Mitchell who seemed to have researched only one question: 'Where do you field?' and goes on to report a conversation with King George VI when he paid the customary royal visit to Lord's. The king revealed that he had seen the TV interview and told Hadlee he thought Mitchell was 'an awful bloody fool'. Hadlee took home to New Zealand as one of his most treasured possessions a telegram from Prince Philip, the then president of MCC, congratulating the New Zealanders on their 'charm and sportsmanship'. Hadlee had achieved his objective.

His philosophy as a captain was to win the confidence of the players in his judgement and to allow them to express their individual talents with as much help from him as it was possible for him to give. When England played in Christchurch in 1951, Hadlee was the captain who brought back Washbrook when the batsman had been given out lbw. He explained to the umpire that the ball had hit the bat before the pad. It is fitting, therefore, that Hadlee's Test Match should be the one he played at Headingley in 1949 against a captain with a similar approach to the spirit of the game, George Mann, who had made 49 in 24 minutes when he deprived himself of the fastest 50 in Test cricket by declaring.

It was the first of Trevor Bailey's 61 Tests for England, as well as the only one in which Alan Wharton, the Lancashire (later Leics) left-hander, played.

ENGLAND v. NEW ZEALAND
Headingley, 1949

ENGLAND

First Innings		
Hutton c Sutcliffe b Cowie	101	
Washbrook c Sutcliffe b Cowie	10	
Edrich c Donnelly b Cowie	36	
Compton st Mooney b Burtt	114	
Wharton lbw b Cowie	7	
Mann c Scott b Burtt	38	
Bailey c Scott b Cowie	12	
Evans c Mooney b Burtt	27	
Bedser c Donnelly b Burtt	20	
Young st Mooney b Burtt	0	
Hollies not out	0	
Extras (b3 lb4)	7	
Total	372	

Second Innings

c Mooney b Cave	0
not out	103
b Cave	70
c Mooney b Cave	26
b Sutcliffe	13
not out	49
Extras (b4 lb 2)	6
Total (4 wkts declared)	267

Bowling: Cowie 43–6–127–5; Cave 27–5–85–0; Rabone 18–7–56–0; Burtt 39.3–16–97–5

Bowling: Cave 26–3–103–0; Rabone 17–4–56–0; Burtt 15–2–56–0; Sutcliffe 4–1–17–1; Scott 1–0–9–0

NEW ZEALAND

First Innings	
Sutcliffe c Evans b Young	32
Scott c Washbrook b Bailey	1
Hadlee c Edrich b Bailey	34
Wallace c Evans b Bailey	3
Donnelly c Young b Bailey	64
Smith c Compton b Edrich	96
Rabone c Evans b Edrich	13
Mooney c Edrich b Bailey	46
Burtt c Bedser b Compton	7
Cave c Edrich b Bailey	2
Cowie not out	26
Extras (b2 lb8 nb7)	17
Total	341

Second Innings

c Bedser b Young	82
c Bedser b Young	43
(4) not out	13
(3) not out	54
Extras (b1 lb2)	3
Total (for 2 wkts)	195

Bowling: Bailey 32.3–6–118–6; Bedser 22–8–56–0; Edrich 9–2–18–2; Young 22–6–52–1; Hollies 25–6–57–0; Compton 8–2–23–1

Bowling: Bailey 9–0–51–0; Bedser 9–1–26–0; Edrich 2–0–13–0; Young 14–3–41–2; Hollies 11–3–33–0; Compton 1–0–5–0; Hutton 3–0–23–0

2
HASSETT TAKES OVER

Australia to South Africa
1949–50

Tour captain: A. L. Hassett

Ellis Park, Johannesburg: *Australia won by an innings and 85 runs*
Cape Town: *Australia won by 8 wickets*
Durban: *Australia won by 5 wickets*
Johannesburg: *Match drawn*
Port Elizabeth: *Australia won by an innings and 259 runs*

This was the start of the post-Bradman era, a significant date in Australian cricket history. Not that The Don was entirely lost to the game by any means. As selector, administrator and contributor to the more thoughtful treatises on the game, he had a part to play for many years yet. His career was an era in its own right because of the immense stature of the man. The comment by R. C. Robertson-Glasgow in *Wisden*: 'So must ancient Italy have felt when she heard of the death of Hannibal,' is not merely an example of the writing that cricket merited and received 40 years ago – it is almost literally true. 'Almost' because even those who feared Bradman the most must have regretted his retirement. I talked a lot to Bill Bowes of his experiences and to have bowled at The Don was a privilege – a memory he cherished above all others.

So Hassett, as the man who took over as Australia's captain, was going to be – at least for his first tour – tackling the hardest job in cricket. Not for one moment did he attempt to copy his predecessor in any way. Temperamentally, anyway, he would probably have found it impossible. Bradman could certainly make people respect him; Hassett could make people love him. He wouldn't have expressed it in that way, of course, and he might not even have considered it in those terms. He would probably have described himself as an easygoing sort of bloke who got on with most people, some better than others. And that would be the truth, if not the whole truth. Bradman positively *inspired* loyalty; Hassett gently *induced* it.

Arthur Lindsay Hassett first came to my juvenile notice on the afternoon of 23 August 1938, and I hated him. He was the man who caught out Len Hutton, bowled O'Reilly, for 364, an innings I hoped would

go on forever. It was not until 42 years and five days had elapsed after
that Tuesday afternoon at The Oval that I met the man and discovered
what countless friends had known for so long – that he is an utterly
delightful chap with a dry, quiet sense of humour which is irresistible.
Lindsay was one of a whole series of guest summarisers who joined us
in the 'Test Match Special' commentary box in the course of the Centenary Test at Lord's in 1980. It was a parade marshalled from the Debrett
of England-Australia Tests and no one entertained listeners more brilliantly than A. L. Hassett; no one fascinated me more during our 40-
minute off-the-air lunchtime chats over a glass of execrable rosé wine
than A. L. Hassett.

He had led, as we have seen, the Australian Services XI in those
immediate postwar matches and the miracle was that he had stayed out
of the glasshouse long enough to play wartime cricket at all. As a
humble gunner with an anti-aircraft unit on Mount Carmel (in what
was then Palestine) in 1941 he had helped to shoot down a Heinkel
bomber and was piqued, no less than his fellow countrymen, to be called
out for an immediate firearms parade by a young British subaltern. On
checking Lindsay's rifle, the lieutenant was moved to remark, 'If you
took the trouble to clean your rifle, Gunner Hassett, you might just
manage to become a good soldier in a long war.'

The solemn features of Gunner VX38843 Hassett showed no reaction, but his mates knew him better than their officer. They waited.
After a pause, timed to exquisite perfection, the private soldier replied:
'If you had cleaned and oiled your bat for twenty years, sir, you'd never
score a run.'

From some experience in those parts of Anglo-Australian relationships at that time I would say that was as typical a response by an
Aussie other rank to a British officer as has ever been recorded. It might
not have been the sort of accord which was likely to speed up a
successful conclusion to hostilities but it established beyond a shadow
of doubt the measure of respect one man felt for the other.

Lindsay Hassett's war would make a book in itself – indeed, I earn-
estly hope someone has written it – and the remarkable thing is that
for someone who was to prove a born leader of men on the cricket
field he utterly shunned responsibility as a serviceman. One of nine
children born to an estate agent, Lindsay learned his cricket at Geelong
College, near Melbourne. He played his first Test at Trent Bridge on
Bradman's 1938 tour (making 1 in the first innings, 2 in the second)
and made his first century for Australia in Brisbane while his brother
Vin was being married around a thousand miles away in Geelong. The
exchange of vows was interspersed with whispered intelligence on the
progress of an innings at The Gabba and while it was taking place,
Lindsay laconically recalled later, 'I had raced from 93 to 96.'

He was a wonderful vice-captain to Bradman on his last tour of

England, working as a kind of social secretary to keep the off-the-field activities ticking over and morale high. It might not have been as necessary a role as on some tours with less successful sides to less congenial climes but prolonged absence from home creates its own problems. Bradman retired at the end of the tour and Hassett's appointment to succeed him and to skipper the 1949–50 tour to South Africa was ungracious in its lack of unanimity. Nor was he granted the side he wanted since the selectors, incredibly, left out Miller who at that time was undoubtedly the best all-rounder in the world (and not many who followed have equalled him). It was only an injury to Bill Johnston which enabled the captain to insist upon the arrival of Miller as a replacement.

In his first Test as Australia's captain, at Ellis Park, Johannesburg, Lindsay went to the wicket with a scoreboard reading 2 for 2 wickets. He hit 112 and Australia won by an innings. They won four out of five Tests (the other was drawn) including that astonishing third Test in Durban where 'Tooey' Tayfield (7 for 23) bowled out the tourists for 75 in their first innings and Australia still won by five wickets. Even more than the results, Hassett's party is remembered by more senior South African aficionados as possibly the most welcome and popular party ever to tour the country. The Hassett magic, self-effacing but ever present, had worked again.

From a most distinguished career and a colourful cricket life which straddled the Second World War, we choose the first Test v. South Africa at Ellis Park on 24, 26, 27 and 28 December 1949 as Lindsay Hassett's tour match:

SOUTH AFRICA v. AUSTRALIA

Ellis Park, Johannesburg, 1949

AUSTRALIA

First Innings

A. R. Morris c Tayfield, b McCarthy	0
J. Moroney run out	0
K. R. Miller b Mann	21
A. L. Hassett b Watkins	112
R. N. Harvey b Watkins	34
S. J. E. Loxton st Wade b Tayfield	101
C. L. McCool b Tayfield	31
I. W. Johnson c Cheetham b Mann	66
R. A. Saggers lbw b McCarthy	14
R. R. Lindwall c Nel b Tayfield	21
W. A. Johnson not out	1
Extras (b5 lb5 w2)	12
Total	413

Bowling: McCarthy 25–2–90–2; Watkins 19–3–56–2; Smith 13–0–70–0; Tayfield 28–3–93–3; Mann 28.4–4–92–2

SOUTH AFRICA

First Innings		Second Innings	
E. A. B. Rowan b Miller	60	lbw b McCool	32
O. E. Wynne lbw b Johnston	3	c Saggers b Johnston	33
J. D. Nel b Johnson	4	c Saggers b Johnston	14
A. D. Nourse c Hassett b Johnson	0	c Saggers b Johnson	36
W. W. Wade b Miller	2	b Johnston	11
J. E. Cheetham lbw b Johnston	10	c Hassett b Johnston	35
J. C. Wakins c Hassett b Miller	36	c Miller b Johnson	0
H. J. Tayfield lbw b Miller	6	c Miller b Johnson	0
N. B. F. Mann b Miller	0	lbw b Johnston	13
V. I. Smith not out	1	c McCool b Johnston	1
C. N. McCarthy b Johnson	0	not out	1
Extras (lb14, nb 1)	15	*Extras* (b9 lb 3 wl nb 2)	15
Total	137	Total	191

Bowling: Lindwall 10–1–22–0; Johnston 12–4–21–2; Miller 15–3–40–5; Johnson 18.2–6–37–3; Loxton 1–0–2–0

Bowling: Lindwall 8–1–25–0; Johnston 20.1–5–44–6; Miller 11–1–27–0; Johnson 14–0–54–3; Loxton 3–0–11–0; McCool 9–3–15–1

West Indies to England
1950

Tour captain: J. D. C. Goddard

Old Trafford: *England won by 202 runs*
Lord's: *West Indies won by 326 runs*
Trent Bridge: *West Indies won by 10 wickets*
The Oval: *West Indies won by an innings and 56 runs*

John Goddard had already made sure of his place in Test history by leading his West Indians to victory in India 18 months earlier; now he consolidated it with a four-Test visit which shook English cricket to its very foundations. Bowlers expected to find Rae and Stollmeyer a difficult opening pair; they were prepared to have to work hard to remove the three Ws (Worrell, Weekes and Walcott) because the talent of these players was, at least in part, known. But the batsmen were most certainly not expecting to be bowled out by an attack consisting of the 40-year-old Hines Johnson, the medium-paced Gerry Gomez and two unknown spinners, aged 21 and 20, called Ramadhin and Valentine whose experience of first-class cricket – never mind Tests – consisted of a handful of matches. England duly won the first Test on a spinner's wicket at Old Trafford, despite Alf Valentine's 8 for 104 while Ramadhin was returning more modest figures of 2 for 90. But in games against the English counties the little man from Trinidad was cleaning up. In all on that tour, Sonny Ramadhin took 135 wickets for only

14.88 runs apiece and stories of his unfathomable variations of spin ran through the dressing-rooms like a prairie fire. In fact, Ramadhin was basically an off-spinner who, without any ostentatious change of action, could make one go the other way. Immediately he was labelled a leg-spinner who didn't employ any wrist movement ... a finger-spinning leg-break bowler! By the time the second Test was played at Lord's, enough rumours had swept round the grounds of England to give Ramadhin a head start, no matter what he bowled. He took 5 for 66 in 43 overs, followed by 6 for 86 in 72 overs (43 of which were maidens). Meanwhile, Valentine was quietly picking up a match aggregate of 7 for 127 at the other end and together they bowled West Indies to their first-ever win in England, following it with others at Trent Bridge and The Oval.

Gilbert Parkhouse, of Glamorgan, joined the ranks at Lord's of those who have been dismissed for 0 in a first Test innings and the future Bishop of Liverpool, batting at number 3 at The Oval as D. S. Sheppard, showed a proper episcopal absence of partiality by getting out to Ramadhin in the first innings and to Valentine in the second. In the four Tests, Valentine took 33 wickets at 20.42 and Ramadhin 26 at 23.23. Goddard, his place in history assured, showed his versatility at The Oval by opening the bowling in the second innings – and getting the wicket of Hutton who had carried his bat for 202 in the first innings.

England to Australia and New Zealand
1950–1
Tour captain: F. R. Brown

Brisbane: *Australia won by 70 runs*
Melbourne: *Australia won by 28 runs*
Sydney: *Australia won by an innings and 13 runs*
Adelaide: *Australia won by 274 runs*
Melbourne: *England won by 8 wickets*

Christchurch: *Match drawn*
Wellington: *England won by 6 wickets*

Frederick Richard Brown shares with the humorist, Michael Bentine, the common (if unusual) birthplace of Lima, the Peruvian capital, though there the resemblance ends. The creation of laughter through conscious and brilliantly created humour (e.g. The Goons) is not what immediately springs to mind when one considers the cricket career of the man who led England in Australia and New Zealand in 1950–1.

That career may be said to fall into three categories. A big, burly man, Brown had a brilliant, two-year career at Cambridge where he headed the batting averages and won the first of his brace of Blues; and in his second year he topped the bowlers as a leg-break and googly merchant. He could also, and did with success, bowl medium-pace seam-up. In short, he was an accomplished all-rounder who did the double in his first full season with Surrey which earned him a place in Jardine's 'bodyline' tour party of 1932–3. His particular talents were not in great demand during that tour and up to the Second World War he played a relatively small number of games each season and his touring was restricted to Hubert Martineau's annual jaunts to Egypt with amateur sides.

He spent three years as a prisoner-of-war and while he remained actively interested in the administration of the game in a behind-the-scenes role he had played very little first-class cricket for 10 years when he accepted an invitation to captain Northants in 1949. At the age of 39 he immediately recaptured much of the form he had shown at Cambridge and Northants jumped from last place in the County Championships table to sixth. Nevertheless, his selection as tour captain was not universally popular. Both Yardley and Mann declined the invitation and they were captains with the gentle touch. Brown, a more brusque and at times abrasive character, was not renowned as a leader 'who looked after the lads' in the mould of (as we shall see) M. J. K. Smith, for instance. Brian Close, touring for the first time as an immature 19-year-old, returned with a virtual hatred of his captain and Jim Laker, in later years, was to conceive a cordial dislike of Freddie Brown who tended to adopt an old-style, distant, amateur stance in his leadership without a leavening of benign paternalism. Nevertheless, he was prepared to lead from the front and was third in the Test batting averages on tour, while he bowled more overs than anyone except Alec Bedser. Effectively, the attack was mounted throughout the tour by just four bowlers, Bailey and Wright shouldering the main burden, with Brown and Bedser. This meant a lot of hard work in the days of eight-ball overs on Test pitches which (the first at Brisbane excepted) were generally good. In these circumstances, Brown's 18 Test wickets at 21.16 are impressive for a leg-spinner. Australia won the first four games of the series but at Melbourne, second time round, Brown led England to their first victory over the old enemy since The Oval in 1938, a win which ended Australia's sequence of 25 Tests without defeat. This, then, is the match which stands as Freddie Brown's monument:

AUSTRALIA v. ENGLAND

Melbourne, 1951

AUSTRALIA

First Innings		*Second Innings*	
Burke c Tattersall b Bedser	11	c Hutton b Bedser	1
Morris lbw b Brown	50	lbw b Bedser	4
Hassett c Hutton b Brown	92	b Wright	48
Harvey c Evans b Brown	1	lbw b Wright	52
Miller c and b Brown	7	c and b Brown	0
Hole b Bedser	18	b Bailey	63
Johnson lbw b Bedser	1	c Brown b Wright	0
Lindwall c Compton b Bedser	21	b Bedser	14
Tallon c Hutton b Bedser	1	not out	2
Johnston not out	12	b Bedser	1
Iverson c Washbrook b Brown	0	c Compton b Bedser	0
Extras (b2 lb1)	3	*Extras* (b2 lb8 wl nbl)	12
Total	217	Total	197

Bowling: Bedser 22–5–46–5; Bailey 9–1–29–0; Brown 18–4–49–5; Wright 9–1–50–0; Tattersall 11–3–40–0

Bowling: Bedser 20.3–4–59–5; Bailey 15–3–32–1; Brown 9–1–32–1; Wright 15–2–56–3; Tattersall 5–2–6–0

ENGLAND

First Innings		*Second Innings*	
Hutton b Hole	79	not out	60
Washbrook c Tallon b Miller	27	c Lindwall b Johnston	7
Simpson not out	156	run out	15
Compton c Miller b Lindwall	11	not out	11
Sheppard c Tallon b Miller	1		
Brown b Lindwall	6		
Evans b Miller	1		
Bedser b Lindwall	11		
Bailey c Johnson b Iverson	5		
Wright lbw b Iverson	3		
Tattersall b Miller	10		
Extras (b9 lb1)	10	*Extras* (lb2)	2
Total	320	Total (for 2 wkts)	95

Bowling: Lindwall 21–1–77–3; Miller 21.7–5–76–4; Johnston 12–1–55–0; Iverson 20–4–52–2; Johnson 11–1–40–0; Hole 5–0–10–1

Bowling: Lindwall 2–0–12–0; Miller 2–0–5–0; Johnston 11–3–36–1; Iverson 12–2–32–0; Johnson 1–0–1–0; Hole 1–0–3–0; Hassett 0.6–0–4–0

Reg Simpson, the Notts amateur, reached his only hundred against Australia on his 31st birthday and was, in fact, second in the England batting averages in Tests to Hutton – but more than 50 runs per innings behind him. Compton, who had a number of injury problems, averaged 7.57 in his eight Test innings. The third part of Brown's cricketing life began after his retirement in 1953 when he became chairman of the selectors, although he had been a member of that committee in 1951 and 1952. He spent five years as chairman of the Cricket Council, 1974–9 and is still a powerful M C C figure at Lord's.

The tour followed the traditional pattern of moving on to New Zealand where the first Test in Christchurch was drawn in a match in which 1,013 runs were scored for the loss of only 21 wickets (Bailey scoring his only Test hundred). The second match, in Wellington, England won despite torrential rain and an earthquake!

South Africa to England
1951
Tour captain: A. D. Nourse

Trent Bridge: *South Africa won by 71 runs*
Lord's: *England won by 10 wickets*
Old Trafford: *England won by 9 wickets*
Headingley: *Match drawn*
The Oval: *England won by four wickets*

Son of a distinguished cricketing father, Dudley Nourse, who led the 10th South Africans in Festival of Britain Year, ended his Test career at The Oval on 18 August after skippering his country in 15 of the 34 Tests he played. A popular cricketer and captain, Nourse had enjoyed wartime competition while on active service in the Middle East with many of the men he met on that tour. There was, in fact, an Army tradition as well as a cricketing strain in the family. His father, Surrey-born, had gone to South Africa as a soldier five years before the outbreak of the Boer War and settled there. His cricket career spanned 40 seasons and his memory remains, as the 'Grand Old Man' of South African cricket. Dudley, no less renowned, made three tours of England, like his father, and was vice-captain to Melville in 1947. His final tour as captain started unfortunately when he sustained a broken thumb against Gloucestershire at Bristol and at the age of 40 found it slow to heal.

Nevertheless, he led South Africa in the opening Test at Nottingham with characteristic courage, batting in severe pain for more than nine hours to score 208 in a total of 483. He was able to take no further part in the match and though he returned to play in all four remaining Tests he never rediscovered his touch with the bat. His problems as captain were exacerbated by a lack of success from his opening bowlers, of whom much had been expected. Michael Melle was plagued by injury and bowled in fewer than half the tour matches; Cuan McCarthy, fast and always aggressive (he was a boxer as well as a cricketer) had problems with line and length and with whispered suspicions about the legality of his delivery. (He was 'called' for throwing the following year.) Nor was Nourse much more fortunate with his spin attack. Athol Rowan, the off-spinner, was continually troubled by a knee injury and

Tufty Mann (slow left-arm) was stricken by an illness from which he died less than a year later. In many ways it was a tragic tour, far from a fitting epitaph to the career of a gallant and most respected captain. His brave innings at Trent Bridge marked the way most of us remember him.

ENGLAND v. SOUTH AFRICA

Trent Bridge, 1951

SOUTH AFRICA

First Innings		Second Innings	
E. Rowan c Evans b Brown	17	c Ikin b Bedser	11
Waite run out	76	c Ikin b Tattersall	5
McGlew b Brown	40	st Evans b Bedser	5
Nourse run out	208	absent hurt	
Cheetham c Ikin b Bedser	31	b Bedser	28
Fullerton c Compton b Tattersall	54	(4) c Brown b Tattersall	13
van Ryneveld lbw b Bedser	32	(6) c Hutton b Bedser	22
A. Rowan b Bedser	2	(7) c Evans b Bedser	5
Mann c Tattersall b Wardle	1	(8) b Tattersall	2
Chubb not out	0	(9) not out	11
McCarthy not out	1	(10) b Bedser	5
Extras (b3 lb17 nbl)	21	Extras (b4 lb9 nbl)	14
Total (9 wkts declared)	483	Total	121

Bowling: Bedser 63–18–122–3; Bailey 45–13–102–0; Brown 34–11–74–2; Tattersall 47–20–80–1; Wardle 49–21–77–1; Compton 2–0–7–0

Bowling: Bedser 22.4–8–37–6; Bailey 2–0–10–0; Tattersall 23–6–56–3; Wardle 4–3–4–0

ENGLAND

First Innings		Second Innings	
Hutton c Waite b A. Rowan	63	c and b A. Rowan	11
Ikin c McCarthy b Chubb	1	c Ikin b Tattersall	33
Simpson c Waite b McCarthy	137	c and b A. Rowan	7
Compton c Waite b McCarthy	112	lbw b A. Rowan	5
Watson lbw b McCarthy	57	lbw b Mann	5
Brown c Fullerton b Chubb	29	(7) c McCarthy b A. Rowan	7
Evans c sub b Chubb	5	(8) c van Ryneveld b Mann	0
Wardle c Fullerton b Chubb	5	(9) c sub b A. Rowan	30
Bailey c Fullerton b McCarthy	3	(6) c Waite b Mann	11
Bedser not out	0	b McCarthy	0
Tattersall did not bat		not out	0
Extras (b4 lb3)	7	Extras (lb5)	5
Total (9 wkts declared)	419	Total	114

Bowling: McCarthy 48–10–104–4; Chubb 46.2–12–146–4; A. Rowan 46–10–101–1; Mann 20–5–51–0; van Ryneveld 3–0–10–0

Bowling: McCarthy 8–1–8–1; Chubb 6–2–9–0; A. Rowan 27.2–4–68–5; Mann 24–16–24–4

The notorious Trent Bridge 'featherbed' pitch was at that time in its most benign state – hence the number of overs bowled by the quicker men on the first three days. Nourse's great innings was the first double century made by a South African against England and Reg Simpson's 137 the first hundred made by a Notts batsman in a Trent Bridge Test.

Nourse started the tour with the considerable advantage of enjoying the respect of his players for a splendid cricketing record, but he also had the vital attribute of being an essentially likeable man who could mix easily without losing any of his authority. Like most tour parties, who invariably form Saturday Night Clubs and establish 'courts' for 'trying' a fascinating variety of esoteric offences, the tenth South Africans were not slow to form their own secret society which was named in honour of their captain: 'The Noursemen Club'.

In view of the tragic destruction of player-media relationships which was to occur in England cricket circles 30 years on, it is interesting to look back on that exclusive club of 22 members which came into being on board the *Arundel Castle* in that spring of 1951. There were 15 players, a manager (Sid Pegler), baggage-master (W. H. 'Fergie' Ferguson), three newspapermen and two broadcasters. Overseas sides, particularly those from South Africa, New Zealand and West Indies, have always enjoyed the enviable situation of a small media following who have been comfortably and happily integrated with the players and management. England, on the other hand, have often been accompanied by Press and broadcasting parties who have outnumbered the practitioners, thus precluding that cosy relationship which can make all the difference between a happy and an unhappy tour – on both sides. It only needs one rotten apple to spoil a barrel; it is relatively easy to sort out one bad tourist in a group of three or four but an entirely different matter when the awkward squad consists of six or seven in a media party of 23 or 24. Then, everyone suffers.

England to India
1951–2
Tour captain: N. D. Howard (D. B. Carr)

Delhi: *Match drawn*
Bombay: *Match drawn*
Calcutta: *Match drawn*
Kanpur: *England won by 8 wickets*
Madras: *India won by an innings and 8 runs*

India were still not accepted as really a Test-standard country and Nigel Howard, the Lancashire captain, took to the sub-continent a party which introduced no fewer than seven new caps in the course of the first three Tests – Howard himself, Donald Carr (Derbyshire), Don Kenyon (Worcs), Fred Ridgway (Kent), Dick Spooner (Warwicks), Eddie Leadbeater (Yorkshire) and Cyril Poole (Notts). Leadbeater, the leg-spinner, was flown out as a replacement for Bert Rhodes, of Derbyshire. After five games (including one Test) the party played a series of five games in the newest cricketing country of Pakistan. Two of the matches, in Lahore and Karachi, were described as Tests but were not officially recognised as such by the I C C. Nevertheless, they introduced to the tourists a 16-year-old batsman called Hanif Mohammad of whom England bowlers were to see much in the future.

Howard's men then returned to India for four more Tests, winning on a spinner's pitch in Kanpur (where his fellow Lancastrians Tattersall [8 for 125] and Malcolm Hilton [9 for 93] did their captain proud) and losing in Madras. This was India's first Test victory in 25 matches but Howard was not involved. An attack of pleurisy caused him to miss the match and Carr led the side.

It was a long and gruelling tour, lasting from early October until the beginning of March and taking in four final games in what was then Ceylon (Sri Lanka). The captain had a major preoccupation in keeping morale at a reasonable level through a five-month tour when travel and accommodation were far from the more sophisticated standards they were to attain in the future. There was much indisposition of the type euphemistically, if vaguely, described as 'stomach trouble' and off-duty boredom had to be attacked in a positive manner. Nigel Howard, son and brother of other Lancashire amateur cricketers, had a relatively limited first-class career because of business commitments and an affection for the game of golf. Nevertheless, he made his mark by overcoming many difficulties on one of the longest of all tours to the Far East and while his batting enjoyed little success he enhanced his reputation as an outstanding fieldsman and cheerful leader.

West Indies to Australia and New Zealand
1951–2

Tour captain: J. D. C. Goddard (J. B. Stollmeyer)

Brisbane: *Australia won by 3 wickets*
Sydney: *Australia won by 7 wickets*
Adelaide: *West Indies won by 6 wickets*
Melbourne: *Australia won by 1 wicket*
Sydney: *Australia won by 202 runs*

Christchurch: *West Indies won by 5 wickets*
Auckland: *Match drawn*

Those who have seen most of their Test cricket in the 1980s may be intrigued by the situation in Australia on this tour – West Indies, as in

England, had very little firepower in attack and skipper Goddard relied to an enormous extent upon the spinning 'twins', Ramadhin and Valentine, while Australia waged what was to all intents and purposes a bumper war through Lindwall and Miller, backed up by the awkward left-arm, over-the-wicket pace of Bill Johnston. It is interesting to speculate that memories of that tour may have lingered in West Indian minds because most of the players who had to bob and weave to dodge the short-pitched deliveries of the best (by far) quick attack in the world were still around, many of them in influential administrative roles, when West Indian retribution on a cosmic scale came in the seventies and eighties . . . Rae and Stollmeyer, Weekes, Walcott and Gomez. Indeed, while Goddard bowled his two spinners for 129 of the 150 overs of the Australian first innings in Brisbane, Miller was warned for intimidation of the West Indies debutant batsman Roy Marshall, later to have a splendid batting career with Hampshire and to become a committee-man with Somerset.

Goddard's opening attack in all five Tests relied heavily on Gerry Gomez who was never really more than medium pace and relied on massive shoulders and a brisk approach to get movement in the air and off the pitch when conditions were right. They were not often right in the clear atmosphere of Australia. Goddard had to pair him with three different opening partners at various stages of the series and the only Test which was won by the tourists was that in Adelaide when, after five opening overs from Gomez, the captain took the ball himself and, in concert with Frank Worrell, bowled out Australia in their first innings for 82 on a rain-affected pitch. This, then, becomes Goddard's match:

AUSTRALIA v. WEST INDIES

Adelaide, 1952

AUSTRALIA

First Innings		*Second Innings*	
Burke c Stollmeyer b Worrell	3	(9) b Valentine	15
Morris b Worrell	1	(5) b Valentine	45
Harvey c Guillen b Gomez	10	(6) c Guillen b Ramadhin	9
Miller c Ramadhin b Worrell	4	(7) lbw b Gomez	35
Hole c Worrell b Goddard	23	(8) c Weekes b Gomez	25
Lindwall b Worrell	2	(10) not out	8
Johnson c Stollmeyer b Worrell	11	(1) c Marshall b Valentine	16
Ring c Christiani b Goddard	5	(4) run out	67
Langley b Worrell	5	(2) b Valentine	23
Noblet b Goddard	8	(3) c Weekes b Valentine	0
Johnston not out	7	lbw b Valentine	0
Extras (lb3)	3	*Extras* (b8 lb4)	12
Total	82	Total	255

Bowling: Gomez 5–3–5–1; Worrell 12.7–3–38–6; Goddard 8–1–36–3

Bowling: Gomez 7–2–17–2; Worrell 9–2–29–0; Goddard 1–0–7–0; Valentine 27.5–6–102–6; Ramadhin 25–4–76–1; Marshall 5–1–12–0

WEST INDIES

First Innings			Second Innings	
Marshall c Burke b Johnson		14	c Langley b Ring	29
Stollmeyer b Johnson		17	c Miller b Ring	47
Goddard c Langley b Lindwall		0		
Worrell b Miller		6	(3) c Noblet b Johnson	28
Weekes b Johnson		26	(4) c and b Ring	29
Gomez c Langley b Johnson		4	(5) not out	46
Christiani c Miller b Johnson		4	(6) not out	42
Guillen b Noblet		9		
Atkinson c Burke b Johnson		15		
Ramadhin not out		5		
Valentine b Noblet		0		
Extras (lb5)		5	*Extras* (b6 lb5 wl)	12
	Total	105	Total (for 4 wkts)	233

Bowling: Lindwall 4–0–18–1; Johnson 12–0–62–6; Miller 5–1–13–1; Noblet 3.5–0–7–2

Bowling: Lindwall 13–1–40–0; Johnson 19–4–50–1; Miller 5–0–12–0; Noblet 13–1–30–0; Ring 16.5–3–62–3; Johnson 7–1–27–0

The eccentric nature of the Australian batting order in the second innings, amounting to a virtual reversal of the first innings, was due to the fact that Arthur Morris (skippering Australia in the absence of the injured Hassett) saw 20 wickets fall on the first day for only 207 runs. Faced with going in a second time on the opening day, Morris gambled on the wicket easing the following day and sent out Ian Johnson and Gil Langley to face the last few overs. The game finished half-way through the third day: Christmas Day.

The Tests in New Zealand were the first between the two countries.

India to England
1952
Tour captain: V. S. Hazare

Headingley: *England won by 7 wickets*
Lord's: *England won by 8 wickets*
Old Trafford: *England won by an innings and 207 runs*
The Oval: *Match drawn*

Few captains have brought tour parties to England with the odds stacked more heavily against them than Vijay Samuel Hazare. This was partly foreseeable, partly a matter of sheer misfortune because while the appointment of Len Hutton – a professional – as captain was always going to bring a serious sense of purpose to England's cricket, no one really could have predicted the extent to which a young fast bowler called Frederick Sewards Trueman was literally going to terrify the Indian batsmen into submission. Hazare was brother, father and uncle of four other first-class cricketers. He played his early cricket in the central area of the sub-continent but his greatest days came when he moved to the princely state of Baroda. First-class cricket in India 40 and 50 years ago often followed a strange pattern with enormous scores being piled up by sides with no thought of ultimately achieving an outright victory. The whole emphasis was on batting and amassing astonishing scores, both individually and collectively. Wickets were so flat – oh *so* flat – with many games played on matting that to get a ball to bounce stump-high was a major achievement. There was little or no point in trying to bowl fast and even good spinners, refining their art in conditions of terrible adversity, had to expect to concede runs heavily.

But these were matters Hazare knew about only too well. What he could not possibly have been prepared for was the abject crumpling of his batting on so many occasions. He was, at the outset, without India's three senior players – Merchant, Amarnath and Mushtaq Ali – and his leading all-rounder, Mankad, was a contracted professional player in northern league cricket in England. He was available when his club commitments permitted which meant he played in only three Tests and none of the other competitive matches of the tour. The selectors had no alternative to picking a team of largely untried young players and the consequences were largely disastrous. The first Test started badly enough with three wickets going down at Headingley for 42 runs and Hazare, with the 20-year-old Manjrekar, saving face by putting on 222 for the fourth wicket. But after England had achieved a first-innings lead of 41, India went in again on Saturday 7 June, and soon the scoreboard showed an historic 0 for 4 wickets. Three fell to Trueman – this was his first Test – in eight balls and the other to Bedser and from that moment Trueman had handed the black spot to most of the front-line batsmen.

The point is perhaps best illustrated by a look at the experience on that tour of one of the most prolific scorers of all Indian Test batsmen – Pahlan ('Polly') Umrigar. Physically, he was outstandingly well-built and during the summer of 1952 he scored 1,688 runs at an average of 48.22 against the English counties, including three double centuries (against Lancashire, Kent and Oxford University). He had a career batting average of 52.28 and in Tests he averaged 42.22. But in the four Tests of 1952 his scores were 8, 9, 5, 14, 3, and 0. He fell to Trueman four times (three clean bowled) and after taking eight Indian wickets for 31 in 52 balls at Old Trafford, Trueman swore that as he ran in to bowl at Umrigar he could see his leg-slip fieldsman, Tony Lock, between the stumps and the batsman! Umrigar's failure in the series and his obvious distaste for Trueman's pace had a disastrous effect upon Indian batting morale.

Hazare, who refused to be intimidated, led bravely from the front. He scored 89, 56, 69 not out, 49, 16 (out of 58), 16 (out of 82) and 38 (out of 98) in his seven Test innings but it was a lost cause.

As with most Indian captains of his era, Hazare lacked the bowlers to make early breakthroughs except when the wicket was turning. Phadkar, Ramchand and Divecha were nowhere near Trueman's pace and Hazare's own medium-pacers were generally as effective as any of those three against very strong England batting. The off-spinner Ghulam Ahmed was by far Hazare's most potent bowler but 15 wickets (even at 24.73) was not Test-winning stuff with little effective support.

Hazare undoubtedly found his own performance affected by the strain of leading a side with its morale effectively destroyed from the third day of the first Test; yet if others had equalled his relative consistency – or shown greater resolution – India's showing on this tour would have looked much better.

Pakistan to India
1952–3

Tour captain: A. H. Kardar

Delhi: *India won by an innings and 70 runs*
Lucknow: *Pakistan won by an innings and 43 runs*
Bombay: *India won by 10 wickets*
Madras: *Match drawn*
Calcutta: *Match drawn*

Pakistan's first day of Test cricket came on 16 October 1952, slightly over five years after the partition of the sub-continent into the states of India and Pakistan and it took international cricket's newest member just 10 days to achieve its first Test win. After an innings' defeat in New Delhi in three days, the teams moved a couple of hundred miles to the east and in the only Test ever played on the University ground in Lucknow, Pakistan bowled out India for 106 and 182 on a matting wicket to win by an innings under the leadership of A. H. Kardar. Pakistan's first captain has been one of the most interesting – and most influential – figures in the game for more than 40 years. Born Abdul Hafeez, in Lahore, in 1925, he was playing representative cricket at 18 and he was 21 when I first saw him in action in Bombay – a slow left-arm bowler who hit the ball hard as a middle-order batsman. After partition, he added 'Kardar' to his name and came to Oxford University in 1947, winning three Blues. Then he had three seasons with Warwick-shire before returning to lead his country in all Pakistan's first 23 Tests.

A disciplinarian, and perhaps a touch autocratic, Kardar faced prob-lems which can only be imagined in instilling into his players not only a sense of identity as cricketers but as citizens of a new country. He had toured England in 1946 as an *Indian* Test player; now he led Pakistan to India (twice), to England and to the West Indies and thus became a trailblazer in three continents. After retiring as a player, Kardar became President of the Board of Control for Cricket in Pakistan and played the leading role in organising the game there. Ever a political figure, he was not (in some of the turbulent periods of Pakistan's short history) for the whole of that time on the 'winning' side but somehow he contrived to retain his influence in a behind-the-scenes role. Undoubt-edly he is the godfather of Pakistan cricket and has presided (either from a front seat or one a little further back) over the emergence of his country as the second most powerful cricketing nation in the world in the 1980s. For his most memorable Test occasion we shall wait for a subsequent tour. It is interesting to note in the meantime that Kardar's first Pakistan Test team included Nazar Mohammed, father of Mudas-sar Nazar who was to become one of his country's most consistent and regular players of the next generation.

South Africa to Australia and New Zealand
1952–3
Tour captain: J. E. Cheetham

Brisbane: *Australia won by 96 runs*
Melbourne: *South Africa won by 82 runs*
Sydney: *Australia won by an innings and 38 runs*
Adelaide: *Match drawn*
Melbourne: *South Africa won by 6 wickets*

Wellington: *South Africa won by an innings and 180 runs*
Auckland: *Match drawn*

To John Erskine Cheetham falls the distinction of having been the first South African captain to play in a shared rubber in Australia and that, to most people, would seem entirely appropriate. Cheetham was a solid, rather than scintillating, batsman but he had a touch of genius as a captain. He was an excellent tactician who also possessed great gifts of man-management. For an example of both it is necessary to look no further than the fourth and fifth Tests on this tour. In Adelaide, the tourists saved the game after being faced with a first innings total of 530 and in Melbourne, second time round, they actually won after Australia had totalled 520 in the first innings.

It was a very young side and very few people indeed outside the tourists' own ranks expected it to make much impression against Hassett's experienced players. Cheetham, starting out without much experience in *his* ranks, introduced four men completely new to Test cricket during the course of the series. Perhaps luck was on Cheetham's side to the extent that Lindwall and Miller broke down during the fourth Test and could not play in the last one yet Australia could still put out a formidable eleven players – and let us not forget that the tourists had already won the second Test. What impressed the Aussies most of all was the tremendous enthusiasm of the young South Africans, especially in the field, and the way they had knitted together as a team by the middle of the tour. That is a clear indication of good captaincy and in particular, good tour captaincy. The no-hopers went home with a 2–2 squared series and one match drawn. Cheetham was to lead South Africa in 15 of his 24 Tests and missed two in 1955 through injury during the tour to England. This meant that he missed the Old Trafford Test on that tour which was the best performance by South Africa that I ever saw, but that, and the fourth Test at Headingley, are really part of the Jackie McGlew story, as we shall see. At the same time, it was a *tour* under Cheetham's captaincy. For his handling and moulding of a relatively inexperienced side in Australia, 'Jack' Cheetham's match is, therefore, the second Test against Australia over Christmas, 1952.

AUSTRALIA v. SOUTH AFRICA
Melbourne, 1952

SOUTH AFRICA

First Innings		Second Innings	
McGlew b Lindwall	46	st Langley b Ring	13
Waite c Lindwall b Miller	0	c Hole b Miller	62
Endean c Benaud b Lindwall	2	not out	162
Funston c Ring b Miller	9	run out	26
McLean c Lindwall b Ring	27	lbw b Miller	42
Cheetham c Johnston b Miller	15	lbw b Johnston	6
Watkins c Langley b Benaud	19	b Johnston	3
Mansell b Lindwall	24	b Miller	18
Murray c Johnston b Benaud	51	st Langley b Ring	23
Tayfield c Langley b Miller	23	lbw b Lindwall	22
Melle not out	4	b Lindwall	0
Extras (b4 lb3)	7	*Extras* (bl lb5 w4 nbl)	11
Total	227	Total	388

Bowling: Lindwall 14–2–29–3; Miller 21–3–62–4; Johnson 12–2–37–0; Ring 18–1–72–1; Benaud 6.6–1–20–2

Bowling: Lindwall 31.5–4–87–2; Miller 22–5–51–3; Johnson 31–9–77–2; Ring 31–5–115–2; Benaud 6–0–23–0; Hole 7–0–24–0

AUSTRALIA

First Innings		Second Innings	
McDonald c sub b Mansell	82	c Mansell b Murray	23
Morris c and b Tayfield	43	c Watkins b Melle	1
Harvey c Cheetham b Tayfield	11	(4) c Watkins b Tayfield	60
Hassett c Melle b Mansell	18	(3) lbw b Tayfield	21
Miller c Endean b Tayfield	52	b Tayfield	31
Hole c Waite b Mansell	13	(7) b Tayfield	25
Benaud b Tayfeld	5	(8) c Melle b Tayfield	45
Lindwall run out	1	(9) b Melle	19
Ring c McGlew b Tayfield	14	(10) c Melle b Tayfield	53
Langley not out	2	(6) b Tayfield	4
Johnson lbw b Tayfield	0	not out	0
Extras (nb2)	2	*Extras* (bl lb6 nbl)	8
Total	243	Total	290

Bowling: Melle 14–0–73–0; Watkins 6–1–15–0; Murray 3–1–11–0; Tayfield 29.4–9–84–6; Mansell 19–3–58–3

Bowling: Melle 11–2–39–2; Watkins 10–2–34–0; Murray 23–7–59–1; Tayfield 37.1–13–81–7; Mansell 14–2–69–0

India to West Indies
1953
Tour captain: V. S. Hazare

Trinidad: *Match drawn*
Barbados: *West Indies won by 142 runs*
Trinidad: *Match drawn*
British Guiana: *Match drawn*
Jamaica: *Match drawn*

Hazare's tourists, like the home side led by Jeff Stollmeyer, were once again much stronger in batting than bowling so that four high-scoring drawn games were interrupted by the West Indian win in Bridgetown where Valentine in the first innings and Ramadhin in the second were able to spin the ball more effectively than Gupte and Mankad. Once again we see Hazare unable to do full justice to his great talents as a batsman of splendid technique, almost certainly because of the cares of skippering the side. He was one of the most imposing batsmen India has produced when playing in domestic competitions or in Tests when he was not in charge. Indian cricket historians tend to rate Hazare as a lesser player than Merchant, yet in spite of his batting failures when captain he still ended with a Test batting average of 47.65. It is interesting to speculate what the figure might have been if Hazare had been free of the responsibilities of leadership in England and the West Indies.

Australia to England
1953
Tour captain: A. L. Hassett

Trent Bridge: *Match drawn*
Lord's: *Match drawn*
Old Trafford: *Match drawn*
Headingley: *Match drawn*
The Oval: *England won by 8 wickets*

Lindsay Hassett's final Test as Australia's captain was the match which cost them the Ashes after just under 19 years. This must be seen as a cruel injustice because not only had the little Victorian been a fine player and a good captain, he had been one of the most popular figures in international cricket over a span of 15 years interrupted by the war. His first innings 115 (out of 249) at Trent Bridge ranks as one of the classic rearguard actions on a ground which has seen a number of outstanding examples of that sort of knock. When Colin McDonald and Graeme Hole failed to make the grade as openers, Hassett took on the job himself after the first Test but too many of his batsmen had a poor tour in a wet summer which no one enjoyed more than Alec Bedser. My outstanding memory of 1953 is of Bedser's bowling at Trent Bridge on Tuesday 16 June, after the penultimate day of the Test had been washed out by rain – 7 for 44, following on his first innings 7 for 55 – and in particular a delivery which bowled the 22-year-old Richie Benaud round his legs at fast-medium pace. England were set to win that game when rain intervened but in the second Test, at Lord's, Australia had a firm grip on a contest which they would have won but for the famous rearguard action by Willie Watson and Trevor Bailey. Rain ruined the Old Trafford Test completely and at Headingley it was Bailey again (with defensive bat and even more defensive bowling) who saved England. By the time the Ashes were won at The Oval, more than half a million people watched the series and if Hassett's farewell to international cricket was not the emotional affair that Bradman's had been, he left behind a host of friends and admirers in this country.

New Zealand to South Africa
1953–4
Tour captain: G. O. Rabone (B. Sutcliffe)

Durban: *South Africa won by an innings and 58 runs*
Johannesburg: *South Africa won by 132 runs*
Cape Town: *Match drawn*
Johannesburg: *South Africa won by 9 wickets*
Port Elizabeth: *South Africa won by 5 wickets*

Geoff Rabone, who led New Zealand on their first-ever tour of South Africa, was not by nature or inclination an opening batsman but he took on that responsibility in the opening Test at Durban and scored his only century in Test matches which took just over six hours, in contrast to his normal style as middle-order player. A tall, pleasant and cheerful cricketer, he led a side unprepared for the fast, hostile and extremely aggressive bowling of Neil Adcock who made his first appearance in Durban. Two of Rabone's men were taken to hospital and two more were dismissed by deliveries which struck them on the chest and dropped on to the stumps in the second Test defeat at Ellis Park. But at Newlands (third Test) Rabone led a spirited reply by scoring 56 and sharing an opening partnership of 126 with Murray Chapple, then took 6 for 68 with his mixture of seamers and spinners. Just before the fourth Test, Rabone broke a bone in his right foot and Bert Sutcliffe, New Zealand's leading batsman of that era, took over the captaincy for the two final matches, chose to bat on both occasions and both games were lost.

Sutcliffe's record as a Test captain may well have been unimpressive but there can be no doubt at all about his stature as a New Zealand Test cricketer. In an age when outstanding Kiwi cricketers were thin on the ground, Sutcliffe was a world-class left-hand batsman.

England to West Indies
1954
Tour captain: L. Hutton

Jamaica: *West Indies won by 140 runs*
Barbados: *West Indies won by 181 runs*
British Guiana: *England won by 9 wickets*
Trinidad: *Match drawn*
Jamaica: *England won by 9 wickets*

Len Hutton took England to the West Indies in 1954 without any inkling of the maelstrom of controversy – political, racial and umpiring – he was to encounter. As a professional captain, a relatively new creature in world cricket, he was acutely conscious of the mistakes which had been made in the selection of the team to tour in 1948 based on a serious underestimation of the developing expertise of West Indian cricketers. What he did not and could not know, was the developing nationalism of the islands fuelled by the insistence of the West Indies Board on picking white (i.e. of European stock) captains of the Test side irrespective of the claims of black players. After the successful West Indies tour to England in 1950, Eric Williams (later to become Prime Minister of Trinidad) had made it a point in his claims for Trinidadian independence. This was to reach a high point at a later stage, bringing to an end the white domination of West Indian captaincy. In 1954 it was at the simmering stage but in an indirect way it was to lead to problems for Hutton, notably during the first Test when Jeff Stollmeyer (a white West Indian) declined to enforce the follow-on after his West Indian side had scored 417 at Sabina Park and bowled out England for 170. An already potentially volatile situation was exacerbated by the 'calling' of Tony Lock for throwing his quicker ball and a decision by umpire Burke that J. K. Holt junior was run out when six runs short of a century in his first Test match. Threats were made against the umpire's family.

Hutton confessed later that the tour left him physically and mentally drained and he felt strongly that it shortened his playing career by a couple of years. This is not in the least surprising when one considers that apart from extraneous influences which no touring captain had experienced previously in the West Indies, he was ludicrously and wrongly accused of having insulted Alex Bustamente, the Chief Minister of Jamaica, and had to handle complaints from the public, rightly or wrongly, levelled against his players Trueman, Lock and Graveney. Tour captains in the past had had their problems but none had ever been in a British colony where a rising tide of nationalism provided a backdrop to a Test series.

Along with his manager, Charles Palmer (who earned full marks from Hutton all along the line), he struggled to prevent the tour from disintegrating into quasi-political chaos while at the same time trying to handle players sickened by what they saw as umpiring mistakes from which the captain himself, as well as seasoned and senior players like Compton, suffered. *Wisden*, in a typically low-key and reasoned assessment of the tour afterwards, rated umpiring mistakes as seven or eight to two in favour of the West Indies.

Despite all these problems and after two defeats in the first two Tests, Hutton's men squared the series and the captain averaged 96.71 in the five Tests and 78 in all matches. It was a monumental achievement by a tour captain with as many dramas as Hutton faced on that trip – riots, umpiring shortcomings, dissent by his own players, off-the-field complaints against them, allegations of 'chucking' against one of his bowlers. In the last Test, a 17-year-old Barbadian called Garfield St Aubrun Sobers made his first international appearance, scoring 14 not out and 26 at number nine and taking four wickets for 81 in the match . . .

Pakistan to England
1954
Tour captain: A. H. Kardar

Lord's: *Match drawn*
Trent Bridge: *England won by an innings and 129 runs*
Old Trafford: *Match drawn*
The Oval: *Pakistan won by 24 runs*

Pakistan's first tour to England started on a damp and depressing note with no play possible for three days at Lord's. Going in with a little more than two hours of play possible on the fourth day, Kardar's tourists managed to extend their first innings of 87 into the fifth day and to take nine England wickets before Hutton declared at 117 for 9 in an attempt to force an improbable victory. Hanif Mohammad, 'the little master', gave a glimpse of the obduracy which was to be his trademark by batting for five hours 40 minutes in scoring 59 runs in his two innings. England scored an easy win at Trent Bridge where Bob Appleyard, Yorkshire's two-in-one bowler, took five for 51. Three more Test days were lost at Old Trafford because of rain in a terrible summer. The previous year, however, a team under the name of Pakistan Eaglets had paid a limited visit to England.

They were coached by Alf Gover at his school in London and one of them, a police officer from Lahore named Fazal Mahmood, developed his ability to bowl in the style of Alec Bedser, whom he had admired from afar. In 1954 he returned as Kardar's vice-captain and on Bedser's home ground, The Oval, he bowled Pakistan to victory in the fourth and final Test which squared the series. Fazal had a match return of 12 wickets for 99 and on the occasions I have talked to him in his native Lahore his great delight has been the recollection of 'bowling like Bedser on Bedser's ground'. For the historic success against a strong England batting side and an attack which fielded, for the first time, Frank Tyson and Peter Loader, this has to be Kardar's crowning achievement.

ENGLAND v. PAKISTAN

The Oval, 1954

PAKISTAN

First Innings		Second Innings	
Hanif Mohammad lbw b Statham	0	c Graveney b Wardle	19
Alim-ud-Din b Tyson	10	(7) lbw b Wardle	0
Waqar Hassan b Loader	7	run out	9
Maqsood Ahmed b Tyson	0	c Wardle b McConnon	4
Imtiaz Ahmed c Evans b Tyson	23	c Wardle b Tyson	12
A. H. Kardar c Evans b Statham	36	c and b Wardle	17
Wazir Mohammad run out	0	(8) not out	42
Fazal Mahmood c Evans b Loader	0	(9) b Wardle	6
Shuja-ud-Din not out	16	(2) c May b Wardle	12
Zulfiqar Ahmed c Compton b Loader	16	c May b Wardle	34
Mahmood Hussein b Tyson	23	c Statham b Wardle	6
Extras (nb2)	2	Extras (b3)	3
Total	133	Total	164

Bowling: Statham 11–5–26–2; Tyson 13.4–3–35–4; Loader 18–5–35–3; McConnon 9–2–35–0

Bowling: Statham 18–7–37–0; Tyson 9–2–22–1; Loader 16–6–26–0; McConnon 14–5–20–1; Wardle 35–16–56–7

ENGLAND

First Innings		Second Innings	
Hutton c Imtiaz b Fazal	14	c Imtiaz b Fazal	5
Simpson c Kardar b Mahmood	2	c and b Zulfiqar	27
May c Kardar b Fazal	26	c Kardar b Fazal	53
Compton c Imtiaz b Fazal	53	c Imtiaz b Fazal	29
Graveney c Hanif b Fazal	1	(6) lbw b Shuja-ud-Din	0
Evans c Maqsood b Mahmood	0	(5) b Fazal	3
Wardle c Imtiaz b Fazal	8	c Shuja-ud-Din b Fazal	9
Tyson c Imtiaz b Fazal	3	c Imtiaz b Fazal	3
McConnon c Fazal b Mahmood	11	(10) run out	2
Statham c Shuja-ud-Din b Mahmood	1	(11) not out	2
Loader not out	8	(9) c Waqar b Mahmood	5
Extras (1bl w1 nbl)	3	Extras (lb2 nb3)	5
Total	130	Total	143

Bowling: Fazal 30–16–53–6; Mahmood 21.3–6–58–4; Zulfiqar 5–2–8–0; Shuja-ud-Din 3–0–8–0

Bowling: Fazal 30–11–46–6; Mahmood 14–4–32–1; Zulfiqar 14–2–35–1; Shuja-ud-Din 10–1–25–1

Gubby Allen — too old at 45

Nawab of Pataudi (snr) and Wally Hammond at The Oval, 1946

John Goddard leads out his 1950 touring West Indians

Don Bradman — great batsman, formidable captain

Hutton and Washbrook, one of England's greatest opening pairs

Dudley Nourse — batted in pain for nearly six hours at Trent Bridge

kie McGlew — happy in 1955, not so in 1960

Jack Cheetham, a popular South African, batting at The Oval in 1955

eddie Brown and Lindsay Hassett in Sydney, 1951. (Australia had won the Jubilee Trophy)

Abdul Hafeez Kardar, perhaps the most influential figure in Pakistan cricket

Ian Johnson, an Australian winner in the West Indies

Simpson v. Sobers during the tied Test at Brisbane in December, 1960

England to Australia and New Zealand
1954–5
Tour captain: L. Hutton

Brisbane: *Australia won by an innings and 154 runs*
Sydney: *England won by 38 runs*
Melbourne: *England won by 128 runs*
Adelaide: *England won by 5 wickets*
Sydney: *Match drawn*

Dunedin: *England won by 8 wickets*
Auckland: *England won by an innings and 20 runs*

Just as Bradman had come to England in 1948 determined to avenge the humiliation at The Oval 10 years earlier, Hutton was no less determined to hold on to the Ashes which had been wrested from Australia in 1953. As captains of their countries, there can be no greater similarity than between those two. Both were thoroughly professional in their philosophy, determined in their attitude, meticulous in their preparation and ruthless in their approach. There was Press criticism at the omission of Trueman from the tour party (echoed by the player himself!) and Laker was disappointed at his omission while Jim McConnon of Glamorgan went as the specialist off-spinner. But in the party was Bob Appleyard and Hutton knew that gave him a double-edged weapon. Appleyard could back up the pace attack of Tyson, Statham, Loader and Bailey, or could switch to off-spinners if required. Speed was going to be his main weapon on the tour.

It was in the belief that The Gabba wicket would be at its liveliest in the early stages of the first Test that Hutton put Australia in to bat – and saw them score 601 for eight declared and win by an innings. Hutton made no bones about his mistake. 'I misread the wicket,' he said, 'and that's all there was to it.' England won the next three Tests and drew the last one in which no play was possible on the first three days in Sydney. The Ashes had been retained – comprehensively – and this was one significant verdict on the series:

Australia reached its lowest depth in the 1954–5 series against England. Let us not minimize the effectiveness of the speed bowling of Tyson and Statham; neither let us make excuses for our failure. We failed because our batsmen gave one of the most gutless exhibitions seen in a Test series. I know the wickets were not always of the best and most durable quality, which factor made the effectiveness of the English fast bowlers even more deadly, but I refuse to believe occasions did not arise when the batsmen went down without showing their customary and expected fight. Their morale was low because they forgot the meaning of courage, or, if they did not forget the meaning of it, they forgot how to apply it.

And whose words are these? None other but the Australian captain, Ian Johnson.

Now if Australian morale was low after their first defeat in Sydney, how much lower might that of the tourists have been after their drubbing in Brisbane when their tour captain, on his own admission, had misread the pitch? And how much more difficult is it to restore the morale of a side which is going to be away from home for nearly six months and which has started so disastrously? Hutton was not a captain who looked for a shoulder to cry on; he was not a man who found it easy to share his burdens. In many ways those contemporaries who have called him a 'loner' have a point. Brisbane was a catastrophe not only in its own context as the opening Test but in terms of his planned strategy for the series. If Leonard had started to doubt his own judgement after misreading The Gabba pitch the entire rubber could well have been a disaster.

He didn't make excuses and he didn't look for scapegoats amongst his five-man pace attack. When I asked him, for the purposes of this book, for the qualities he regarded as important in a tour captain, he replied: 'A sense of humour. Be a good listener. There will be times when you are upset; keep them to yourself. To suffer in silence is a great asset.'

At the beginning of that tour, Hutton knew relatively little about Frank Tyson. They had played together in one Test, the final one against Pakistan three months earlier, and they had encountered each other, fleetingly, in the County Championship. But until they embarked on the SS *Orsova* Hutton had really not much idea what made Tyson tick, as they say. He quickly discovered that the Northants bowler was 'a conscientious and intelligent man' who made a determined effort on board ship to get, and remain fit. He also learned that Tyson recited Wordsworth to himself to concentrate the mind when walking back to his bowling mark! But it was during the second Test, in Sydney, that he really impressed his captain *as a bowler*, which was always going to be the most important factor to Hutton. Tyson had been knocked unconscious by a bouncer from Lindwall and it was only in the dressing-room that he recovered. Hutton recalls:

When he came round I swear there was a new light in his eye. I am not given to fanciful imagination and the fact is that he was a yard, maybe a yard and a half, faster when he bowled the following day. When Lindwall came in to bat Tyson was bowling: a flashpoint situation. Everyone on the ground, probably including Lindwall, expected Tyson to finger the bump on his head and let fly a retaliatory bumper. Instead, Frank slipped in the perfect, spot-on yorker which utterly deceived and bowled Lindwall.

That strikes one as coming straight from the heart of a captain who was not always lost in admiration at the thinking of fast bowlers.

From his vast experience of Tests in two different ages, before and after the war; from his own tremendous repertoire of heroic perform-ances, Sir Leonard Hutton chooses the third Test of that series, at Melbourne, as *his* Test to remember. Why?

Because it was played on two pitches – the one at the start of the match and the one which was waiting for us when we reached the ground on Monday morning after the rest day. I was a little concerned when I saw the wicket at the start. It was very dry and cracks had already started to appear before the end of the first day. By close of play on Saturday (second day) I had never seen so many cracks on a pitch, some of them almost three-quarters of an inch wide and the colour was not far from the shade of Bondi Beach.

The weather was hot and I would say ideal for watching cricket, apart from the flies. They were plentiful. Flies like cricket at Melbourne. Rest day was a scorcher with no breeze at all and the team stayed indoors as the sun beat down from a cloudless sky. My thoughts were all about that pitch and what the sunshine was doing to those cracks. What sort of wicket would we find on Monday morning?

I knew as soon as I looked out from the pavilion that something had happened over the weekend and when I went out to the middle I was staggered by what I saw. The cracks had gone. Not one could be seen. It was a new wicket.

It is now a matter of record, of course, that the pitch had been illegally watered during the rest day and that Tyson, bowling faster than ever according to those closest to him, returned seven wickets for 27 as Australia were dismissed for 111 on the final day. It was a victory made up of many factors which Hutton savoured:

I saw the finest catch I have ever seen a wicket-keeper take. Neil Harvey glanced Tyson firmly off his legs, hitting the ball hard. How Godfrey (Evans) managed to get his right hand to the ball I shall never know. This catch was largely responsible for England's victory in a vital match. I had a battle-royal with Keith Miller, whose hostile bowling was quite remarkable. I wished so often that he was a member of my team. On his day, and when he was trying, he was the finest cricketer I played against.

A remarkable tribute from a man not given to over-indulgence in superlatives.

Amongst the many touches of staff work that General Hutton under-took in the course of that tour was an adjustment to Tyson's run-up which proved a decisive factor:

At Brisbane [Tyson: 29–1–160–1] it was blindingly obvious that unless he cut his run-up by at least three or four yards he would soon be on his knees, a spent and useless force. My problem was to change virtually overnight the habits he had formed over the years from his Manchester schooldays, Durham University and Northants without putting at risk his speed, rhythm and accuracy.

Tyson was put on a crash course and Alf Gover, the highly-rated coach who was travelling as a member of the Press party, was recruited to help. Fortunately, Tyson willingly co-operated and adapted to a shortened run with surprising ease. The results exceeded our expectations and after he was streamlined he had lost none of his pace and gained in accuracy. Frank and I had an excellent rapport and the natural understanding of two Northerners counted for much.

There is more to that final remark than the Northerner's natural independence of thought and sometimes feigned inability to understand his southern colleagues, especially in matters of humour. Leonard's essentially dry wit was not always understood, notably by Cowdrey and Compton on two particular occasions. And certainly the Australian Press did not know what to make of England's first professional captain at the earlier conferences with newspapermen on that tour – were his deadpan remarks to be taken seriously or was there a gently ironic smile hidden there, somewhere?

But the man who lists 'a sense of humour' as an essential in a touring captain rarely if ever did anything in a cricket match without a sense of purpose. Thus, in the fourth Test, at Adelaide, when Cowdrey played a couple of rash shots in the middle of an important fourth-wicket partnership with Compton, Leonard sent out the twelfth man, Vic Wilson, with a couple of bananas from a bowl of fruit in the dressing-room. 'What are they for?' demanded a mystified Cowdrey when Wilson reached the middle. 'The skipper thought you might be hungry after seeing those two shot from you just now,' replied Vic. 'I think he wants you to stay here and get your head down.'

Hutton quietly explained later: 'I thought it might make a bigger impact than the usual ploy of changing a bat or gloves.' There was more than a touch of the psychologist in Hutton's approach to captaincy. And while he was a Northerner to his fingertips, the North-South divide played no part in his attitude to players. Of the two young public school and Oxbridge men in his party he said, 'I hope the deeds of May and Cowdrey will never be overlooked in assessing England's triumphs in Sydney and Melbourne. Without their quite brilliant batting, a base would not have been set up for Tyson's dramatic assaults.'

AUSTRALIA v. ENGLAND
Melbourne, 1955

ENGLAND

First Innings			*Second Innings*	
Hutton c Hole b Miller	12		lbw B Archer	42
Edrich c Lindwall b Miller	4		b Johnston	13
May c Benaud b Lindwall	0		b Johnston	91
Cowdrey b Johnson	102		b Benaud	7
Compton c Harvey b Miller	4		c Maddocks b Archer	23
Bailey c Maddocks b Johnston	30		not out	24
Evans lbw b Archer	20		c Maddocks b Miller	22
Wardle b Archer	0		b Johnson	38
Tyson b Archer	6		c Harvey b Johnston	6
Statham b Archer	3		c Favell b Johnston	0
Appleyard not out	1		b Johnston	6
Extras (b9)	9		*Extras* (b2 lb4 wl)	7
	Total	191		Total 279

Bowling: Lindwall 13–0–59–1; Miller 11–8–14–3; Archer 13.6–4–33–4; Benaud 7–0–30–0; Johnston 12–6–26–1; Johnson 11–3–20–1

Bowling: Lindwall 18–3–52–0; Miller 18–6–35–1; Archer 24–7–50–2; Benaud 8–2–25–1; Johnston 24.5–2–85–5; Johnson 8–2–25–1

AUSTRALIA

First Innings			*Second Innings*	
Favell lbw b Statham	25		b Appleyard	30
Morris lbw b Tyson	3		c Cowdrey b Tyson	4
Miller c Evans b Statham	7		(5) c Edrich b Tyson	6
Harvey b Appleyard	31		c Evans b Tyson	11
Hole b Tyson	11		(6) c Evans b Statham	5
Benaud c sub b Appleyard	15		(3) b Tyson	22
Archer b Wardle	23		b Statham	15
Maddocks c Evans b Statham	47		b Tyson	0
Lindwall b Statham	13		lbw b Tyson	0
Johnson not out	33		not out	4
Johnston b Statham	11		c Evans b Tyson	0
Extras (b7 lb3 nb2)	12		*Extras* (bl lb13)	14
	Total	231		Total 111

Bowling: Tyson 21–2–68–2; Statham 16.3–0–60–5; Bailey 9–1–33–0; Appleyard 11–3–38–2; Wardle 6–0–20–1

Bowling: Tyson 12.3–1–27–7; Statham 11–1–38–2; Bailey 3–0–14–0; Appleyard 4–1–17–1; Wardle 1–0–1–0

Moving on to New Zealand for the usual two Test matches after Australia, Hutton's tourists crushed the home country by eight wickets in the first Test to be played in Dunedin despite losing two complete days to rain and by an innings and 20 runs in Auckland where New Zealand were dismissed in their second innings for the lowest total in history – 26, of which Bert Sutcliffe made 11. England nevertheless (a little light-heartedly) used four bowlers: Tyson 7–2–10–2; Statham 9–3–9–3; Appleyard 6–3–7–4; Wardle 5–5–0–1. Hutton was England's top scorer with 53 in what was to be his last Test innings.

India to Pakistan
1955

Tour captain: M. H. Mankad

Dacca: *Match drawn*
Bahawalpur: *Match drawn*
Lahore (Bagh-i-Jinnah): *Match drawn*
Peshawar: *Match drawn*
Karachi: *Match drawn*

Returning the compliment of Pakistan's 1952 tour, India played a five-match series in November and December 1953, under the captaincy of Mulwantrai Himatlal Mankad whom I have never heard referred to in any other way than 'Vinoo' Mankad. In the 1950s he was probably as well-known in northern England as he was in his own country through playing league cricket with great success. A most talented and versatile cricketer, he took 162 Test wickets with his slow left-arm deliveries and could bat anywhere in the order – as he demonstrated on the first official tour to Pakistan undertaken by any country. In the first Test he went in at number 8, in the second at number 3, the third at number 8, the fourth at number 7 and in the last at number 5. Yet in previous series, to England and at home to Pakistan, he had been an opening batsman. His movements within Indian cricket were even more extensive than his movements around English league clubs and he played at one time or another for no fewer than eight different first-class sides in India. During the English summers of the 1950s he played a lot of Festival cricket in various 'Commonwealth' elevens and was an entertaining and attractive batsman as well as one of the leading spin bowlers in world cricket.

His tour to Pakistan was as much concerned with national prestige as establishing new Test cricket territory and all four drawn Tests were played with sternly defensive attitudes on both sides. At one point (fourth Test) the run-rate deteriorated to 1.61 an over and set the pattern for many Tests to follow in Pakistan and India.

Australia to West Indies
1955
Tour captain: I. W. Johnson

Jamaica: *Australia won by 9 wickets*
Trinidad: *Match drawn*
British Guiana: *Australia won by 8 wickets*
Barbados: *Match drawn*
Jamaica: *Australia won by an innings and 82 runs*

In the opinion of Ian Johnson, captain on this tour, it marked a turning point in Australian cricket. Purely on results this seems a strange view to take since the Aussies had so recently been beaten by Hutton's tourists to Australia and just over a year later they lost by two Tests to one, with two drawn, in England. Yet to win three matches in the West Indies and not to lose one in the five-Test series was a remarkable achievement, particularly as they had been 'assured' by their England visitors and their own Press that West Indies would be too strong for them, that they would be cheated by the umpires and regarded with hostility by the crowds. It was a very satisfied Johnson indeed who was able to comment at the end of the tour: 'We were *not* thrashed on the field, we had *no* trouble with the umpires and most certainly we were not hooted by the crowds. Quite the contrary. In fact we were accepted so well that I rate them the most wonderful people before whom I have ever played cricket.'

West Indian cricket was, in fact, developing in a somewhat strange manner. New and exciting batsmen were emerging all the time (O. G. 'Collie' Smith was the latest genius to appear in this series) but they were almost invariably middle-order players; a settled opening partnership had not yet been achieved and whereas one opening bowler was generally available, he rarely found a partner of comparable ability. Sobers was still only 18 years old, generally used as a fourth- or fifth-choice bowler and not yet revealing his immense potential as a batsman with any degree of consistency. And all the time, simmering just beneath the surface, was the political issue of the invariable choice of a white West Indian as the captain, and it was exacerbated by the appointment of Denis Atkinson as vice-captain in this series against Australia. The object of this was abundantly clear. Atkinson had already been named as captain of the modest-strength party to tour New Zealand and that was not due to take place for another 10 months. He was now being given a degree of experience in captaincy.

In the event, Atkinson was given very much more experience than he had expected because Jeff Stollmeyer (against whose experience as player *and* captain there could be no complaint although he was of European stock) injured a finger in practice and had to withdraw from the first Test. Atkinson was thus thrown in at the deep end and the Australians then listened with interest to the jibes of the ever-volatile Jamaicans directed not at them but the home captain, who was urged 'to get back to Barbados and peddle his insurance policies'. The overwhelming body of public opinion, and of the players themselves, was that the West Indies should have been led by Frank Worrell but the Board of Control was clearly not yet ready for the radical change from white to black captaincy. Johnson's tour was made to some extent easier by this dissension within the opposition ranks. In the first Test he injured a foot while batting and it was Miller who took over to lead Australia to victory by 10 wickets. While the rubber was won by a comfortable three-nil margin, the West Indies contributed some notable batting with Walcott (a leading figure in the 'Worrell for captaincy' lobby) twice scoring two centuries in a match – the second and fifth Tests. Johnson took on a lot of work as a bowler with 7 for 44 in Georgetown as his best return and more than once he scored good runs in the lower reaches of the batting order. It is interesting that despite the punishment he took from Clyde Walcott on that tour, he rated Everton Weekes as one of the best batsmen he ever bowled to.

Johnson was never going to be a darling of the Press; he was too lacking in what is known in modern journalism as 'charisma' but it is a fair bet that he enjoyed the respect of the contemporary newspapermen to a far greater extent than he would have done 30 years later. His style of captaincy would be classed as dour in the extreme by a 1980s writer and yet this is what Ian Johnson thought of Len Hutton:

He is dour by nature and suspicious of all opponents. That is not meant as a criticism of Len; it is merely his attitude to life. I respect him for it but I feel he tends to carry his intensity to play to win – an intensity with which I agree entirely on the field – far too much off the field so that he cannot relax. The Australian approach is 'The day's play is over, now let's enjoy ourselves.' Len never seemed able to do that. When one day's play ended he settled down to plan out the next and fraternisation with the opposition did not enter his scheme of things at all.

There is no doubt that Johnson, a highly intelligent and articulate man, thought deeply about all aspects of his cricket and he was a considerable student of character – particularly the English character! In the last analysis, however, he may be thought to have lacked the ruthless efficiency of a Bradman or a Chappell, the cricket brain of a Benaud or the endearing personal charm of a Hassett. Nevertheless, his place in history is secure: he took the first Australian side to the West Indies, and he won. Johnson's Test has to be the third, in British Guiana.

WEST INDIES v. AUSTRALIA
British Guiana, 1955

WEST INDIES

First Innings		Second Innings	
Holt c and b Miller	12	c Langley b Miller	6
Stollmeyer c Archer b Miller	16	c and b Johnson	17
Walcott c and b Archer	8	hit wkt b Lindwall·	73
Weekes c Archer b Benaud	81	c Langley b Johnson	0
Worrell c Johnson b Archer	9	hit wkt b Benaud	56
Sobers c Watson b Johnson	12	(8) b Johnson	11
Atkinson b Lindwall	13	st Langley b Johnson	16
Depeiza not out	16	(6) st Langley b Johnson	13
N. Marshall b Benaud	0	c sub b Johnson	8
Ramadhin c Archer b Benaud	0	st Langley b Johnson	2
King c Langley b Benaud	13	not out	0
Extras (bl lb1)	2	*Extras* (b1 lb2 nb2)	5
Total	182	Total	207

Bowling: Lindwall 12–0–44–1; Miller 9–1–33–2; Archer 10–0–46–2; Johnson 9–1–42–1; Benaud 3.5–1–15–4

Bowling: Lindwall 18–1–54–1; Miller 9–3–18–1; Archer 12–3–43–0; Johnson 22.2–10–44–7; Benaud 14–3–43–1

AUSTRALIA

First Innings		Second Innings	
McDonald b Atkinson	61	b Atkinson	31
Morris c Sobers b Atkinson	44	c Walcott b Marshall	38
Harvey c Holt b Ramadhin	38	not out	41
Watson c and b Ramadhin	6	not out	22
Miller c Depeiza b Sobers	33		
Benaud c sub b Marshall	68		
R. Archer st Depeiza b Sobers	2		
Johnson c Stollmeyer b Sobers	0		
Lindwall b Atkinson	2		
Langley not out	1		
Johnston absent hurt	0		
Extras (lb2)	2	*Extras* (nb 1)	1
Total	257	Total (for 2 wkts)	133

Bowling: King 12–1–37–0; Worrell 9–2–17–0; Ramadhin 26–9–55–2; Atkinson 37–13–85–3; Marshall 33.3–16–40–1; Stollmeyer 1–0–1–0; Sobers 16–10–20–3

Bowling: King 3–0–10–0; Worrell 7–2–20–0; Ramadhin 9–1–29–0; Atkinson 15.5–5–32–1; Marshall 13–6–22–1; Sobers 11–4–19–0

Johnson's figures were his best in Tests and he had in this particular game the problem of being a bowler short because of Bill Johnston's injury. He was, perhaps, fortunate in having the all-round ability of Benaud, Miller and Ron Archer in the side; on the other hand, he must take credit for skippering a side in which his role was that of a specialist bowler as opposed to an all-rounder. Few players of any country have done that successfully; very few, in fact, have been appointed.

3
FAREWELL TO HUTTON

South Africa to England
1955

Tour captain: J. E. Cheetham (D. J. McGlew)

Trent Bridge: *England won by an innings and 5 runs*
Lord's: *England won by 71 runs*
Old Trafford: *South Africa won by 3 wickets*
Headingley: *South Africa won by 224 runs*
The Oval: *England won by 92 runs*

Jack Cheetham returned to England at the head of a South African team with, for the first time, a pair of genuinely quick and hostile opening bowlers. In fact, Neil Adcock and Peter Heine would probably be rated, by men who faced them, as one of the more aggressive partnerships in the history of the game. It was a mixed season for captains because Hutton, who had been named as England's leader for the series, scored a brilliant 194 for Yorkshire against Notts at Trent Bridge, moved on for the next game at Bournemouth and woke up on the first morning of the game crippled by back trouble which had haunted him for 16 years. Lumbago had been followed by arthritis and in the 1955 season he was taking up to 16 painkilling pills a day. Nevertheless, he soldiered on, looking forward to skippering England against South Africa for the first time and going on tour to that country the following winter. Sadly, he returned to Leeds from Bournemouth, was put into a plaster cast and announced his retirement from the game.

He was still not 40 and he handed over the marshal's baton to Peter May with this tribute from Cardus:

As Old Masters go, Hutton was young enough; the sadness is that physical disability put an end to his career in his prime . . . As a captain he was shrewd but courteous; he knew the game's finer points and though he was unlikely to give anything away [he] was too proud to take anything not his due. Sometimes he may have turned thoughtfulness to worry but this is a natural habit in the part of the world which Hutton comes from. He certainly showed that a professional cricketer can wear the robes of leadership with dignity. At first, no doubt, he appeared at the head of his troops not wearing anything like a Caesarian toga but rather the uniform of a sergeant-major but he moved up in rank and prestige until he became worthy of his command.

So one great captain retired and another who was to achieve greatness took over. By a huge coincidence, Cheetham chipped an elbow during the second Test at Lord's where England went two up in the series. Jackie McGlew took over at Old Trafford and began his captaincy with a win in one of the most dramatic Tests I personally have ever seen. McGlew's captaincy will be reviewed in more detail in due course but it must be recorded that his team won both Tests in the summer of 1955 when he led South Africa. Destiny was to deal less kindly with Cheetham who returned from injury at The Oval in time to see Laker and Lock, at the very height of their powers, find a pitch to suit them in the ground they knew best. The result was a 3–2 win for England in the rubber which produced five definite results for the first time in this country. The summer saw two notable retirements from Test cricket, in addition to Hutton's. Alec Bedser played his 51st and last match at Old Trafford and Frank Chester stood as a Test umpire for the last time in the Headingley match.

Since umpiring will play a more prominent part in our story during later chapters, it is worth noting at this point that Chester was universally regarded as the best in the world for much – most certainly the postwar years – of a career which had begun during the first Test against South Africa in 1924! Chester, an all-rounder with Worcestershire between 1912 and 1914, lost an arm in the Great War and stood for 31 years (interrupted, of course, by the Second World War).

For most of his career he was a member of a profession in which the cult of personality had not yet developed. There were no television close-ups to cast doubts upon umpiring decisions, no intense Press scrutiny, no ostentatious dissent by players. It was an era in which mutual respect between practitioners and adjudicators held together the dignity and discipline of the game and no one was more highly respected amongst the practitioners than Frank Chester. It is difficult to believe, of course, that he never made a mistake but his reputation clearly rested on the fact that in the eyes of those who played at that time he made fewer mistakes than anyone else. As players began to write autobiographical books and memoirs, tributes to the accuracy and fairness of Chester became more frequent and thus were brought home to a wider public who had been accustomed to taking judicial accuracy for granted, certainly at Test level. Even though Bradman and his 1948 team thought him 'theatrical and egocentric', Frank Chester's name is still respected as a monument to impartiality.

New Zealand to Pakistan and India
1955–6
Tour captain: H. B. Cave

Karachi: *Pakistan won by an innings and 1 run*
Lahore: *Pakistan won by 4 wickets*
Dacca: *Match drawn*

Hyderabad: *Match drawn*
Bombay: *India won by an innings and 27 runs*
Delhi: *Match drawn*
Calcutta: *Match drawn*
Madras: *India won by an innings and 109 runs*

The first double tour to the Indian sub-continent was undertaken by a
New Zealand party under the leadership of a man who was a specialist
bowler, though a highly respected figure in New Zealand cricket, Henry
Butler Cave, who found (as others had done and more were to do in
the future) that tour leadership is particularly difficult when it is combined with the duties of heading the attack. All-rounders have proved
to be some of the most successful captains – Benaud, Illingworth, Close,
Hammond, Worrell, although the two latter might more accurately be
described as outstanding batsmen who were more-than-useful bowlers
– but fast or medium-fast bowlers who were *not* batsmen have rarely
been on consistently winning sides.

Harry Cave, a tall, pleasant and thoughtful cricketer, started this long
and difficult tour – few good hotels, long journeys on slow, dusty trains
– at number 7 in the batting order, perhaps in an effort to convince
himself that he possessed an all-rounder's qualities, but after being
bowled for 0 quickly retreated to a more realistic position. He had to
open the bowling a lot of the time, though occasionally he relegated
himself to third and even fourth seamer. Along with his more seasoned
players like Sutcliffe, Hayes and Reid, he had to nurse a group of
inexperienced men and no fewer than six new caps were introduced
during the first leg of the tour. Cave saw Sutcliffe and Reid enhance
their reputations with some big scores but his bowlers suffered heavy
punishment, notably at the hands of Imtiaz Ahmed (Lahore), 'Polly'
Umrigar (Hyderabad) and Mankad (Bombay and Madras) who all
scored double centuries.

West Indies to New Zealand
1956

Tour captain: D. St. E. Atkinson

Dunedin: *West Indies won by an innings and 71 runs*
Christchurch: *West Indies won by an innings and 64 runs*
Wellington: *West Indies won by 9 wickets*
Auckland: *New Zealand won by 190 runs*

Denis St Eval Atkinson, as we have seen, was a controversial selection in some West Indian eyes as captain on this tour and there is a tendency amongst those critics to forget the first three Tests of the series which brought huge wins by the tourists and to linger on the fact that the fourth and final match saw New Zealand score their first victory in any official Test. No one, in fact, could have fought harder to prevent it than the skipper whose 28 at Eden Park was his side's second highest score in a total of 145 while he took seven wickets for 53 in New Zealand's second innings. Atkinson was a much-better-than-average batsman in the middle order and he bowled off-breaks and cutters at a brisk medium pace. He was a good friend and hospitable host to many English cricketers and visitors to Barbados.

Australia to England
1956

Tour captain: I. W. Johnson

Trent Bridge: *Match drawn*
Lord's: *Australia won by 185 runs*
Headingley: *England won by an innings and 42 runs*
Old Trafford: *England won by an innings and 170 runs*
The Oval: *Match drawn*

Ian Johnson's 1956 tourists were unlucky to the extent that it was a wet and miserable summer and produced pitches of the type they particularly disliked. They were unfortunate, too, in that their three spinners – Wilson (slow left-arm), Benaud (leg spin) and Johnson himself with off-breaks – did not perform as well as England's bowlers, though that would have been difficult in view of Laker's phenomenal success, especially at Old Trafford, where he took 19 wickets for 90 runs. And they suffered most of all because their batsmen for the most part were out of touch in the series as a whole. Lindwall, at 34, was not at his best but Miller, approaching 37, bowled his heart out in a way which excited the admiration of his captain in the second Test, at Lord's, which the Australians won: 'I asked a lot of Keith in that match, more by far than any captain is entitled to ask of a player. He gave it to me in much larger quantities than I expected, let alone was entitled to receive.'

Going to Headingley one up in the rubber, Johnson felt that if he had won the toss and batted first the result would have gone the other way. A calculated risk was taken by the three tour selectors (Langley, the wicket-keeper, Miller and the captain) to play Miller simply as a batsman because he had a knee injury, though Johnson secretly hoped that the all-rounder might decide to risk bowling once the game was under way. In fact, as Australia took the field, Johnson asked Miller if he would like to try an over or two but the refusal was firm. If it had been a deciding match, Miller might well have given it a go but they were one up and it seemed to him foolish to take a chance when he might be more urgently needed at a later stage of the tour. When England were 17 for 3 after an hour's play (Archer, who had opened the bowling in place of Miller, had taken all three) it seemed that the gamble had succeeded; but May was now joined by Cyril Washbrook who had been persuaded, at the age of 41, to return to Test cricket after a five-year absence.

May and Washbrook put on 187 for the fourth wicket and according to Johnson the wicket broke up completely after tea on the second day. 'It was the worst wicket we had in the Tests, wet ones included,' he claimed. Laker and Lock bowled out Australia twice between long interruptions for rain, and so the teams met at Old Trafford with the rubber all square.

Enough has been written elsewhere about Laker's astonishing performance but apart from Johnson's lamentations on losing the toss yet again, it is interesting to consider his comment on the pitch: 'My own guess is that the groundsman was asked to prepare a pitch which would take spin in the later stages. This he set out to do but inadvertently went too far and the pitch broke up too early. This just goes to show that we should not tamper with wickets. The ideal, surely, is to prepare a good, hard, fast surface and let nature take its course.'

Johnson, by his own definition, was an off-spinner who relied as much, if not more, on flight as opposed to turn and so it was a particular embarrassment to have figures of 4 for 151 in the Test compared with Laker's 19 for 90. He claimed that 'Laker's two short legs were the secret of his success', which seems a fairly superficial view of the most remarkable spell of bowling in Test history. Most contemporary experts take the view that pin-point accuracy, allied to an ability to spin the ball on good wickets, were the reasons why Laker was able to *employ* those two short legs and that seems to put things in the right order.

The plain fact is that by 1956 Laker had become a master bowler after ten thoughtful years in first-class cricket and quite apart from not liking the weather or the pitches, the Australians had the bowler very much on their minds. His 10 for 44 for Surrey against the tourists earlier in the season had seen to that.

Despite all his disappointments, Johnson's verdict on the tour was that the spirit on the field between the two sides was as good as it should be. 'Tough? Yes, but mean? Decidedly not.'

Australia to Pakistan and India
1956–7
Tour captain: I. W. Johnson (R. R. Lindwall)

Karachi: *Pakistan won by 9 wickets*

Madras: *Australia won by an innings and 5 runs*
Bombay: *Match drawn*
Calcutta: *Australia won by 94 runs*

This tour enabled Johnson to complete his captaincy career with Australia on a winning note, although the inaugural Test between the two sides, in Karachi, produced a shock first day in which only 95 runs were scored on the matting wicket – 80 all out by the tourists, 15 for 2 by Pakistan. Australia's first Test in India, however, was won and the captain shared with Pat Crawford a record ninth-wicket partnership.

England to South Africa
1956–7
Tour captain: P. B. H. May

Johannesburg (New Wanderers): *England won by an innings and 131 runs*
Cape Town: *England won by 312 runs*
Durban: *Match drawn*
Johannesburg: *South Africa won by 17 runs*
Port Elizabeth: *South Africa won by 58 runs*

Leading England abroad for the first time, Peter May had a disappointing tour if it is viewed simply in the context of his own batting in the drawn Test series. He was the outstanding batsman of his generation and remains, arguably, England's most gifted postwar batsman. A prodigy at Charterhouse where he headed the school's batting averages when only 14, he hit a superb 146 for Public Schools v. Combined Services at Lord's when he was 17, had three years of rapid development at Cambridge and made his debut for Surrey in 1950, followed by his first England cap in 1951 when he made 138 on his debut against South Africa at Headingley.

May's reputation has been handed down as that of a 'tough' Test captain which at first glance seems a trifle incongruous in a man of great personal charm and courtesy who has always seemed rather boyishly shy. Indeed when Press criticism – at least that of the most crude and vulgar nature – of his chairmanship of Test selection became intense in 1988, his distaste for being in the public gaze was obvious.

We shall look at this period in more detail in a later chapter but it was painfully clear that May had pursued his career in a different age in which dignity and good manners played a very much more prominent part than was the case 30 years later. It was, I have to confess, something of a surprise to hear May tell me, 'I enjoyed handling people,' but an elaboration of the point followed immediately: 'I didn't have to go to players who arrived for a Test and ask, "Are you fit?" I *knew* they were fit. I have been amazed in recent years [this said in 1989] at the number of players who came to Tests who were *not* fit.' 'Amazed' is a pretty strong word for Peter May to use; he is not given to hyperbole. It went a long way to explaining the air of faint bewilderment which seemed to linger permanently about him during the later, controversial days of his selection chairmanship.

'Loyalty' is an oft-used word in his vocabulary. Loyalty of his players to each other and to the side was always of paramount importance to him and his attitude to all teams he skippered was to take it for granted that they had all 'done their nuts and bolts' and merited the professional respect of their captain. 'The main thing was not to be concerned with who got the runs or took the wickets so long as we won. I tried to remember that everyone is an individual and needs to be regarded as different from everyone else in one way or another. Yes, I enjoyed handling people in my sides. You have to remember that I usually had a pretty good one.'

What about his reputation for toughness? 'I insisted upon certain standards in practice, in play and in behaviour. I don't think that is necessarily to be classed as being "tough". Surely it is simply standard practice?'

P. B. H. May played in 66 Tests and led England in 41 of them, including tours to South Africa, Australia and New Zealand. They were largely successful years for England and, 30 years on, loyalty is still an important word to him. At no time have I ever heard him utter an uncharitable word about the men he played with and against.

His South African tour of 1956–7 saw May have a relatively unsuccessful series in which he only topped 50 in one innings and the cricket in all five games fell some way short of the inspiring. Batting was 'cautious' on both sides with May no doubt anxious to avoid mistakes and his opposite number in a difficult position. Jackie McGlew had been appointed as South Africa's captain for the rubber but before the first Test had to withdraw because of a shoulder injury. Clive van Ryneveld took over as captain – an old adversary of May's for Oxford v. Cambridge and a notable all-round sportsman – then gave way when McGlew was able to play at Newlands. In that second Test, however, McGlew again experienced shoulder trouble and did not play again that summer while undergoing surgery. Van Ryneveld was thus left as a locum captain and was equally anxious to avoid defeat, if possible. The result was, according to Jim Laker, 'the worst series of Test matches in which I have ever played'. The pitches were slow and much of the bowling on both sides was of a negative nature. Indeed in the two Trevors – Bailey of England and Goddard of South Africa – each team had an outstanding specialist in negative bowling and both were heavily employed during the rubber in that particular role.

The series also included the first dismissal for 'handled the ball' in Test cricket – Russell Endean was the batsman.

It is interesting that May chooses as a favourite Test one in which he was not captain – the Second, in Sydney, during Hutton's 1954–5 tour to Australia – but it is equally interesting that his reason for choosing this match indicates just how he viewed matters with a shrewd tactical eye: 'After the disaster of Brisbane, where Tyson had not been at all effective, Australia had to make 222 to win in Sydney. An off-side field was set and Frank was instructed to bowl at the off stump. He did so at very great pace and in fact he hit the off stump three or four times. And Brian Statham gave him ideal support into a strong wind.' May omitted to mention his own second innings century, or his partnership of 116 with Cowdrey, which earned the admiration of their experienced captain.

AUSTRALIA v. ENGLAND

Sydney, 1954-5

ENGLAND

First Innings			Second Innings	
Hutton c Davidson b Johnston	30		c Benaud b Johnston	28
Bailey b Lindwall	0		c Langley b Archer	6
May c Johnston b Archer	5		b Lindwall	104
Graveney c Favell b Johnston	21		c Langley b Johnston	0
Cowdrey c Langley b Davidson	23		c Archer b Benaud	54
Edrich c Benaud b Archer	10		b Archer	29
Tyson b Lindwall	0		b Lindwall	9
Evans c Langley b Archer	3		c Lindwall b Archer	4
Wardle c Burke b Johnston	35		lbw b Lindwall	8
Appleyard c Hole b Davidson	8		not out	19
Statham not out	14		c Langley b Johnston	25
Extras (lb5)	5		*Extras* (lb6 nb4)	10
Total	154		Total	296

Bowling: Lindwall 17-3-47-2; Archer 12-7-12-3; Davidson 12-3-34-2; Johnston 13.3-1-36-3

Bowling: Lindwall 31-10-69-3; Archer 22-9-53-3; Davidson 13-2-52-0; Johnston 19.3-2-70-3; Benaud 19-3-42-1

AUSTRALIA

First Innings			Second Innings	
Favell c Graveney b Bailey	26		c Edrich b Tyson	16
Morris c Hutton b Bailey	12		lbw b Statham	10
Burke c Graveney b Bailey	44		b Tyson	14
Harvey c Cowdrey b Tyson	12		not out	92
Hole b Tyson	12		b Tyson	0
Benaud lbw b Statham	20		c Tyson b Appleyard	12
Archer c Hutton b Tyson	49		b Tyson	6
Davidson b Statham	20		c Evans b Statham	5
Lindwall c Evans b Tyson	19		b Tyson	8
Langley b Bailey	5		b Statham	0
Johnston not out	0		c Evans b Tyson	11
Extras (b5 lb2 nb2)	9		*Extras* (lb7 nb3)	10
Total	228		Total	184

Bowling: Statham 18-1-83-2; Bailey 17.4-3-59-4; Tyson 13-2-45-4; Appleyard 7-2-32-0

Bowling: Statham 19-6-45-3; Bailey 6-0-21-0; Tyson 18.4-1-85-6; Appleyard 6-1-12-1; Wardle 4-2-11-0

West Indies to England
1957
Tour captain: J. D. C. Goddard

Edgbaston: *Match drawn*
Lord's: *England won by an innings and 36 runs*
Trent Bridge: *Match drawn*
Headingley: *England won by an innings and 5 runs*
The Oval: *England won by an innings and 237 runs*

John Goddard completed his 22 Tests as captain of the West Indies on a downbeat note when influenza prevented him from completing the final match of the series in which England won three Tests handsomely and the West Indies none. This was due in part to a fairly modest performance by the three Ws and to the eclipse (after the first Test innings of the series) of Ramadhin and Valentine. Without Rae and Stollmeyer, the tourists were still struggling to find an effective opening partnership and tried no fewer than five different permutations in ten innings.

Ramadhin took 7 for 49 in the first Test and the England team then sat down and worked out a tactical plan for playing him. It involved, in the main, treating him as an off-spinner and playing him outside the off stump with the pads as much as possible. In the second innings, the little Trinidadian took two of the first three wickets to fall and then, in his own words, he was '*kicked* out of the game by May and Cowdrey'. May, 285 not out, and Cowdrey 154, put together 411 for the fourth wicket and Ramadhin (98–35–179–2) was never the same threat again. Meanwhile, the clamour for an end to 'white' captaincy was growing back home, particularly in Trinidad where the campaign was led by the most distinguished of all West Indian writers, C. L. R. James.

Australia to South Africa
1957–8
Tour captain: I. D. Craig

Johannesburg: *Match drawn*
Cape Town: *Australia won by an innings and 141 runs*
Durban: *Match drawn*
Johannesburg: *Australia won by 10 wickets*
Port Elizabeth: *Australia won by 8 wickets*

Ian David Craig was only 17 years old when the Australian selectors sent him on the 1953 tour to England. He averaged a modest 16.5 with the bat and did not play in any of the Tests. He came back in 1956, averaging 36.33 in 20 matches and played a noteworthy innings of 38 against Laker at Old Trafford. From the first, he was clearly in the minds of the selectors – both for New South Wales and Australia – as 'captaincy material'.

Craig had a first-class double century to his name before he was 18 – and against the touring South Africans of 1952–3, too, which earned him his first Test cap – and his potential as a batsman was obvious from the first. Somehow, it was never fulfilled. Nevertheless, for five years he was quietly groomed as a captain of Australia and when he led a side to New Zealand in the 1956–7 antipodean summer he had noticeably built up a good team spirit even though he was only 21. Still, a few eyebrows were raised around the world when he was appointed tour captain for the visit to South Africa the following winter with a side which included experienced players like Harvey, McDonald, Burke, Mackay and two men destined to become outstanding captains – Richie Benaud and Bobby Simpson, who made his Test debut in the first Test, in Johannesburg. It was a series marked by much aggressive, short-pitched bowling by Adcock and Heine who felled a number of Australian batsmen. In such circumstances morale in a touring side can easily be damaged. Writing reflectively, years later, Benaud admired the way it had been sustained. These were the only Tests in which Craig captained Australia. His career was cut short by ill-health and it may be that we did not see the best of him.

Pakistan to West Indies
1958
Tour captain: A. H. Kardar

Barbados: *Match drawn*
Trinidad: *West Indies won by 120 runs*
Jamaica: *West Indies won by an innings and 174 runs*
British Guiana: *West Indies won by 8 wickets*
Trinidad: *Pakistan won by an innings and 1 run*

This series completed Abdul Hafeez Kardar's leadership of his country in its first 23 Tests and he ended on a high with Pakistan's first win over West Indies in the final match of the rubber. It was a historic series in a number of ways. In the first Test, Hanif Mohammad surpassed Hutton's record of the longest innings (1938) by batting for 16 hours 10 minutes for his 337; in the third Test, Garfield Sobers passed Hutton's record Test score (364) by one run before the new West Indies captain, Gerry Alexander, declared. It was Sobers' first three-figure innings in Tests. In the first of the two Trinidad Tests, Fazal Mahmood bowled a total of 101 overs and at Kingston, Jamaica, he bowled 85.2 overs in one innings.

New Zealand to England
1958
Tour captain: J. R. Reid

Edgbaston: *England won by 205 runs*
Lord's: *England won by an innings and 148 runs*
Headingley: *England won by an innings and 71 runs*
Old Trafford: *England won by an innings and 13 runs*
The Oval: *Match drawn*

Although the results of New Zealand's first five-match series of five-day Tests in England were nothing short of disastrous, John Richard Reid was destined to become the outstanding all-round cricketer the country produced until the arrival of Richard Hadlee. He was, in fact, more versatile in that apart from being an aggressive middle-order batsman he could open the bowling with seamers, switch to off-spinners and, when required, he could be an accomplished wicket-keeper. He was a highly popular figure in league cricket in Lancashire where he was a renowned big-hitter. In New Zealand's domestic first-class season he once hit 15 sixes in an innings for Wellington.

He was probably the most combative and competitive cricketer New Zealand has ever produced, describing himself with modest inaccuracy as a 'rough bugger'. He saw his main task as a tour captain as 'keeping 16 assorted personalities happy' and rated as one of his favourite opponents the West Indian spin bowler Ramadhin: 'I could never pick him until I played against him for Heywood in the Central Lancashire League and that was when I decided to play him as an off-spinner.' (May, Cowdrey and England had got it right in 1957.) He admired Ted Dexter for his brisk approach to Test cricket and his immense natural ability and had a great personal liking for Peter May. This was probably tinged with gratitude for, as he once confided to me: 'I stayed with Peter during a weekend at a time when I was having a bad run in 1965 and he asked what the problem was. I told him I just didn't know but I couldn't see where my next run was coming from. Peter said, "When I get into that sort of trot I try to hit the stumps at the other end with every shot I play." So in the next match, against Kent at Maidstone, I hit the stumps five times and scored 165.'

Reid paused for a moment, then added, 'I don't know why I mentioned that. I've never told anybody before.'

He batted against most of the great bowlers of the world in his era and bowled against most of the great batsmen in his 58 Tests but regretted not having the chance to tour West Indies. He had the immense

satisfaction, however, of skippering his country when the first-ever
Test victory was achieved, despite the gallant resistance of the tourists'
captain, Denis Atkinson, in Auckland in 1956. It had taken New Zealand 26 years (and 45 Tests) to taste victory for the first time and that
series was Reid's first experience of Test captaincy. He had taken over
from Harry Cave after the first of the four Tests of 1956, the start of
a record run of 34 Tests in that role.

How does Reid justify his claim to have been a 'rough bugger' of a
captain? He had a more colourful turn of phrase than many of his
predecessors (and successors), it is true. It is equally true that he was
known, on occasions, to change the bowling with the comment, 'Piss
off down to long leg; I can do better myself.' But his players knew there
was no malice in such comments and they were not to be taken too
seriously. It was Reid's way – a way which commanded the respect of
his side.

For a choice of a favourite Test, he is torn between the initial win
over West Indies and New Zealand's first win against South Africa, at
Newlands in January 1961, a match in which he played a notable part
as a batsman, made one telling intervention as a bowler and made two
tactical decisions on which the result hinged.

SOUTH AFRICA v. NEW ZEALAND

Newlands, Cape Town, 1961

NEW ZEALAND

First Innings		*Second Innings*	
McGregor b Burke	68	run out	20
Dowling lbw b Lawrence	0	c Barlow b Burke	12
Sparling c Elgie b Burke	19	c Waite b Burke	9
Reid c Bromfield b McKinnon	92	c Bromfield b Burke	14
Harris st Waite b Bromfield	101	c Bland b Burke	30
Chapple c Waite b Burke	69	b Burke	33
Dick c Waite b Burke	4	(8) not out	50
Bartlett c Waite b Burke	12	(7) st Waite b McKinnon	29
Motz b Burke	0	c Barlow b Bromfield	0
Alabaster c Farrer b Bromfield	1	st Waite b McKinnon	4
Cameron not out	2	not out	10
Extras (lb8 nb9)	17	Extras (b1)	1
Total	385	Total (9 wkts declared)	212

Bowling: Burke 53.5–19–128–6; Lawrence 23–7–46–1; McKinnon 19–6–42–1; Barlow 9–0–40–0; Bromfield 46–11–94–2; Elgie 7–2–18–0

Bowling: Burke 27.1–10–68–5; Barlow 20–2–53–0; McKinnon 17–7–32–2; Bromfield 24–3–58–1

SOUTH AFRICA

First Innings

McGlew c Barlett b Motz	14
Barlow c Harris b Alabaster	51
Farrer c Dick b Alabaster	11
Waite c Chapple b Cameron	33
McLean c Dick b Cameron	20
Bland b Alabaster	32
Elgie c Chapple b Alabaster	6
Burke c Dick b Cameron	0
Lawrence c Reid b Cameron	4
McKinnon not out	9
Bromfield lbw b Cameron	1
Extras (b6 lb2 nb1)	9
Total	190

Bowling: Motz 11–2–30–1; Cameron 24.4–10–48–5; Alabaster 21–4–61–4; Bartlett 5–1–17–0; Sparling 6–1–22–0; Chapple 1–0–3–0

Second Innings

c Dick Bartlett	63
c Reid b Alabaster	16
c Dowling b Alabaster	20
lbw b Alabaster	21
c Harris b Bartlett	113
lbw b Reid	42
c Harris b Cameron	12
c Motz b Sparling	12
c Harris b Reid	0
b Alabaster	4
not out	0
Extras (b14 lb13 w4 nb1)	32
Total	335

Bowling: Motz 24–9–69–0; Cameron 26–14–42–1; Alabaster 50–12–119–4; Bartlett 22–8–40–2; Sparling 6–3–12–1; Reid 14–2–8–21–2

West Indies to India and Pakistan
1958–9
Tour captain: F. C. M. Alexander

Bombay: *Match drawn*
Kanpur: *West Indies won by 203 runs*
Calcutta: *West Indies won by an innings and 336 runs*
Madras: *West Indies won by 295 runs*
Delhi: *Match drawn*

Franz Copeland Murray Alexander, known universally as Gerry, had succeeded uneasily to the West Indies' captaincy ten months earlier with cricketing storm-clouds gathering. The issue of a white or black captain of the Caribbean side was in step with a rising tide of nationalism and claims for the right of self-government in the colonies, particularly in Trinidad, and the loudest voice was still that of C. L. R. James, who wanted to see Frank Worrell as captain.

This was to reach its high point a little later, but Alexander fuelled the fires of discontent by sending home from India the fiery character of Roy Gilchrist after a personal disagreement between the two and although West Indies won the series with great ease after some prolific scoring the captain returned home to find himself in the midst of more blazing controversy.

Gilchrist, let it be said, was an excessively volatile character much given to intimidatory bowling in the northern leagues of England. He was regularly involved in on-the-field trouble and in one of his more spectacular adventures pulled out a stump to do battle with an Australian professional in a Central Lancashire League game in which the Aussie objected to Gilchrist's bowling of beamers. The Alexander–Gilchrist row centred on the bowling of beamers.

Gilchrist was not a popular figure in English cricketing circles by any means. Apart from his notoriety in the leagues as a bowler of very fast, head-high deliveries (of the non-bouncing variety) he incurred the wrath of none other than F. S. Trueman during the fourth Test at Headingley in 1957. Trueman threatened dire retribution and was bent on exacting it when Peter Loader polished off the first West Indian innings with a hat-trick. Gilchrist was the third victim. And the spinners were operating when Gilchrist batted in the second innings. Gilchrist's enforced return from India, therefore, was noted with a certain satisfaction in this country. That was altogether all-too-simplistic to West Indian eyes as Trevor McDonald, ITN newscaster and biographer of Clive Lloyd 27 years later, observed: 'Gilchrist was a wiry young man with a fiery temper. He had been brought up in rural Jamaica. He might have found it difficult to accept the decisions of any captain, but many people writing at the time saw the affair as a clash between "plebeian" Gilchrist and the light-skinned Cambridge graduate, Alexander.' Racial issues were plainly involved before Alexander had held the captaincy for a year. Nevertheless, Gilchrist returned home and Alexander stayed in charge as the tour moved on to Pakistan.

Karachi: *Pakistan won by 10 wickets*
Dacca: *Pakistan won by 41 runs*
Lahore: *West Indies won by an innings and 156 runs*

Alexander had none of the three Ws available in his party but Sobers (who batted magnificently in India), Kanhai, Butcher, Collie Smith and Joe Solomon still represented formidable strength in the middle order and the two defeats were attributable largely to superb bowling by Fazal Mahmood, leading Pakistan for the first time. Thus the sides were captained by a wicket-keeper and a specialist fast bowler, neither of them combinations which have been outstandingly successful in cricket history. Alexander shunted himself up and down the batting order (numbers 8, 4, 2, 1) in an effort to lead by example and achieve some consistency. A little respectability was restored by victory in Lahore where a 15-year-old boy, destined to become a Pakistan skipper, made his Test debut – Mushtaq Mohammad.

Despite all the fulminations of nationalist-minded writers and orators, Alexander retained the captaincy for the West Indies' next home series but the agitation against him had to have some bearing on the troubled nature of part of England's tour. And the selectors still picked him as wicket-keeper with West Indies to Australia in 1960–1 but now he served under Frank Worrell. The dynasty of 'light-skinned' captains had come to an end; C. L. R. James, who had fought the good fight, was able to lay down his pen – on that issue at least.

England to Australia and New Zealand
1958–9
Tour captain: P. B. H. May

Brisbane: *Australia won by 8 wickets*
Melbourne: *Australia won by 8 wickets*
Sydney: *Match drawn*
Adelaide: *Australia won by 10 wickets*
Melbourne: *Australia won by 9 wickets*

Christchurch: *England won by an innings and 90 runs*
Auckland: *Match drawn*

Peter May's tour, with Freddie Brown as manager, was an unfortunate one, plagued by injuries, controversies and, at times, sagging morale and, of course, the results amounted to comprehensive defeat. Even before the tour began the signs were inauspicious. Johnny Wardle, the Yorkshire slow left-arm bowler who was selected as a member of the party, was involved in a dispute with his county and a series of articles written by him in the *Daily Mail* led to his invitation to tour being withdrawn by M C C. Jim Laker, the Surrey off-spinner, was involved in a dispute with his county (and tour) captain and refused to join the party until a compromise was reached. Even so he went on tour with a certain reluctance and was at odds not only with his captain but the manager as well. Yet he topped the tour bowling averages despite the Australians' resolve to 'get after him' following their humiliations in England in 1956. With Tyson now over the hill, the fast bowling burden fell on Trueman (back in favour again), Statham and Loader but the two latter players missed the final Test after being involved in a car accident. And on top of all this England were chronically short of a settled opening partnership to their batting. May led from the front with 1,512 tour runs and was well supported in the Tests by Cowdrey but there was a running controversy concerning the suspect bowling action of Meckiff (whose 6 for 38 was largely responsible for England's defeat in the second Test), of Burke (the opening batsman who was an occasional off-spinner), and of Slater (who played only in the third Test). In addition, Rorke, who made his debut in the fourth Test, had a pronounced drag (at a time when no-balls were judged on the position of the *back* foot at the moment of delivery) which in English eyes meant he was bowling off about 18 yards! Of the quality and legality of Benaud and Davidson, the two leading wicket-takers, however, there could be no complaint.

An interesting sidelight on the 'chucking' controversy was provided for the author 30 years later by Keith Slater, the Western Australian, who also played in Lancashire League cricket. 'When I next visited Adelaide,' he told me, 'I was invited to dinner by (Sir) Don Bradman and after the meal he set up his cinematograph equipment and showed the actions of all the leading bowlers in the world. I didn't class myself amongst them, of course, but he had shots of my action as well and he pointed out all too clearly what the fuss was about.'

Controversy extended to English criticism of the Australian umpires and in just about every way this was an unhappy tour. The first Test of the series was the first one to be televised in Australia and Trevor Bailey indulged his highly individual sense of cricketing humour by compiling the slowest 50 in cricket history – three minutes short of six hours – for the benefit of viewers!

As ever, the tour became a more pleasant and relaxed affair when the party reached New Zealand where Ted Dexter scored his first century for England and Trueman took his 100th wicket in his 25th Test.

India in England
1959
Tour captain: D. K. Gaekwad (P. Roy)

Trent Bridge: *England won by an innings and 59 runs*
Lord's: *England won by 8 wickets*
Headingley: *England won by an innings and 173 runs*
Old Trafford: *England won by 171 runs*
The Oval: *England won by an innings and 27 runs*

To Dattajirao Krishnarao Gaekwad fell the unhappy distinction of skippering an Indian tour party which lost all five Tests – the first time England had enjoyed such a success. Gaekwad was an adequate player in Indian domestic cricket but rarely showed real class at the highest level. Consequently, he lacked stature and authority as a Test captain.

In a good, dry summer with plenty of sunshine the Indians topped 200 only three times in 10 Test innings with the batsmen plainly demoralised by the pace of Trueman and Statham, Alan Moss of Middlesex and Harold Rhodes of Derbyshire. In the first Test, Borde – one of the more experienced Indian batsmen – had a finger broken by a ball from Trueman, and in the second Test Statham fractured one of Nari Contractor's ribs. Fielding was often sloppily untidy and Gaekwad's only tactical weapon seemed to be to slow down play. Crowds, however, were entertained by some high-class leg-spin bowling by Subash Gupte. In the absence of May, who was undergoing surgery, England were captained for the first time by Colin Cowdrey at Old Trafford.

Australia to Pakistan and India
1959–60
Tour captain: R. Benaud

Dacca: *Australia won by 8 wickets*
Lahore: *Australia won by 7 wickets*
Karachi: *Match drawn*

Delhi: *Australia won by an innings and 127 runs*
Kanpur: *India won by 119 runs*
Bombay: *Match drawn*
Madras: *Australia won by an innings and 55 runs*
Calcutta: *Match drawn*

Richie Benaud is almost certainly better known to the modern generation of cricket followers as a television commentator than a player but history will rate him as one of the outstanding captains in the game. In the sense that he knew what he wanted and was determined to get it if it was humanly possible he could be rated as tough as Bradman or (later) Ian Chappell, but there were extra dimensions to Benaud. As a professional journalist he had a built-in sense of public relations; he knew instinctively what the media communicators wanted (even if he was not always prepared to give it!). He had, and has, a highly developed sense of humour and an acute understanding of human nature. Most important of all, he possessed a shrewder tactical sense than most captains. We see this immediately on his first tour as leader of an Australian side abroad.

His men arrived in Dacca (then the capital of East Pakistan, later the independent state of Bangladesh) expecting to play on a newly-laid turf wicket and were told immediately that because of heavy rainfall the pitch was not ready and the first. Test would have to be played on matting – a new experience for most of the tourists. The Australians were highly suspicious of this change as they observed a vast area of grass with only one bare patch – where the mat was to be laid!

Benaud put Pakistan in when he won the toss to give his batsmen a chance to see how the ball performed on matting and went into the game with four specialist bowlers and the intention of using the medium-pace seamers of 'Slasher' Mackay to complete the attack. Mackay was called upon to bowl 45 second-innings overs, took 6 for 42 and thus played a major part in Australia's first win in Pakistan.

'For the captain,' Benaud recalls, 'the unsung hero was Lindsay Kline (twelfth man) who went to the ground every morning well in advance of the main party to watch while the matting was laid and to make sure it was stretched as tightly as it was possible to make it, both lengthways and sideways.' Benaud knew the spells of eastern magic which could be woven on a mat with any trace of slackness or a wrinkle, however minute.

This attention to detail is something which occurs time and time again in Benaud's career as a captain and is highlighted in the Test he chooses as his favourite – Old Trafford in 1961, which we shall look at shortly. His views on captaincy (as expressed in his book *Benaud on Reflection* [published by Collins Willow 1984]) must, therefore, be looked at with the greatest respect:

I believe the man in charge of a cricket team, or any team, must have the conviction that he can, at the very least, do anything he sets out to do; on top of this he needs to believe that occasionally he can achieve the impossible. This will never come about without your players being one hundred per cent behind you, so one of the first things you must do is establish respect from those players. Likewise, you must have respect for them and an enormous amount of faith in them. All this adds up to the need for a good captain to have an air of tremendous confidence about him and that is one of the yardsticks for which I would look.

In addition, a captain must give visible signs of deriving pleasure from the game. It's no good – no matter what you're feeling or what might have gone wrong at home or at work before you set out for the ground – going round the field with a face as long as a wet week. It doesn't have to be contrived but it should be there – the impression of deriving pleasure from being out on the ground for six hours every day. It's not always easy because, in adverse circumstances, there is the temptation to grouse about things, no matter how sunny your personality might be. The temptation must be resisted.

As a journalist, Benaud naturally enough took more than a passing interest in what was written about his men and himself. On the dressing-room wall at Old Trafford in 1961 he pinned a cutting, relating to a previous match and headed 'Benaud for the Chop'. 'I looked at it for inspiration every time I came in or went out of the room,' he grinned, recalling a match which is still seared on the souls of a number of Englishmen who took part.

Let us jump ahead to that match at Old Trafford in 1961, Benaud's favourite Test memory. England achieved a lead of 177 on the first innings and although Australia batted much better in their second effort they were only 157 ahead on the last morning when their final pair, Davidson and McKenzie, came together. To the complete frustration of May and his bowlers, they added another 98 runs to give their side a glimmer of hope. Even so, with Subba Row resisting stubbornly and Dexter striking the ball brilliantly, England reached 150 for the loss of only one wicket. Benaud called for drinks he didn't really want and used the break for an impromptu conference with his team. There was general agreement that simply saving the match was out of the question; they had either to go boldly for a win or go tamely to defeat. Benaud went round the wicket with his leg-spinners, pitching into the bowlers' rough outside the leg stump – and the left-handers' (Subba Row and Close) *off* stump. He took 5 for 12 in 25 balls and England were beaten by 54 runs; Australia won the rubber by two Tests to one and so retained the Ashes. Small wonder that the Old Trafford match is remembered by Richie Benaud with such affection.

ENGLAND v. AUSTRALIA

Old Trafford, 1961

AUSTRALIA

First Innings			*Second Innings*	
Lawry lbw Statham	74		c Trueman b Allen	102
Simpson c Murray b Statham	4		c Murray b Flavell	51
Harvey c Subba Row b Statham	19		c Murray b Dexter	35
O'Neill hit wkt b Trueman	11		c Murray b Statham	67
Burge b Flavell	15		c Murray b Dexter	23
Booth c Close b Statham	46		lbw b Dexter	9
Mackay c Murray b Statham	11		c Close b Allen	18
Davidson c Barrington b Dexter	0		not out	77
Benaud b Dexter	2		lbw b Allen	1
Grout c Murray b Dexter	2		c Statham b Allen	0
McKenzie not out	1		b Flavell	32
Extras (b4 lb1)	5		*Extras* (b6 lb9 w2)	17
Total	190		Total	432

Bowling: Trueman 14–1–55–1; Statham 21–3–53–5; Flavell 22–8–61–1; Dexter 6.4–2–16–3

Bowling: Trueman 32–6–92–0; Statham 44–9–106–1; Flavell 29.4–4–65–2; Dexter 20–4–61–3; Allen 38–25–58–4; Close 8–1–33–0

ENGLAND

First Innings		*Second Innings*	
Pullar b Davidson	63	c O'Neill b Davidson	26
Subba Row c Simpson b Davidson	2	b Benaud	49
Dexter c Davidson b McKenzie	16	c Grout b Benaud	76
May c Simpson b Davidson	95	b Benaud	0
Close lbw b McKenzie	33	c O'Neill b Benaud	8
Barrington c O'Neill b Simpson	78	lbw b Mackay	5
Murray c Grout b Mackay	24	c Simpson b Benaud	4
Allen c Booth b Simpson	42	c Simpson b Benaud	10
Trueman c Harvey b Simpson	3	c Benaud b Simpson	8
Statham c Mackay b Simpson	4	b Davidson	8
Flavell not out	0	not out	0
Extras (b2 lb4 w1)	7	*Extras* (b5 w2)	7
Total	367	Total	201

Bowling: Davidson 39–11–70–3; McKenzie 38–11–106–2; Mackay 40–9–81–1; Benaud 35–15–80–0; Simpson 11.4–4–23–4

Bowling: Davidson 14.4–1–50–2; McKenzie 4–1–20–0; Mackay 13–7–33–1; Benaud 32–11–70–6; Simpson 8–4–21–1

England to West Indies
1960

Tour captain: P. B. H. May (M. C. Cowdrey)

Bridgetown: *Match drawn*
Trinidad: *England won by 256 runs*
Jamaica: *Match drawn*
British Guiana: *Match drawn*
Trinidad: *Match drawn*

For a series in which so much trouble developed and so many personal problems arose, this is remembered with considerable pleasure by most of the men who took part. Two notable exceptions are May, whose health broke down completely just before the fourth Test in Georgetown, and Statham who had to fly home to Manchester immediately after that Test because of the illness of his son. England were put to the bouncer-test by Wesley Hall, then at his peak as one of the greatest-ever West Indian fast bowlers, by the controversial Charlie Griffith (of whom more later) and by Chester Watson who later figured prominently in league cricket in England. England, however, were well-equipped to retaliate with Trueman in particularly good form and Statham, until his return home.

The only Test which produced a clear result was the one in which most trouble occurred, predictably in the volatile atmosphere of Queen's

Park, Port of Spain. Alexander was still captain, C. L. R. James was still campaigning vigorously for his removal and the appointment of Worrell, and nationalist fervour was high in Trinidad. A record crowd for any sporting event anywhere in the West Indies of 30,000 packed the ground and were not pleased by warnings to Hall and Watson for intimidatory bowling. They were even less pleased when Trueman and Statham reduced the West Indies to 98 for 7 on the first grass wicket used at Queen's Park. At this point a young local spin bowler, Charan Singh, was run out for nought in his first Test innings. It was highly unlikely that he was going to change the course of the game as a number 9 batsman but the big Saturday crowd took violent exception to the decision and threw stones and bottles on to the ground, causing the abandonment of play for the day. Appeals by the Prime Minister (Dr Williams) and the legendary Learie (Lord) Constantine were in vain and riot police had to be called in. Significantly (even if it cannot really be seen as relevantly), the nationalist campaign was taken up in earnest immediately after this Test by *The Nation*, organ of the People's National Party.

The remainder of the tour was played without riots and although the Tests were drawn they produced much thrilling cricket – and a number of injuries on both sides. With the departure of the sick May, the captaincy was taken over by Colin Cowdrey who batted with distinction in British Guiana and on the second visit to Trinidad; while Sobers had a magnificent series for the West Indies.

South Africa to England
1960
Tour captain: D. J. McGlew

Edgbaston: *England won by 100 runs*
Lord's: *England won by an innings and 73 runs*
Trent Bridge: *England won by 8 wickets*
Old Trafford: *Match drawn*
The Oval: *Match drawn*

Sadly, Jackie McGlew (touring for the last time) remembers this tour as one he did not enjoy and that will not surprise those who remember the controversy which dogged it from the start. In stark contrast McGlew remembers the 1955 tour with great affection for a 'golden summer' in which all five Tests were taken to a clear result. Five years later, the tour party was greeted by a crowd of 300 anti-apartheid demonstrators, the first time this had happened and it had a depressing effect upon McGlew's party. Then, relations between the sides – usually cordial – were soured by the 'calling' of one of the opening bowlers, Geoff Griffin, for throwing. Through the earlier games of the tour Griffin's action dominated the headlines in most newspapers and after the drawn match with M C C at Lord's a meeting was held by M C C officials together with the umpires, Frank Lee and John Langridge, and the South African manager, Dudley Nourse. Mr Nourse believed that following these discussions Griffin's bowling would be accepted as fair by English umpires but the Press did not take this view and the touring journalists were told that Gubby Allen, at that time chairman of the England selectors, had said to the tour manager: 'You are doing the wrong thing in playing Griffin. I don't think you will get away with it.' The headlines in the popular Press were predictable; it was when *The Times* expressed the view that M C C were condoning throwing that Charles Fortune, South Africa's best-known cricket writer and broadcaster, cabled home a report warning that rapid developments could be expected. A further statement was then issued at Lord's, saying that the M C C Committee was 'giving constant attention to the problem of unfair bowling. The Committee is determined to eradicate such bowling and emphasize they will give their full support to any action umpires may take to further this end.' As Charles Fortune put it: 'The grammar might be a little uncertain but the message was not. This was a clear directive to umpires to be after Geoff Griffin.'

Griffin himself, the baby of the side (he was not quite 21 when the controversy arose), behaved with commendable dignity through it all. Against Notts at Trent Bridge he was called five times for throwing and six times for dragging but somehow retained his composure and his captain was proud of the way he did it. After the Notts match Griffin went to Alf Gover's School to try to sort out his problem. He got through the first Test without problems as far as the umpires (John Langridge and Eddie Phillipson) were able to judge and then came the astonishing second Test at Lord's where Griffin performed the first hat-trick in a Test at Headquarters – and was no-balled out of the game as a chucker!

What made the tourists bitter about the fate of their young bowler was the belief that he had been 'called' on the instructions of M C C top brass behind the scenes. As Charles Fortune put it:

Before lunch and with the old ball Frank Lee paid no particular attention to Griffin's delivery action. Immediately after lunch and with the new ball commissioned, Lee at once condemned Griffin. Why after lunch and not during the morning? If Lee sought some directive from M C C before calling Griffin in the M C C match earlier in the tour – which in fact both he and John Langridge did – then it is not surprising if the South Africans were inclined to the view that for Lee the lunch-time break on this second day entailed more than refreshment and relaxation. When Lee called Griffin immediately after players and umpires came out of the Lord's pavilion after lunch, every South African intimately informed on the full course of events knew at once that Griffin's fate was being decided not by the umpires in the field but by people inside Lord's pavilion. Griffin's bowling I have always contended before ever he was chosen to come to England would be unacceptable to umpires prepared to apply Law 26 (as it then was) in accord with the exact wording of that Law. But what is one to conclude about umpiring in England when evidence steadily accumulates that umpires do not in this matter follow their own judgement? There is to my mind no doubt at all that Griffin was sentenced, not by those appointed to be M C C's judges of fair and unfair delivery, but by the authority who gave these umpires their official appointments.

Those are the words of no tabloid muck-raker but South Africa's most respected cricket correspondent over the past 50 years.

John Waite, the South African wicket-keeper-batsman and one of the senior players on the tour was one who believed Griffin's action 'suspect', like Charles Fortune had done, and felt he should not have been selected for the tour. And he, too, felt strongly that – once he was here – Griffin had been the victim of a conspiracy by people other than the men whose specific job it was to decide what was fair, or unfair, bowling. Waite went so far as to name Gubby Allen (who, apart from his selectorial role, was also chairman of the M C C Cricket Sub-committee) as one who played 'too forceful a part'.

'I understand he told some people,' said Waite, 'and certainly he told me of his belief that Griffin threw every ball. He also let it be known that he held much the same opinion of Ian Meckiff's bowling action.'

History records that Griffin got through the first Test without being called – except for dragging – by umpires Langridge and Phillipson. In the second Test, however, with Syd Buller and Frank Lee officiating, he was called ten times for throwing on the first two days of the match and on the third day he recorded the first hat-trick in a Test at Lord's without complaint from the umpires. On Monday (the fourth day) he was called four times for throwing and then no-balled again when, in desperation, he bowled underarm. He had omitted to give notice of his intention to change!

He did not bowl on the tour again and never played Test cricket again. The balance of the South African attack was damaged but the blow to team morale was something far worse. It is therefore not surprising that skipper McGlew lists the trip to England in 1955 as his most enjoyable tour and that of 1960 as the least enjoyable. Does he, in view of all this, take the view once expressed by Bradman that touring sides always get the worst of the deal from umpires?

'Not altogether – but I would guess it is largely true.'

Jackie McGlew, a popular captain and cricketer at home and abroad, feels that the most important qualities required of a tour captain are these: 'He must lead by example (i.e. his own performances), have the respect of his team and a good relationship with the media.' He chooses as a favourite Test the 1953 game against New Zealand in Wellington.

NEW ZEALAND v. SOUTH AFRICA
Wellington, 1953

SOUTH AFRICA

First Innings		Second Innings
McGlew not out	255	
Waite c Mooney b Blair	35	
Watkins c Reid b Blair	14	
Funston b Fisher	2	
Endean c Mooney b Blair	41	
McLean b Blair	5	
Cheetham b Burtt	17	
Murray st Mooney b Burtt	109	
Mansell run out	10	
Tayfield not out	27	
Fuller did not bat		
Extras (b5 lb4)	9	
Total (8 wkts declared)	524	

Bowling: Blair 36–4–98–4; Fisher 34–6–78–1; Reid 24–8–36–0; Burtt 44–7–140–2; Moir 35–4–159–0; Sutcliffe 1–0–4–0

NEW ZEALAND

First Innings		Second Innings	
Sutcliffe c McGlew b Watkins	62	b Murray	33
Leggat b Fuller b Tayfield	22	c Endean b Watkins	47
Fisher b Fuller	9	(9) c Waite b Watkins	14
Wallace c Waite b Murray	4	(3) b Tayfield	2
Meuli c Endean b Murray	15	(4) b Fuller	23
Miller c Endean b Tayfield	17	(5) c Waite b Watkins	13
Reid b Murray	1	(6) c Waite b Murray	9
Mooney not out	27	(7) b Tayfield	9
Moir run out	1	(8) c Fuller b Watkins	0
Burtt lbw b Fuller	10	lbw b Tayfield	0
Blair b Fuller	0	not out	6
Extras (b3 nb1)	4	*Extras* (b16)	16
Total	172	Total	172

Bowling: Fuller 10.4–7–29–3 Watkins 27–17–29–1; Tayfield 38–15–53–2; Mansell 11–3–27–0; Murray 28–15–30–3

Bowling: Fuller 27–8–43–1; Watkins 23.5–14–22–4; Tayfield 32–12–42–3; Mansell 13–2–30–0; Murray 23–16–19–2

Pakistan to India
1960–1
Tour captain: Fazal Mahmood

Bombay: *Match drawn*
Kanpur: *Match drawn*
Calcutta: *Match drawn*
Madras: *Match drawn*
Delhi: *Match drawn*

Fazal Mahmood had led Pakistan in home series against West Indies and Australia; now he captained his country on tour even if the trip was just across the border to meet Pakistan's next-door neighbours. Fazal was a big, cheerful man with a delightful sense of humour who achieved high rank in the police force. As we have seen, he bowled much on the lines of Alec Bedser and he was a keen student of the game; but once again we find a specialist bowler – and opening bowler, too – coming up against difficulties as a leader. He was not afraid to shoulder the burdens of attack – indeed, he bowled a lot of overs on unresponsive wickets – but as by far the most potent Pakistan attacker of his generation it is possible that he gave long spells to others in his side when it might have been more effective to bowl himself.

Once again in this series we find national prestige taking precedence over a purely cricketing approach, and a defensive attitude on both sides of avoiding defeat at all costs resulted in five high-scoring but sterile draws. Something like 4,700 runs were scored in the series without a result being achieved and the only real attempt to force one came from Fazal in the third Test where he set India to score 267 to win in three hours – an unprecedented striking rate on the sub-continent.

4

A GREAT WEST INDIAN CAPTAIN

West Indies to Australia
1960–1

Tour captain: F. M. M. Worrell

Brisbane: *Match tied*
Melbourne: *Match drawn*
Sydney: *West Indies won by 222 runs*
Adelaide: *Match drawn*
Melbourne: *Australia won by 2 wickets*

With Frank Worrell at last in charge of the West Indians and Australia led by Richie Benaud, whose philosophy of cricket we have already explored briefly, the result was one of the greatest series of all time.

Worrell was already 36 years old when he at last succeeded to the West Indies captaincy and he was destined to lead them in 15 more Tests. The immense prestige he achieved in this time – even in losing series – and the enormous affection with which he was regarded in England and Australia, in particular, suggests that those who campaigned so energetically for his appointment had been absolutely right. His age, and the experience of almost 13 years in Test cricket, meant he started with the built-in respect of his tourists; the whole of the party had come into Test cricket during the course of Worrell's career and he at once achieved the status of a father-figure, much as Clive Lloyd (the West Indies' other outstanding leader) was to do in the future.

Richie Benaud has a particularly vivid memory of Worrell calming and consoling Wes Hall when he dropped a catch at Brisbane in 1960; I have an equally clear picture of him playing the psychiatrist to the same bowler at Lord's in 1963 when Hall, incredulous and almost distraught, observed Brian Close advancing down the pitch to play him as the bowler came in off that long, long run. Worrell had already won renown as one of the great batsmen; very quickly in Australia he advanced his stature as a splendid leader of men. He was also a tactician in a way in which few West Indian captains had previously been seen. The Test sides from the islands had relied for the most part on the individual ability which they had in plenty. Worrell saw as his first duty as a tour captain the need to weld it together into a *team* performance while retaining that individual brilliance. The extent to which he succeeded on his first tour as captain is clearly indicated by the results of the 1960–1 Tests and the crowd of 100,000 which lined the streets of Melbourne as the tourists left for home.

The rubber could not, in any way, have got off to a more magnificent start, with the only tied Test in the history of the game. Who better to describe its most critical stages than the opposition captain, Benaud:

I had to bat for much of the time with Alan Davidson in what was akin to a limited overs situation. We knew roughly how many overs we would receive, even off Wes Hall's longest, longest, longest run, and how many runs were needed, and we made our plans accordingly. Frank made *his* plans which involved the use of the new ball, taken at 200 runs in those days, and the careful use of Wes Hall and Gary Sobers mixed in with Ramadhin and Valentine. You could tell the West Indies were under pressure by some of their throwing in the field and from the tension in the centre. You could also tell there was little likelihood of them crumbling under that pressure because of one incident. When Joe Solomon threw down the stumps to run out Davidson, Alexander was up *over the stumps* for the throw – not on the run but actually over the stumps – and there were two men backing up.

Benaud was caught behind, Grout and Meckiff run out, the last wicket falling with the scores level off the seventh ball (eight-ball overs at that time) of the final over. The breathtaking finish set up the whole tour. Australia won the second Test, West Indies the third; the fourth Test saw Australia escape defeat by the skin of their teeth because Lindsay Kline (scoring his Test-best 15 not out) kept Mackay company for the last 100 minutes of the match; Australia won the rubber (with Mackay again at the crease) by two wickets in Melbourne where nearly 91,000 people watched the second day's play. Worrell left to a hero's farewell, returned home to a hero's welcome.

For his qualities of clear head in a crisis and outstanding handling of a Test side, the tied Test in Brisbane stands as Frank Worrell's monument. He was knighted in 1964 and died in 1967. He was only 42 years old. The greatest innings I saw him play was at Trent Bridge in 1950 but his contribution to great cricket and true sportsmanship was a massive one.

AUSTRALIA v. WEST INDIES

Brisbane, 1960

WEST INDIES

First Innings		Second Innings	
Hunte c Benaud b Davidson	24	c Simpson b Mackay	39
C. W. Smith c Grout b Davidson	7	c O'Neill b Davidson	6
Kanhai c Grout b Davidson	15	c Grout b Davidson	54
Sobers c Kline b Meckiff	132	b Davidson	14
Worrell c Grout b Davidson	65	c Grout b Davidson	65
Solomon hit wkt b Simpson	65	lbw b Simpson	47
Lashley c Grout b Kline	19	b Davidson	0
Alexander c Davidson b Kline	60	b Benaud	5
Ramadhin c Harvey b Davidson	12	c Harvey b Simpson	6
Hall st Grout b Kline	50	b Davidson	18
Valentine not out	0	not out	7
Extras (lb3 w1)	4	Extras (b14 lb7 w2)	23
Total	453	Total	284

Bowling: Davidson 30–2–135–5; Meckiff 18–0–129–1; Mackay 3–0–15–0; Benaud 24–3–93–0; Kline 17.6–6–52–3; Simpson 8–0–25–1

Bowling: Davidson 24.6–4–87–6; Meckiff 4–1–19–0; Mackay 21–7–52–1; Benaud 31–6–69–1; Simpson 7–2–18–2; Kline 4–0–14–0; O'Neill 1–0–2–0

AUSTRALIA

First Innings		Second Innings	
McDonald c Hunte b Sobers	57	b Worrell	16
Simpson b Ramadhin	92	c sub b Hall	0
Harvey b Valentine	15	c Sobers b Hall	5
O'Neill c Valentine b Hall	181	c Alexander b Hall	26
Favell run out	45	c Solomon b Hall	7
Mackay b Sobers	35	b Ramadhin	28
Davidson c Alexander b Hall	44	run out	80
Benaud lbw b Hall	10	c Alexander b Hall	52
Grout lbw b Hall	4	run out	2
Meckiff run out	4	run out	2
Kline not out	3	not out	0
Extras (b2 lb8 w1 nb4)	15	Extras (b2 lb9 nb3)	14
Total	505	Total	232

Bowling: Hall 29.3–1–140–4; Worrell 30–0–93–0; Sobers 32–0–115–2; Valentine 24–6–82–1; Ramadhin 15–1–60–1

Bowling: Hall 17.7–3–63–5; Worrell 16–3–41–1; Sobers 8–0–30–0; Valentine 10–4–27–0; Ramadhin 17–3–57–1

Australia to England

1961

Tour captain: R. Benaud

Edgbaston: *Match drawn*
Lord's: *Australia won by 5 wickets*
Headingley: *England won by 8 wickets*
Old Trafford: *Australia won by 54 runs*
The Oval: *Match drawn*

Benaud, an enthusiast throughout his career, had brought something of the spirit of his epic series at home to the West Indians with him. Every tour to Richie was something of a crusade, with the aim of lifting the standards of the game and in particular the level of enjoyment by both the participants and the observers. He believed firmly that the one communicated its philosophy and atmosphere to the other. Cricket in England at the time was sinking into the doldrums. Attendances were down at County Championship matches and this, inevitably, was being reflected in the Test crowds. Benaud's first public utterance at the start of the tour indicated that he wanted to get away from dull, remorseless cricket, with a quick over-rate and no dawdling in the field. Many captains have gone abroad and said something similar; Benaud meant it. He wanted no controversies and he kept his word with the result that the editor of *Wisden* commented: 'Good fellowship and friendliness pervaded the tour and for once the importance of winning a game or a series was not allowed to impinge upon the true spirit of cricket. I have been watching Test cricket for 40 years and I cannot recall a more pleasant atmosphere. I am sure that all cricket-lovers will say: "Long may it continue." '

Australia had the better of the first Test in which Dexter made 180 with some brilliant stroke-play and Subba Row scored 59 and 112 in his first Test against Australia. Brittle batting by England and splendid bowling by 'Garth' McKenzie (later to prove a popular figure in Leicestershire cricket) on his Test debut saw England beaten at Lord's and May, after playing under Cowdrey's captaincy in the first two games, was restored to the leadership. Immediately Cowdrey's personal batting form returned at Headingley where Trueman, asking his captain's permission to bowl largely experimental cutters at medium-fast pace, took five wickets for no runs in the second innings after opening in his usual style.

I remember being asked to write a preview of this Test and noting that the pitch had a pattern of cracks unlike anything I had ever seen there. After a wet spring, a warm, dry summer had developed, and the character of the pitch had not gone unnoticed by 'F S T'. He had played there in May and now returning to Leeds for the first time he had, as he put it, 'just a feeling' that he might be able to get movement by bowling off-cutters. He did. Australia, after passing 100 with three wickets down, were all out 120 in their second innings.

The interesting fourth Test at Old Trafford is detailed elsewhere. At The Oval, Australia might well have won again but for the rain which returned to spoil the end of that season. A certain degree of ill-health and increasing business cares meant it was the last of Peter May's 66 Tests. He had captained England in 41 with dignity and honour – 20 victories, 10 defeats and 11 draws.

Four of *Wisden*'s 'Five Cricketers of the Year' were members of the Australian touring party – Benaud, Lawry, Davidson and O'Neill. The fifth, incidentally, was an Australian who never played for his country; my old friend Bill Alley, who that summer scored 3,019 as a Somerset county cricketer when he was in his forties.

Benaud started his newspaper career as a clerk and, even though he was a Test cricketer he only won a transfer to the editorial side of the business after much pleading with the executive editor of the Sydney *Sun*. And he turned down the easy option of writing a sports column for pounding the police calls beat as a junior. He went through other departments, learning the basics of his trade thoroughly, before turning to a sports column which he wrote for 13 years. In 1969, a well-rounded journalist, he set up a freelance writing and sports consultancy with his wife, Daphne – a former B B C production assistant and secretary to E. W. Swanton. They make a great team.

From 1958 to 1963 Richie was in the unique position of Test captain with a full-time job as a journalist when he was not playing. And he brought his party to England in 1961 hard on the heels of the controversial South African tourists and the 'Griffin Affair' in which the English Press had played no small part. With that perverseness which often invades English newspaper columns, Benaud's 1961 side were promptly labelled as one of the weakest to leave Australia's shores – because the controversial figures of Meckiff, Rorke and Burke had been left behind! It appealed greatly to Richie's sense of humour that no fewer than *eight* bowlers on the tour took at least 50 wickets.

His dual role of captain and media man has always enabled him to look generously on the faults, foibles and shortcomings of both parties. In 1984 he wrote: 'Newspaper writers and television and radio men now are no different from my playing time, in the sense of needing a story and at times going to great lengths to do so. It would do no harm if players and captains had a better appreciation of problems facing the media . . . some of which can be of their own making.'

That was in 1984. I wonder what his view would be after some of the excesses of 1987, 1988 and 1989? It would undoubtedly be thoughtful, perhaps enigmatic, probably drily humorous. But I doubt if it would be exactly the same.

England to Pakistan and India
1961–2
Tour captain: E. R. Dexter

Lahore: *England won by 5 wickets*

Bombay: *Match drawn*
Kanpur: *Match drawn*
Delhi: *Match drawn*
Calcutta: *India won by 187 runs*
Madras: *India won by 128 runs*

Dacca: *Match drawn*
Karachi: *Match drawn*

If Edward Ralph Dexter had been born 35 years earlier he would probably have won a DSO (perhaps even the VC) as a teenage second lieutenant by leading his men over the top in Flanders armed with nothing more lethal than a swagger-stick. He was brilliant sportsman of the most dashing type, his batting generously endowed with élan which he showed to full effect in the Old Trafford innings of Benaud's favourite Test.

On his first trip abroad as captain Dexter scored a career-best 205 against Pakistan in Karachi on the long and curiously split tour, but the tortuous nature of much of the cricket must have been irksome in the extreme to a man of his restless nature. Those who played alongside Dexter vouch for his great gifts but do not rate patience highly amongst them. If things were not going to plan – and he was a great planner – or if a match drifted towards stalemate, he had a tendency to lose concentration. Various members of his teams provide instances of this but perhaps the most notable was at The Oval on the morning of 15 August 1964, when Australia, one-up in the series, were heading towards a big first-innings lead. The story is told, with deep emotion, by F. S. Trueman whose total of Test wickets at that time stood at 297. 'He didn't know what to do next,' recalls Fred. 'We were getting shut out of the game and we were coming up to lunchtime on the Saturday when I saw he was going to give the ball to Parfitt.' (At this point in the narrative, Fred's voice rises in a crescendo of incredulity. He and Peter Parfitt were to become great friends in their post-playing days but Fred never rated Peter's bowling – 12 Test wickets at 47.83 – very highly.) 'To *Parf*! I snatched the bloody ball from him and put myself on.' The rest is history – two wickets in two balls and the 300th Test victim duly acquired after lunch.

Although Dexter was clearly destined to lead England at some stage of his career, he became captain during the winter of 1961–2 almost by default. Eight of the 29 players questioned about their availability said they could not make the trip and two of these, May and Cowdrey, would undoubtedly have been given precedence as leader. Dexter's tourists were, therefore, some way short of being a full-strength party and it required an outstanding innings by the captain to win the first Test against Pakistan. In India, the tourists encountered an old oriental custom of flashing mirrors to dazzle the England batsmen. By way of diversion, fruit was thrown at boundary fieldsmen and the crowd further amused themselves by starting fires and staging pitched battles. The tourists suffered chronically from boredom off the field and sometimes too much excitement on it! But in Dacca, not the most exotic cricketing centre of the sub-continent, they watched Hanif Mohammad score a century in each innings which together occupied nearly 15 hours at the crease.

If keeping 16 assorted individuals happy and in good heart is high on a tour captain's list of priorities, Dexter's first experience must have been daunting in the extreme. Even after the two later Tests in Pakistan the party's travails were not ended. There was still a three-match visit to Ceylon to be completed. When the tourists returned home they had been away for nearly five months and had played many games in places where accommodation and catering were far from first-class.

New Zealand to South Africa
1961–2
Tour captain: J. R. Reid

Durban: *South Africa won by 30 runs*
Johannesburg: *Match drawn*
Cape Town: *New Zealand won by 72 runs*
Johannesburg: *South Africa won by an innings and 51 runs*
Port Elizabeth: *New Zealand won by 40 runs*

John Reid again led New Zealand on tour and batted with great consistency throughout the series in which both countries carried out team-building exercises. South Africa introduced no fewer than seven new caps in Durban, three of whom – Eddie Barlow, Colin Bland and Peter Pollock – were to reach great prominence in the future. New Zealand had five men new to Test cricket in the first match and another, Graham Dowling (later to become secretary of the N Z Board of Control) in the second. The final Test, which gave New Zealand a historic second victory and a shared rubber, marked the end of Jackie McGlew's distinguished international career. He had suffered a great deal with injuries and completed his final Test with a thumb in splints and a shoulder in plaster!

India to West Indies
1961–2

Tour captain: N. J. Contractor (The Nawab of Pataudi jun.)

Trinidad: *West Indies won by 10 wickets*
Jamaica: *West Indies won by an innings and 18 runs*
Barbados: *West Indies won by an innings and 30 runs*
Trinidad: *West Indies won by 7 wickets*
Jamaica: *West Indies won by 123 runs*

This was a series in which India lost a captain and acquired their youngest ever leader in dramatic, almost tragic, circumstances. Nari Contractor had skippered India in two home series and in the first two Tests of this tour when, batting against Barbados in Bridgetown, he was struck on the head by a ball from Charlie Griffith. It was one of those deliveries which made Griffith's bowling suspect by batsmen wherever he played – one which came without warning and was very much faster than anything else he bowled. Contractor, according to his team-mates, had no chance to play a shot. At the very last minute he tucked his head into his shoulder but was struck a sickening blow on the side of the head.

After being helped to the dressing room, Contractor sat dazed and sick until bleeding started from his nose and ears. An ambulance was called and the captain was whipped into hospital where, that evening, he underwent an operation for a fractured skull. A blood transfusion was necessary – in fact, a series of them – and when he finally left hospital, with a plate in his head, Contractor's blood mingled with that of three team-mates, an Indian Press man . . . and Frank Worrell!

The whole of the Indian party visited their captain in hospital on that first night where they found him, still anaesthetised, cursing fluently in Gujerati. And in one of those strange meetings of old and new, of modern medical science and ancient superstition, Chandu Borde reported hearing an owl hooting outside the hospital and several members of the party were filled with foreboding at this sign of ill omen.

As the Barbados match continued, Vijay Manjrekar was struck on the bridge of the nose by a delivery from Griffith and lost his sight for a period of about 20 minutes. Small wonder, therefore, that the tourists' emergency captain, the 21-year-old Mansur Ali Khan (son of Nawab of Pataudi who had led India to England in 1946), confessed ruefully: 'He bowled me in each innings for my first "pair" in first-class cricket and I never saw either ball.'

The third Test of the series followed on the same ground a few days later. Contractor, when he was fit to leave hospital, returned home to India and never played Test cricket again. Griffith, however, continued his career and was to hit many more batsmen who were wholly unprepared for deliveries which were suddenly and astoundingly quicker. 'Young' Pataudi, at the age of 21 years, two months and 18 days, became the youngest Test captain in history and went on to lead his country in 40 matches. We shall look at him in more detail later; in that series, even without Griffith bowling in any of the Tests a dispirited and demoralised side lost all five games.

Pakistan to England
1962
Tour captain: Javed Burki

Edgbaston: *England won by an innings and 24 runs*
Lord's: *England won by 9 wickets*
Headingley: *England won by an innings and 117 runs*
Trent Bridge: *Match drawn*
The Oval: *England won by 10 wickets*

Having tried, with mixed results, a captain who had been promoted from the ranks (Fazal Mahmood), the Pakistan selectors reverted to the officer-class in choosing their leader in England in 1962 and the outcome was a total disaster. Javed Burki had the right pedigree (three Blues at Oxford, 1958–60) and the right family background (two little boys destined for great things in the future were his cousins – Imran Khan, whose mother was a Burki, and Majid Jehangir Khan), but he was not an inspiring leader and the tourists never seemed to get together as a team. Management by an army brigadier with a major as his assistant did not inspire much confidence in the future of Pakistan as a military force and it was no help at all to the captain that a spate of injuries resulted in much traffic between England and Pakistan. In all, 21 players were used at some stage of the tour including the 35-year-old Fazal Mahmood. One tourist who probably looks back upon his visit with affection was the medium-pace bowler Antao D'Souza who at Bradford twice took the wicket of a Yorkshire Colt named Geoffrey Boycott (each time for four runs) little knowing that his victim would, in due course, score more than 8,000 runs for England. Another tourist who made progress was Mushtaq Mohammad (still only 18) with 1,614 runs, though his leg-spin bowling was rarely seen. With an apparent lack of either strategic or tactical planning and a threadbare attack, Pakistan were crushingly defeated in four Tests and drew in Nottingham only because of rain.

England to Australia and New Zealand

1962–3

Tour captain: E. R. Dexter

Brisbane: *Match drawn*
Melbourne: *England won by 7 wickets*
Sydney: *Australia won by 9 wickets*
Adelaide: *Match drawn*
Sydney: *Match drawn*

Auckland: *England won by an innings and 215 runs*
Wellington: *England won by an innings and 47 runs*
Christchurch: *England won by 7 wickets*

The composition of this side was intriguing to Australian eyes with 'Lord Edward' Dexter as captain, the Duke of Norfolk, Earl-Marshal of England, as manager, and the future Bishop of Liverpool in the ranks. The Rev. David Sheppard landed at Freemantle wearing his clerical 'dog-collar', while the other members of the party sported their M C C touring ties. In the context of leading by example, Dexter batted brilliantly in the series with splendid support from Ken Barrington and Cowdrey, the vice-captain. The fielding, however, left much to be desired and far too many catches were dropped at important stages of the Tests. This was partly due to an element of disgruntled rebellious-ness and one or two tour bonuses were 'docked' when the party returned home. Several aspects of this tour have found their way into the reper-toire of after-dinner speakers, not all of them the sort of stories by which a tour captain ideally wishes to be remembered.

The first-choice wicket-keeper at the start of the tour, John (J. T.) Murray lost his place in the first two Tests to the amateur A. C. Smith – subsequently to become Chief Executive of the T C C B – and when he regained it for the third Test, Murray injured a shoulder so that Smith resumed the role in the last two. Statham, at that time the world's leading fast bowler in terms of Test wickets, was not at his best and the 6ft 7½ ins Larter could not force his way into the Test side. Trueman, however, who celebrated his 32nd birthday between the last two matches of the series, took 20 wickets and played a major part in the victory in Melbourne.

It was easier going on the other side of the Tasman Sea where Barrington continued to score heavily and was joined as a centurion by Parfitt, Cowdrey and the Essex all-rounder Barry Knight, while Trueman overtook Statham's 242 Test wickets to come home with a total of 250. Dexter had not had the most comfortable of tours but in terms of results it had been largely satisfactory.

West Indies to England
1963
Tour captain: F. M. M. Worrell

Old Trafford: *West Indies won by 10 wickets*
Lord's: *Match drawn*
Edgbaston: *England won by 217 runs*
Headingley: *West Indies won by 221 runs*
The Oval: *West Indies won by 8 wickets*

Such was the regard in which Frank Worrell was held that the rumblings of discontent which echoed around the county grounds of England about the bowling of Charlie Griffith never became a front-line issue in the Test series. Despite England's defeat for the Wisden Trophy by three games to one, this series is still remembered for the brilliance of the cricket, mingled with a certain amount of drama.

Worrell's side was similar to the one which had made a great impact in Australia (1960–1) and such was the team spirit forged on that tour that it seemed the selectors had made a conscious effort to see it continued. If the side had a weakness it was in not being assured of a good start because while Conrad Hunte made good runs, his partners – at various times Carew, McMorris and Rodriguez – rarely did. The middle order was extremely strong with Sobers, at 26, now at the height of his all-round powers and his versatility as a bowler was a tremendous help to the captain.

Griffith took 119 wickets on tour, 32 of them in Tests, and was never called for throwing even though the extra pace of certain deliveries seemed inexplicable to county batsmen. Griffith for the most part appeared to be a fairly ordinary fast-medium bowler – not of the same class and quality or pace as his partner, Hall – until a delivery suddenly flew far faster than the others. As this was usually a yorker or a bouncer it presented problems few batsmen had ever encountered before. A trail of batsmen in county sides were laid low and one of them, John Hampshire from Yorkshire (now a first-class and Test umpire) still feels the effects of being knocked out by Griffith at Middlesbrough – more than a quarter of a century later! There were rumours around the circuit that umpires had been briefed by the powers at Lord's *not* to call Griffith to avoid a 'political' furore but this was never brought into open debate as in the case of Griffin, a white South African, three years earlier.

The second Test at Lord's must go down as the most tense in which Dexter, or anyone else involved in it, has ever played. It involved probably the greatest bowling performance of the 32-year-old Trueman's career which left England needing to score 233 to win. The first three wickets were lost for 31, then Cowdrey retired hurt after being hit on the left forearm which was found to be fractured. Barrington and Close then played an astonishing partnership of 99. Barrington scored 60 by his own methods which were different from those of Close. The Yorkshire captain countered the pace of Hall by walking down the pitch to meet him, to the utter astonishment of the bowler. The duel between these two was one of the great moments of cricket through all its ages. The Lord's 'ridge' – real or imagined – was real enough to Close with bowling of Hall's pace and the ball flying around his ears from a length. Close has always had a kamikaze approach to matters of physical danger and if he could not hit Hall's fastest deliveries he took them on the body, reasoning with simple but near-suicidal logic that he couldn't be bowled and he couldn't be lbw a couple of yards down the pitch.

Parks, Titmus and Trueman were out while Close was reaching 70 and then Griffith returned to the attack, with 16 needed in the last 18 minutes. The description of what followed is Close's own:

> In came Charlie with that same casual, easy run-up and then suddenly it was the bouncer. Not only that but it came up the hill like an off-break – a very, very fast, bouncing off-break. It just caught the bottom edge and squeezed between my arm and my body as it screamed up. Murray took the catch standing 20 yards back. Of course the ball was thrown. No one on earth could have bowled at that speed from that approach.

In came Derek Shackleton, only to be run out as England still tried for a now-improbable win and as the players started to leave the field they saw Cowdrey, left arm in plaster, emerge from the Lord's pavilion. He intended to bat one-handed, using only his right arm, if he had to take strike. Mercifully, he did not; David Allen faced the last ball of the match. England could have won with a six or lost if he had been out. They settled for a draw!

ENGLAND v. WEST INDIES

Lord's, 1963

WEST INDIES

First Innings		*Second Innings*	
Hunte c Close b Trueman	44	c Cowdrey b Shackleton	7
McMorris lbw b Trueman	16	c Cowdrey b Trueman	8
Sobers c Cowdrey b Allen	42	(5) c Parks b Trueman	8
Kanhai c Edrich b Trueman	73	(3) c Cowdrey b Shackleton	21
Butcher c Barrington b Trueman	14	(4) lbw b Shackleton	133
Solomon lbw b Shackleton	56	c Stewart b Allen	5
Worrell b Trueman	0	c Stewart b Trueman	33
Murray c Cowdrey b Trueman	20	c Parks b Trueman	2
Hall not out	25	c Parks b Trueman	2
Griffith c Cowdrey b Shackleton	0	b Shackleton	1
Gibbs c Stewart b Shackleton	0	not out	1
Extras (nb10 lb1)	11	Extras (b5 lb2 nb1)	8
Total	301	Total	229

Bowling: Trueman 44–16–100–6; Shackleton 50.2–22–93–3; Dexter 20–6–41–0; Close 9–3–21–0; Allen 10–3–35–1

Bowling: Trueman 26–9–52–5; Shackleton 34–14–72–4; Allen 21–7–50–1; Titmus 17–3–47–0

ENGLAND

First Innings		*Second Innings*	
Stewart c Kanhai b Griffith	2	c Solomon b Hall	17
Edrich c Murray b Griffith	0	c Murray b Hall	8
Dexter lbw b Sobers	70	b Gibbs	2
Barrington c Sobers b Worrell	80	c Murray b Griffith	60
Cowdrey b Gibbs	4	not out	19
Close c Murray b Griffith	9	c Murray b Griffith	70
Parks b Worrell	35	lbw b Griffith	17
Titmus not out	52	c McMorris b Hall	11
Trueman b Hall	10	c Murray b Hall	0
Allen lbw b Griffith	2	not out	4
Shackleton b Griffith	8	run out	4
Extras (b8 lb8 nb9)	25	Extras (b5 lb8 nb3)	16
Total	297	Total	228

Bowling: Hall 18–2–65–1; Griffith 26–6–91–5; Sobers 18–4–45–1; Gibbs 27–9–59–1; Worrell 13–6–12–2

Bowling: Hall 40–9–93–4; Griffith 30–7–59–3; Sobers 4–1–4–0; Gibbs 17–7–56–1

Worrell brushed aside defeat at Edgbaston, read the pitch accurately at Headingley and saw his prediction that spin would be decisive in the later stages justified by Lance Gibbs and Sobers. He went out of Test cricket in triumph at The Oval and it was tragic that he did not enjoy a longer retirement. He had been one of the great batsmen and great gentlemen of cricket and, arguably, West Indies' outstanding captain.

South Africa to Australia
1963–4
Tour captain: T. L. Goddard

Brisbane: *Match drawn*
Melbourne: *Australia won by 8 wickets*
Sydney: *Match drawn*
Adelaide: *South Africa won by 10 wickets*
Sydney: *Match drawn*

If someone started researching cricketing genealogy and discovered that Trevor Goddard of South Africa and Trevor Bailey were related it would not surprise me in the least, even though one was a left-hander and the other right. Both could be obdurate as batsmen or play with delightful freedom; both were masters of negative, leg-theory bowling and both could be incisive wicket-takers. Goddard was by nature an *opening* batsman, while Bailey's place was normally in the middle order although he had some experience in opening a Test innings, too. Goddard had been playing first-class cricket for 10 years and opening in Tests for seven when he was chosen to lead his country in Australia in what was Benaud's last series and he took with him a largely untried party which was to enjoy remarkable success.

The Springboks were a harmonious and popular group of tourists and most of the major problems were on the Australian side. Indeed, it must have afforded Goddard (who had been in England in 1960) a certain grim satisfaction to observe the complete upheaval of a 'chucking' controversy in the opening Test. We have noted much of the Benaud character in previous chapters; what we have not examined so far is the tougher side of the man's personality, a resolution and integrity which would not allow him to compromise any of his principles.

Clearly the question of bowling with suspect, or obviously illegal, actions was a matter of serious concern to cricket's administrators during the period of the late fifties and early sixties; in fact, during the visit by England in 1962–3 Sir Donald Bradman had invited all the Sheffield Shield captains to his home and shown them his film of bowlers with questionable actions. Benaud then resolved not to continue to use a bowler who was called for throwing by an umpire and he made a mental note not to carry on with a bowler he himself considered suspect.

He had put this into practice by not bowling Gordon Rorke in a N S W v. South Australia match after a couple of deliveries which Benaud thought looked 'unusual'. He was asked about this by the chairman of the N S W selectors, Dudley Seddon (who was also a national selector), and here we get a glimpse of the steel beneath

Benaud's soft-spoken exterior. When he heard Richie's explanation (1: the pitch was taking spin and Rorke's bowling was not required; 2: a couple of deliveries had been thought to be not quite legitimate), Mr. Seddon responded with a bit of good, old-fashioned, Aussie-type frankness: the selectors picked the side and they would make sure the bowlers were legitimate. Benaud's job was to skipper the side that was picked and would he remember that? I rejoice in the answer from Benaud: if he found in his N S W side a man whose action was suspect he wouldn't bowl him at all. But he *would* open the batting with him and how did Mr Seddon like that? Magnificent!

This, then, was the background against which the Australian selectors put Ian Meckiff into the team for the first Test in Brisbane under Benaud's captaincy. In his first over he was called by Colin Egar for throwing his second, third, fifth and ninth deliveries. He did not bowl again in the match, in Test or any other kind of cricket. Benaud did not skipper Australia again after that game but this requires elaboration. He had already discussed with Bradman what might be the right time for him to step down from the Test captaincy and he had also announced that he would be unavailable to tour England in 1964. Probably Benaud would have seen through the series with South Africa and bowed out, tidily, at the end of that Australian summer.

Between the first and second Tests, however, playing in a grade (i.e. league) match in Sydney, he broke his spinning finger in three places whilst fielding at slip and thus Bobby Simpson took over the captaincy of both N S W and Australia. Benaud returned to play under Simpson's captaincy in the remaining three Tests and retired at the end of the season.

Goddard, meanwhile, was leading from the front with a series of solid scores and watching with interest the 19-year-old Graeme Pollock scoring 122 in Sydney and 175 in Adelaide. He was to become one of the finest left-hand batsmen of all time and it is little short of tragic that so few people around the world were able to see him play because of political issues. Goddard had been noted by Jim Laker as one to watch for the future when he coached him as a schoolboy in Durban in the South African summer of 1959–60. He was more of a solid and reliable player than one who showed outstanding gifts but his all-round ability made him a more-than-useful member of any side and drawing a series in Australia with so many young and inexperienced players in his party stamps him as a good tour captain. His match, for all-round contributions and effective leadership, is the fourth Test of this series, in Adelaide.

AUSTRALIA v. SOUTH AFRICA
Adelaide, 1964

AUSTRALIA

First Innings		Second Innings	
Simpson b Goddard	78	c Lindsay b Halse	34
Lawry c Partridge b P. Pollock	14	c Goddard b P. Pollock	38
O'Neill c Goddard b P. Pollock	0	c Partridge b Halse	66
Burge c Halse b P. Pollock	91	run out	20
Booth c Lindsay b Goddard	58	lbw b P. Pollock	24
Shepherd lbw b Goddard	70	c Lindsay b Barlow	78
Benaud b Partridge	7	b Barlow	34
McKenzie c Lindsay b Goddard	12	c and b Barlow	4
Grout c P. Pollock b Goddard	0	(10) c Pithey b Halse	23
Hawke not out	0	(9) c Carlstein b Seymour	0
Extras (b1 lb8 nb5)	14	Extras (lb4 w1 nb3)	8
Total	345	Total	331

Bowling: P. Pollock 21–1–96–3; Partridge 22–4–76–1; Halse 13–1–54–0; Goddard 24.6–4–60–5; Seymour 12–2–38–0; Bland 1–0–7–0

Bowling: P. Pollock 14–1–73–2; Partridge 17–3–76–0; Halse 13.3–0–50–3; Goddard 21–3–64–0; Seymour 19–1–54–1; Barlow 5–2–6–3

SOUTH AFRICA

First Innings		Second Innings	
Goddard b Hawke	34	not out	34
Barlow lbw b Hawke	201	not out	47
Pitchey c Grout b Hawke	0		
G. Pollock b Hawke	175		
Bland c Grout b Gaunt	33		
Carlstein c Benaud b Gaunt	37		
Lindsay b Simpson	41		
P. Pollock c Benaud b Hawke	21		
Seymour c Simpson b Hawke	3		
Partridge b McKenzie	6		
Halse not out	19		
Extras (b7 lb8 w3 nb7)	25	Extras (w1)	1
Total	595	Total (no wicket)	82

Bowling: Gaunt 24–2–115–2; McKenzie 30.1–2–156–1; Hawke 39–5–139–6; Benaud 20–1–101–0; Simpson 10–1–59–1

Bowling: Gaunt 4–0–22–0; Hawke 6–0–22–0; Benaud 3–1–17–0

England to India
1963–4
Tour captain: M. J. K. Smith

Madras: *Match drawn*
Bombay: *Match drawn*
Calcutta: *Match drawn*
Delhi: *Match drawn*
Kanpur: *Match drawn*

Ask any cricketer who toured under Michael John Knight Smith (universally referred to as 'M J K') what he was like as a skipper and the answer, without any doubt at all, will be, 'Great . . . looked after the boys.' No captain can ask for a more appealing accolade than that, surely? Mike Smith was a fine all-round sportsman, winning a Blue as a fly-half for Oxford in 1954–5, an England cap against Wales in 1956 and he started in first-class cricket with Leics when only 18. After gaining cricket Blues in all three years (1954–6) at Oxford he joined Warwickshire and skippered them from 1957 to 1967. He was a forcing batsman with an impressive repertoire of on-side strokes and was particularly good against quicker bowling in spite of the fact that he wore spectacles. This did not prevent, either, his becoming one of the outstanding short-leg fieldsmen of his day and most of his 592 catches were held there.

His contemporary, namesake and fellow amateur (although everyone had become simply 'cricketers' when the distinction was abolished after 1962) at Edgbaston was Alan Christopher Smith and today the same differentiation is observed between them as bestowed by their colleagues in the 1950s – M J K and A C.

M J K was more self-effacing than A C and perhaps 'quietly efficient' would be a reasonable description of his approach to captaincy in which he was exactly the opposite of Dexter if one follows an analogy of officers in trench warfare. Ted would have gone over the top with a swagger stick; Smith's first concern would have been for the welfare and safety of his troops. Much the same comparison can be made between Brian Close and Ray Illingworth, to whom we shall come in due course. M J K's preoccupation in 'looking after the boys' excited the approval of Geoffrey Boycott, no less, on his tour to South Africa with Smith in 1964–5 and Geoffrey does not dispense compliments lightly, especially to Public School and Oxbridge recipients.

Smith could scarcely have had a more difficult first tour. He would have been second-in-command to Cowdrey who, however, was forced to cry off with a shoulder injury before the party set out. It was not exactly an enthusiastic band of volunteers since no fewer than 36 candidates had been sounded out for their availability by M C C who had also cut down the length of the trip to eight weeks. The dietary hazards of the sub-continent were by this time well-known and the subject of hair-raising anecdote whenever two or three former tourists were gathered together; accommodation had not improved dramatically in some centres and long-distance travel could not be avoided: e.g. Madras to Ahmedabad, Bombay to Calcutta were scheduled trips on this itinerary. Even so, M J K cannot possibly have been prepared for the scale of his injury and illness problems. After the first Test, Barrington broke a finger in Ahmedabad and the management sent an urgent signal for reinforcements. Cowdrey, happily recovered from his shoulder injury, was dispatched together with Parfitt; but before they could arrive, Smith had to nominate his side for the second Test in Bombay. Roll-call revealed that Edrich, Sharpe and Mortimore were definitely unavailable because of 'stomach trouble' and Barrington had not recovered from his broken finger. That meant that the captain could muster ten men reasonably fit to take the field and one, Mickey Stewart, just about able to give it a go. At tea-time on the first day Stewart collapsed with dysentery and took no further part in the match or the tour.

It is in circumstances like this that a tour party collapses completely or is welded together by its corporate spirit. England, never knowing what sort of team they would be able to field from one game to the next, carried on to make a draw in each of the remaining Tests and were unbeaten in the minor matches. They had even managed a win against South Zone in the second match of the tour, so the party returned home with honour intact and the survivors with a warm regard for their captain.

South Africa to New Zealand
1963–4
Tour captain: T. L. Goddard

Wellington: *Match drawn*
Dunedin: *Match drawn*
Auckland: *Match drawn*

Goddard again led South Africa against Reid's New Zealanders in a disappointing series marred by much rain and other cold and cheerless conditions. There was damage to the pitch in Auckland by anti-apartheid demonstrators and the greatest excitement came in chilly Dunedin where South Africa tried, unsuccessfully, to score 65 to win in the final 27 minutes.

Australia to England
1964
Tour captain: R. B. Simpson

Trent Bridge: *Match drawn*
Lord's: *Match drawn*
Headingley: *Australia won by 7 wickets*
Old Trafford: *Match drawn*
The Oval: *Match drawn*

Nine of Bobby Simpson's tourists were touring England for the first time, while the captain was leading for the first time abroad. It seemed strange to be watching an Australian side without Harvey, Benaud and Davidson in particular; while England, back under Dexter's direction, knew that some of their senior players were nearing the end of the line . . . young Australia, ageing England. Simpson was helped in getting the Test series off on the right note of highly competitive but personally pleasant rivalry by his wicket-keeper Wally Grout. Fred Titmus, improvising as an opener (as Geoffrey Boycott's first Test partner), could have been run out but Grout declined to break the wicket when the ball was returned to him because batsman and bowler had collided as the opening pair went for a quick single. The incident, at the very beginning of the series, set the tone and a number of friendships developed between the players which are still in existence today.

Simpson had learned the trade of captaincy from Benaud, who in turn had studied under Miller. Although he had considerable all-round ability, Simpson (unlike the other two) was an *opening* batsman by inclination. On the 1961 tour he had to take a place in the middle order until Colin McDonald was injured. From the third Test of that series onwards, Simpson became a regular opening batsman and therefore is generally regarded as a batsman who bowled (leg-spin) rather than an all-rounder in the Miller/Benaud mould. As one of the finest slip fieldsmen of all time he took upon himself the extra burden of concentrating hard in a highly specialist position, as well as skippering the side. Like Benaud in particular, he was a great student of the game and an analyst of the strengths and weaknesses of the opposition. Those who did not see him play may recall that these qualities were reflected in his *management* of later Australian sides, notably the 1989 tourists to England. If ever a captain led from the front, it was Robert Baddeley Simpson – opening batsman, first-slip catcher and breaker of partnerships.

The summer of 1964 was a wet one and most of the Tests were

interrupted with, ironically, the exception of Old Trafford where Simpson shared an opening partnership of 201 with Lawry, and scored a record (for a Test captain) 311 which started with his maiden Test century after 54 previous Test innings.

Simpson has been one of the leading figures in Australian cricket over the past 35 years, captaining his country in 39 Tests and playing a major part in the reconstruction of the international side after, first, Kerry Packer's World Series and later, the so-called 'rebel' tours to South Africa. After leading Australia for a record 29th time in the first two Tests (v. India) of 1967–8, Simpson handed over the reins to Bill Lawry and retired from Test cricket. Ten years later, however, he emerged to lead a side of players, mostly unknown outside Australia (12 of the previous summer's tourists to England having joined the World Series), to a 3–2 successful rubber against India. It was on Bobby Simpson's 42nd birthday that he took the last Indian wicket to ensure victory in the fifth and deciding Test, having scored 100 with the bat and this must stand as Simpson's cricketing monument – above all his double and triple hundreds, his average of 46.81 and his 110 catches in 62 Tests.

ENGLAND v. AUSTRALIA

The Oval, 1964

AUSTRALIA

First Innings			*Second Innings*	
Wood st Kirmani b Chandrasekhar	39		c Vengsarkar b Bedi	8
Darling c Vengsarkar b Chandrasekhar	65		b Bedi	56
Yallop c Gavaskar b Amarnath	121		b Bedi	24
Toohey c Gavaskar b Chandrasekhar	60		c Kirmani b Prasanna	10
Simpson c Viswanath b Ghavri	100			
Gosier b Ghavri	1		lbw b Ghavri	51
Rixon b Bedi	32		st Kirmani b Bedi	34
Yardley c and b Ghavri	22		run out	13
Thomson c Ghavri b Chandrasekhar	24		c Vengsarkar b Ghavri	26
Clark b Chandrasekhar	0		(11) c Amarnath b Ghavri	3
Callen not out	22		(9) lbw b Ghavri	1
			(10) not out	4
Extras (b4 lb14 nb1)	19		Extras (b5 lb15 w3 nb3)	26
Total	505		Total	256

Bowling: Ghavri 22–2–93–3; Amarnath 12–0–45–1; Bedi 34–1–127–1; Prasanna 10–1–48–1; Chandrasekhar 29.4–0–136–5; Gaekwad 5–0–37–0

Bowling: Ghavri 10.5–2–45–4; Amarnath 4–0–12–0; Bedi 20–3–53–4; Prasanna 34–7–68–1; Chandrasekhar 14–0–52–0

INDIA

First Innings		Second Innings	
Gavaskar c Toohey b Thomson	7	c Rixon b Callen	29
Chauhan c Cosier b Clark	15	c Wood b Yardley	32
Amarnath c Cosier b Thomson	0	c Callen b Yardley	86
Viswanath c Rixon b Callen	89	c Simpson b Clark	73
Vengsarkar c Rixon b Callen	44	c Toohey b Yardley	78
A. D. Gaekwad c Rixon b Callen	27	c and b Yardley	12
Kirmani run out	48	b Clark	51
Ghavri c Simpson b Clark	3	c sub b Callen	23
Prasanna not out	15	not out	10
Bedi c sub b Clark	6	c Cosier b Callen	16
Chandrasekhar c and b Clark	2	c Rixon b Simpson	2
Extras (b4 lb1 nb8)	13	Extras (b6 lb11 nb16)	33
Total	269	Total	445

Bowling: Thomson 3.3–1–12–2; Clark 27.7–6–62–4; Callen 22–0–83–3; Cosier 4–3–4–0; Yardley 23–6–62–0; Simpson 9–0–33–0

Bowling: Clark 29–6–79–2; Callen 33–5–108–3; Cosier 13–6–21–0; Yardley 43–6–134–4; Simpson 23.4–6–70–1

India's spin attack was at its best at this time and the first five batsmen provided, arguably, the greatest strength they have ever had in those positions. Simpson lost the services of his main strike bowler, Thomson, who pulled a hamstring after only 27 deliveries. The substitute fieldsman was, incidentally, Kim Hughes, later to captain Australia.

Australia to India and Pakistan
1964
Tour captain: R. B. Simpson

Madras: *Australia won by 139 runs*
Bombay: *India won by 2 wickets*
Calcutta: *Match drawn*

Karachi: *Match drawn*

After a tour of England from late April to mid-September, the Australians then moved on for four more Tests in India and Pakistan so they did not return home until the beginning of November. The Australian Board asked a lot of their players in those days and placed overwhelmingly heavy burdens upon their captains and managers.

Pakistan to Australia
1964

Tour captain: Hanif Mohammad

Melbourne: *Match drawn*

After skippering his country against Australia in Karachi 36 days earlier, Hanif Mohammad was again captain in this one-off match which saw the first Test appearance of Ian Chappell. Hanif, at 29, was now a veteran of 12 years of Test cricket, having been in the Pakistan side from the first when he started as a batsman-wicket-keeper. He had long since abandoned the stumper's duties and concentrated (a most appropriate word in his case) on his batting. In the course of a career spanning 18 years (55 Tests), Hanif achieved the reputation of one of the hardest batsmen to dismiss in the history of the game. Apart from his longest-ever innings in the West Indies (1957–8) he had to his credit a score of 499 in domestic first-class cricket. His captaincy followed the lines of his batting with a preoccupation in avoiding the possibility of error and seven of his 11 Tests as captain were drawn. He was, however, a pleasant and friendly little man with whom I worked extensively on commentary in Pakistan in 1977–8.

England to South Africa
1964–5

Tour captain: M. J. K. Smith

Durban: *England won by an innings and 104 runs*
Johannesburg: *Match drawn*
Cape Town: *Match drawn*
Johannesburg: *Match drawn*
Port Elizabeth: *Match drawn*

Following his successful stand-in captaincy in India the previous winter, M. J. K. Smith once more came to the selectors' rescue when the party for South Africa was being picked. Ted Dexter had decided to stand as a Parliamentary candidate in the autumn General Election and Colin Cowdrey was not available, so Smith took with him a party which was the subject of fairly sharp Press criticism. Contemporary reports noted with severe disapproval the choice of Mike Brearley in preference to the more experienced Tom Graveney, Eric Russell and Mickey Stewart.

Future events would indicate selectorial perspicacity in looking to the future in Brearley's case and the critics might well have concentrated on the inexperience of the fast bowling department where the main support for Price (Middlesex) was likely to come from Ian Thomson, of Sussex, as yet uncapped. In the event, Dexter's venture into politics proved unsuccessful and he then joined the party as Smith's vice-captain and batted well, along with Boycott, Barrington and Smith himself, but it was the two off-spinners, Allen and Titmus, who bore the brunt of the attack. Although England won the first Test, catching the opposition on a turning wicket after Smith had fortunately won the toss, South Africa were never again bowled out twice in the series. For the final Test, when Price was injured together with David Brown, the Warwickshire quick bowler, England were forced to call in Ken Palmer, of Somerset, who was in South Africa on a coaching engagement.

Smith, then, had his problems with an attack which was never incisive enough in normal conditions and on Test wickets so that his opposite number (Goddard), Barlow, Pithey, Bland and, above all, the brilliant younger Pollock scored heavily. The England captain was forced therefore on occasions to fall back on a strategy which was becoming increasingly fashionable in the game – slowing down the over-rate. The young Brearley, who was newly down from Cambridge after a brilliant academic (and cricketing) three years, did not get into the Test side and in fact had to wait for almost another 12 years before making his international debut, watched with more than passing interest from the dressing-room.

He was, he observed many years later, 'appalled and embarrassed' when England bowled only 29 overs in one two-hour period. One likes to believe, however, that Brearley learned something of man-management on his first tour – an aspect of captaincy at which he was to excel but in a different way from Mike Smith.

Pakistan to New Zealand
1965
Tour captain: Hanif Mohammed

Wellington: *Match drawn*
Auckland: *Match drawn*
Christchurch: *Match drawn*

Hanif Mohammad's policy of avoiding defeat at all costs was seen at its worst in Auckland where Pakistan, batting first, managed slightly over one run per over on the opening day. The first and third Tests were badly affected by rain and the batting on both sides did little to stimulate the small crowds.

New Zealand to India and Pakistan
1965
Tour captain: J. R. Reid

Madras: *Match drawn*
Calcutta: *Match drawn*
Bombay: *Match drawn*
Delhi: *India won by 7 wickets*

Rawalpindi: *Pakistan won by an innings and 64 runs*
Lahore: *Match drawn*
Karachi: *Pakistan won by 8 wickets*

Within 11 days of completing their home series against Pakistan, New Zealand were playing the first match of their Indian tour, once again with Reid as captain. One of his opening bowlers, Bruce Taylor, scored a maiden first-class hundred in his first Test appearance in Calcutta, then went on to take five wickets for 86. It was, however, a fruitless tour for Reid who then led his troops on to Pakistan where he experienced a two-nil defeat in the three-match series.

Reid, after making four and nought in the first Test, scored 88, 128 and 76 in his three other innings and after watching Hanif bat for nearly 7½ hours in Lahore, had the intense satisfaction of bowling his rival captain for one in Karachi. It was, Reid grimly observed, one of the greater moments of his life! There was no time to rest and contemplate the achievement, however. By the end of the month (April), the New Zealanders were in England for a three-Test series. We shall look at that summer in a moment, but during that crowded period of the first four months of 1965, Australia visited the West Indies.

Australia to West Indies
1965
Tour captain: R. B. Simpson

Jamaica: *West Indies won by 179 runs*
Trinidad: *Match drawn*
British Guiana: *West Indies won by 212 runs*
Barbados: *Match drawn*
Trinidad: *Australia won by 10 wickets*

Simpson's opposition captain was another man who led from the front, a man whose leadership we shall consider in more detail shortly but it is worth noting that in this series Garfield Sobers did not score one century and that had not happened for a long time. Is this, perhaps, an example of captaincy affecting personal performance? Sobers was later to adopt a less intense attitude to leadership but in five Tests which saw some prolific run-making his personal best was 69. Simpson, now an experienced captain, felt no such inhibitions and in Barbados he and Lawry both scored double centuries and shared an opening partnership of 382 in a match which was drawn, with a total of 1,640 runs scored.

Like English batsmen 18 months earlier, the Australians on that tour were convinced that Charlie Griffith 'chucked' his quicker ball and there was a strong feeling – shared by English and South African cricketers – that the legislators had spent too much time trying to produce an acceptable definition of what constituted a throw while there was no universally acknowledged definition of what was a *fair* delivery.

There was deep concern in the Australian camp about the physical dangers presented by Griffith but, as ever with their tour teams, they refused to allow it to dampen their off-duty spirits. From every Australian tour abroad there has always come a rich fund of entertaining anecdotes and the one I like best from this trip was passed on by my friend Neil Hawke. En route from the first Test to the island of St Kitts, the party had to break their journey in Puerto Rico. Now the Australians, all part-timers and officially *amateur* cricketers, had pretty modest daily allowances for meals and while waiting for their connection in St Juan they were given five dollars each to feed themselves. As this, according to Hawke (or 'Ghoul' as he was known to his teammates) would merely have bought them a hamburger or a milk shake, half a dozen of them decided to pool their resources and invest them in a casino.

Barry Jarman was entrusted with the 30 dollars of which he gambled two bucks on red on the roulette wheel. It won; he doubled up and won again. By letting the stake and winnings 'ride' on red, he quickly

erry Alexander and Peter May at the Queen's Park
val, Port-of-Spain

Nari Contractor, who almost died in the West Indies

ohn Reid, a tough New Zealander

Richie Benaud hits F.S. Trueman high . . . 'It's alright,
sunshine, it were a no-ball'

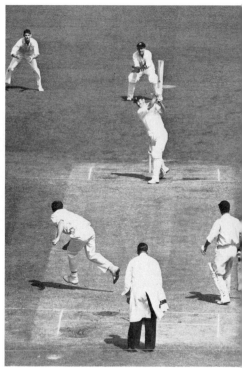

'Young' Pataudi batting for Oxford University, 1962

A typical lordly drive by Ted Dexter

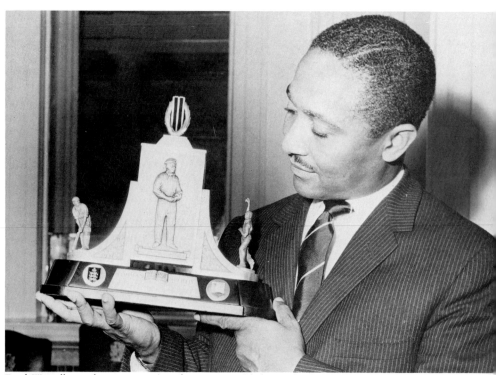

Frank Worrell, great batsman, captain and sportsman, with the Wisden Trophy

M.K. Smith — 'looked after the boys'

A glass of bubbly for the friendly rivals: Ian Chappell and Ray Illingworth

Two New Zealand skippers together: Glenn Turner (completing 1000 runs before the end of May, 1973) and Mark Burgess

The artistry of Bishen Singh Bedi

Triumph in India for Tony Greig

Wasim Bari and Geoff Boycott toss at Karachi in 197
watched by Ken Barrington

Two Pakistan captains in action together — Intikhab Alam (hooking Chris Old's no-ball) and Mushtaq
Mohammed. The umpire is Tommy Spencer

found himself with winnings of 128 dollars plus the 28 of their original pool. Food was forgotten and the party adjourned to the nearest bar . . . for champagne!

Despite the problem of Griffith, this was again a happy and enjoyable tour in spite of a losing rubber. Australians seem to have been able to enjoy cricket and touring in the West Indies more than the players of any other country. This is not to say that no other country enjoys going there but with other tourists there has been at one time or another a drama, a controversy, a riot, a disaster. Conversations with Aussies who have been to the Caribbean invariably invoke a huge smile and an outpouring of joyous reminiscence.

New Zealand to England
1965
Tour captain: J. R. Reid

Edgbaston: *England won by 9 wickets*
Lord's: *England won by 7 wickets*
Headingley: *England won by an innings and 187 runs*

The emerging force and drawing-power of West Indian cricket had prompted the ICC to give sympathetic consideration to their request for more frequent tours, particularly to England and Australia where the profits helped the development of their domestic cricket. Consequently a reshuffling of the scheduled tours brought about the first *double* tour to England in 1965 with New Zealand and South Africa each playing three Tests. As a result, the West Indies, who were not due in England until 1971, were now able to tour in 1966.

As the guinea pigs of this experiment, New Zealand, with Reid as captain and Walter Hadlee as manager, lost all three Tests and were on the receiving end of some heavy scoring by Cowdrey, Dexter and in particular John Edrich, whose 310 not out at Headingley was the first triple century by an Englishman since Hutton's 364 in 1938. Hutton had hit his on Surrey's ground; Edrich made his at Hutton's head-quarters. Two fine cricketers ended their Test careers during this series in a way which was rather sadly linked. Bert Sutcliffe, the fine left-hander who had made his Test debut 18 years earlier, came out of retirement to add a little experience to Reid's relatively young side. At Edgbaston he was hit on the ear by a bouncer from the 34-year-old Trueman and retired hurt. He played a gallant innings of 53 second time round but that was his last Test appearance. No 'successful' strike against a batsman distressed 'F S T' more than this one. He followed

Sutcliffe into Test retirement after the second Test, after taking his 307th wicket in 67 matches.

The final Test of the series was John Reid's 34th and last as captain of New Zealand. He had captained his country through one of the leaner periods of their history, rarely finding himself in charge of a settled side but always leading by example as batsman, bowler and, if necessary, wicket-keeper. His was always a battle against the odds but he had seen history made when he skippered New Zealand in their first Test victory and he was never less than one hundred per cent competitive in any game he played.

South Africa to England
1965
Tour captain: P. L. van der Merwe

Lord's: *Match drawn*
Trent Bridge: *South Africa won by 94 runs*
The Oval: *Match drawn*

To Peter Lawrence van der Merwe fell the unhappy role of skippering the last South African tour team. After this visit they went into cricketing isolation for political reasons, although Australia paid two more visits to that country before its final excommunication from international cricket. At least South Africa went out with a bang in 1965 (overseas tours) as they were to do in their 1970 home series and thereafter their only players to enjoy Test cricket were those who came to play in the English County Championship (Greig, Lamb, Chris and Robin Smith) or who went to Australia (Keppler Wessels). Van der Merwe's captaincy followed the pattern of his personal batting – thoughtful, cautious, painstaking – but he had in his ranks men whose cricket was substantially different. The reasons for allocating only three Tests in a double series were not clearly understood in South Africa and although the team was not vastly experienced it arrived with a determination to make England pay for what was regarded as something of a slight. Thus van der Merwe had nationalist feeling on his side in building up a formidable team effort. The Pollock brothers, whom I had met as teenagers at their home in Port Elizabeth five years earlier, had a brilliant tour, together with Bland and Barlow.

Barlow, bespectacled like his captain, was an aggressive opening batsman, accomplished slip fielder and an extremely useful change bowler; Bland, apart from his batting, set new standards of excellence in the field at cover point or mid-wicket and made as many headlines in this role as anyone else in the party with bat or ball. At Lord's he ran out both Barrington and Parks with direct hits on the stumps and it was calculated that he saved as many as 30 runs a match. South Africa's win at Trent Bridge was England's first defeat under Mike Smith's captaincy and it was enough to secure the rubber.

The team played with great determination, shrugging off the occasional demonstration by anti-apartheid factions to play attractive cricket. One personal memory brings an ironical smile. The first game of the tour was against Derbyshire at Queen's Park, Chesterfield – a public park where the staff traditionally set out a flower-bed in the form of the national arms of the season's touring side. Having renewed my acquaintance with the Pollock brothers, I watched while they photographed the floral coat-of-arms of the Republic of South Africa. Looking back 25 years, one wonders what the reaction of the current Member of Parliament for Chesterfield would have been to the efforts of the Council's Parks Department!

England to Australia
1965–6
Tour captain: M. J. K. Smith

Brisbane: *Match drawn*
Melbourne: *Match drawn*
Sydney: *England won by an innings and 93 runs*
Adelaide: *Australia won by an innings and 9 runs*
Melbourne: *Match drawn*

Mike Smith's party was the first to fly all the way to Australia and it looked thin in the bowling department since Statham had followed Trueman into Test retirement. Nevertheless, once again Smith achieved a good team spirit and despite both sides being stronger in batting than bowling and stoppages for rain in two Tests, a clear result was achieved in Sydney and Adelaide. The final match was notable for Cowper's 12-hour innings of 307 and the retirement of Wally Grout after 51 Tests. Some authorities rate Grout as the greatest Australian wicket-keeper. For sheer quality my preference is for Tallon but there is no doubt that Grout was a highly-skilled operator behind the stumps as well as being one of the most popular Australians with opposition teams.

England to New Zealand
1966
Tour captain: M. J. K. Smith

Christchurch: *Match drawn*
Dunedin: *Match drawn*
Auckland: *Match drawn*

Smith's declaration at Lancaster Park gave New Zealand a chance to score 196 in 139 minutes for their first win over England. This had to be seen as generous since it was difficult to see a Test side being bowled out in less than 2½ hours but Smith had calculated well. In going for a tempting target, Murray Chapple's men almost brought about their own undoing and were 48 for 8 at the end. Vice-captain Cowdrey, ever a popular figure in New Zealand, held his 100th slip catch and played his record 141st innings for England during the series. Smith came home destined to play only one more Test as captain.

For holding his side together in the face of crippling difficulties, Smith's greatest achievement must be the drawn second Test in India in 1964.

INDIA v. ENGLAND
Bombay, India 1964

INDIA

First Innings		Second Innings	
Mehra lbw b Knight	9	lbw b Titmus	35
Kunderan c Wilson b Price	29	c Titmus b Price	16
Sardesai b Price	12	run out	66
Manjrekar c Binks b Titmus	0	(8) not out	43
Nawab of Pataudi jnr	10	(4) b Price	0
Jaisimha c Price b Titmus	23	(5) c Larter b Knight	66
Borde c Binks b Wilson	84	c Smith b Titmus	7
Durani c Binks b Price	90	(6) c Knight b Titmus	3
Nadkarni not out	26	lbw b Knight	0
Rajinder Pal lbw b Larter	3	not out	3
Chandrasekhar b Larter	0	did not bat	
Extras (b2 lb9 nb3)	14	Extras (lb4 wl nb5)	10
Total	300	Total (8 wkts declared)	249

Bowling: Knight 20–3–53–2; Larter 10.3–2–35–2; Jones 13–0–48–0; Price 19–2–66–3; Titmus 36–17–56–2; Wilson 15–5–28–1

Bowling: Knight 13–2–28–2; Larter 5–0–13–0; Jones 11–1–31–0; Price 17–1–47–2; Titmus 46–18–79–3; Wilson 23–10–41–0

ENGLAND

First Innings		Second Innings	
Bolus c Chandrasekhar b Durani	25	c Pataudi b Durani	57
Smith c Borde b Chandrasekhar	46	(4) not out	31
Parks run out	1	(5) not out	40
Knight b Chandrasekhar	12		
Titmus not out	84		
Wilson c and b Durani	1	(3) c Pataudi b Chandrasekhar	2
Binks b Chandrasekhar	10	(2) c Borde b Jaisimha	55
Price b Chandrasekhar	32		
Larter c Borde b Durani	0		
Jones run out	5		
Stewart absent ill			
Extras (b4 lb7 nb6)	17	*Extras* (b12 lb7 wl nbl)	21
Total	233	Total (for 3 wkts)	206

Bowling: Rajinder Pal 11–4–19–0; Jaisimha 3–1–9–0; Durani 38–15–59–3; Borde 34–12–54–0; Chandrasekhar 40–16–67–4; Nadkarni 4–2–8–0

Bowling: Rajinder Pal 2–0–3–0; Jaisimha 22–9–36–1; Durani 29–12–35–1; Borde 37–12–38–0; Chandrasekhar 22–5–40–1; Nadkarni 14–11–3–0; Sardesai 3–2–6–0; Mehra 2–1–1–0; Pataudi 3–0–23–0

West Indies to England
1966
Tour captain: G. St. A. Sobers

Old Trafford: *West Indies won by an innings and 40 runs*
Lord's: *Match drawn*
Trent Bridge: *West Indies won by an innings and 139 runs*
Headingley: *West Indies won by an innings and 55 runs*
The Oval: *England won by an innings and 34 runs*

Gary Sobers ushered in a new era of Test captaincy when his tenth West Indians flew in to the rain-soaked spring of 1966. His party was weak in opening batting and the pace attack of Hall and Griffith seemed to have been around for a long time although they were in fact 28 and 27 years old respectively. Again there were rumblings around the counties about Griffith's quicker deliveries but again he was not 'called'. It is interesting to note that contemporary newspaper critics complained of Sobers' cavalier attitude to matches with the counties – 'treating them as practice games'. If the critics were justified, then Sobers was acting as a trail blazer because 'other' fixtures on tours have for a long time now been regarded simply as warm-up games. Indeed, in England the policy is to rest senior players in such matches but in 1966 Sobers was perhaps being a little avant garde. About his own cricket there were no complaints for the greatest all-rounder the world has seen (if one discounts the statistical claims of Wilfred Rhodes [1898–1930],

39,969 runs, 4,204 wickets) set the most spectacular standards by averaging 103 in Tests, taking 20 wickets and fielding quite brilliantly in close-catching positions. When one talks of leading by example, thoughts turn immediately to Sobers who played his cricket with an air of joyous exuberance which was infectious. That he was a competitor in every sense of the word there is no doubt.

Nothing delighted him more than a battle against the odds – in any context. He would happily have played Jack Nicklaus, Arnold Palmer or Nick Faldo, off level golf handicaps, for a fiver; he loved a race meeting and was not exactly the bookmaker's least favourite punter; and no target set by a cricket captain could be resisted.

Sobers was not a studious, deep-thinking leader; for him, cricket captaincy was a straightforward matter of 'our' ability against 'theirs' and *ours* usually meant *his*. He was the most magnificent and glorious of cricketers and yet he carried his God-given ability lightly. It was something to be enjoyed rather than glorified. He was one of the most friendly and pleasant West Indian cricketers I have ever known and was equally popular wherever he played. His contribution to the West Indies' success in this series, and to the enjoyment of the cricketing public, was immense. His scores were 161, 46 and 163 not out, 3 and 94, 174, 81 and 0. After replacing M. J. K. Smith as captain after the first Test, the selectors then relieved his successor, Cowdrey, after the fourth and appointed Brian Close, a skipper who combined flair and amateur psychology with one of the shrewdest cricketing minds in the game.

At The Oval, England achieved a first-innings lead of 259 due to some astonishing tail-end batting by Murray (112), Higgs (63) and Snow (59). They lifted England from 166 for 7 to 527 all out. West Indies were three up in the series and almost any other captain would have fought to the end to avoid defeat. It seemed that Sobers had this thought at The Oval when he held himself back to number 7 and went to the wicket with his side at 137 for 5. Close (as keen a follower of the Turf as Gary Sobers but with a little more Yorkshire caution in his cricketing make-up) knew his man. He ostentatiously discussed the field-placing with Snow, then England's fastest bowler, and as he took his own place at short leg Close signalled to John Murray to stand a little wider on the off side. Sobers didn't need it spelling out to him – he knew he was to be tried out with a bouncer. As he was probably the best hooker in the world at that time the challenge was irresistible. He was fractionally late on the shot but what he had not bargained for was short leg, crouching and alert waiting for the catch instead of taking rapid evasive action. The ball flew from bottom edge, via thigh pad or 'box', into Close's hands.

Sobers stood for a moment, observed Close's grim smile and companionable wink, and realized in that moment that one gambler had outsmarted another. He could not help it – he *laughed* as he returned to the dressing-room. England had the last laugh by winning the Test.

West Indies to India
1966–7
Tour captain: G. St. A. Sobers

Bombay: *West Indies won by 6 wickets*
Calcutta: *West Indies won by an innings and 45 runs*
Madras: *Match drawn*

The first Test of this series was significant in that it introduced to international cricket Ajit Wadekar, a future Indian captain, and Clive Lloyd who was destined to lead West Indies to their pre-eminent position as the finest team, by far, in the world. Lloyd observed Sobers' captaincy with interest, even though at that point he had no thoughts of leading the side himself. Lloyd had a cautious streak which was completely alien to Sobers' nature but for the moment the cavalier approach to captaincy was the West Indies' policy. Some of Gary's decisions in the field mystified his senior players, but in terms of individual and collective ability the tourists were so far ahead of the home side that he had few problems until the final innings in Madras where the spinners, Prasanna and the newly emerging Bishen Singh Bedi, put West Indies in danger of unthinkable defeat. Sobers was forced to play a totally out-of-character defensive innings with the unlikely partner of Griffith to save the game. Rioting and the firing of stands marked the second Test where Gary demonstrated the versatility of his bowling by using both slow left-arm orthodox and back-of-the-hand bowling, after sharing the new ball.

Australia to South Africa
1966–7

Tour captain: R. B. Simpson

Johannesburg: *South Africa won by 233 runs*
Cape Town: *Australia won by 6 wickets*
Durban: *South Africa won by 8 wickets*
Johannesburg: *Match drawn*
Port Elizabeth: *South Africa won by 7 wickets*

The first ever defeat of Australia on South African soil in 64 years and the subsequent losing of the rubber seem largely inexplicable if one looks at an immensely powerful batting line-up. Simpson's problems arose largely from his bowlers' inability to dismiss South Africa twice, or cheaply enough to get into a position to win except at Newlands. And even there South Africa scored a total of 720 runs before losing. They were put in by Simpson in Durban and lost Barlow to the first ball of the match yet still won it comfortably. Putting in the opposition after winning the toss has happened a little more frequently in recent years but in the mid-sixties it was still an event – and one to be kept very much in mind when it led to defeat by eight wickets. It was not a tour Simpson recalls with particular delight.

India to England
1967

Tour captain: The Nawab of Pataudi jun.

Headingley: *England won by 6 wickets*
Lord's: *England won by an innings and 124 runs*
Edgbaston: *England won by 132 runs*

It was five years since the younger Pataudi had been pitchforked into Test captaincy in the West Indies and now he was an experienced and natural leader. Additionally, he had played a lot of cricket in this country – at school (Winchester), three years at Oxford and in the County Championship with Sussex, skippering them in 1966. He was therefore a cosmopolitan character with a sense of humour which was distinctly European. He had overcome the immense handicap of losing an eye in a road accident in 1961 and has so far spent the rest of his life making light of an injury which would have caused most people to abandon all hope of continuing to play cricket. He thought at first he had merely injured a hand in the crash but a splinter of glass had entered his eye. After its removal he never again had full sight in the damaged eye but within four weeks he was back in the nets. He found difficulty in adjusting the focus of his good eye to tasks like lighting a cigarette, or pouring a glass of water from a jug, so cricket had to be adjusted to as well. George Cox, the Sussex coach, spent hours bowling to him in the nets until a new technique had been evolved which served him well enough.

While he played his cricket and led his country in a thoroughly efficient manner, laughter was never far from 'The Noob's' lips. That nickname, by which he was most generally referred to in English cricket, was one of several thought to have been bestowed by his fellow student and team-mate at Oxford, David Green, in a Press interview conducted on the Nawab's behalf while he was batting. Green smilingly disclaims 'credit' for this but the origins are of no great importance; 'The Noob' or 'Tiger' was ever a popular figure in cricketing circles everywhere.

Pataudi somehow found a smile in everything . . . in the inability of his team sometimes to communicate with each other without the aid of an interpreter; in the fact that his princely family found favour in the eye of the Raj through not fighting against the British in the Indian Mutiny; in his obligatory tiger-hunt, aged eight, firing his first shot 'which scared me more than the tiger'. I have long suspected that it was the Pataudi humour which led to an hilarious mix-up when the tourists played Yorkshire at Bramall Lane. Fred Trueman, skippering the home side, insisted he had indicated to the Indian captain that he required them to follow-on; 'The Noob' gravely maintained that he had received no such invitation. And the two sides started to emerge from the pavilion side by side . . .

Pataudi in 1967 needed all his sense of humour to remain cheerful on a tour dogged by wet weather, by injuries to his bowlers and by fragile batting. Notwithstanding his personal 64 and 148 at Headingley, the game was lost and indeed India were never in contention. Yet he lost none of his natural courtesy with interviewers and, I am sure, he never lost his smile.

Pakistan to England
1967
Tour captain: Hanif Mohammad

Lord's: *Match drawn*
Trent Bridge: *England won by 10 wickets*
The Oval: *England won by 8 wickets*

Hanif Mohammad was again Pakistan's captain in the second half of a wet and miserable summer and it is interesting to note that his team at Lord's included one past and seven future captains. The Pakistanis were a much stronger side than India had proved in the first half of the summer with three of them – Mushtaq, Ibadulla and Nasim-ul-Ghani – experienced in English conditions but Hanif's lack of enterprise and unimaginative approach stifled the initiative of his side. Even his record (at that time) 187 at Lord's seemed designed as a match-*saving* effort and Pakistan's response to a challenge to score 257 in 210 minutes to win was to reach 88 for 3.

England to West Indies
1968
Tour captain: M. C. Cowdrey

Trinidad: *Match drawn*
Jamaica: *Match drawn*
Barbados: *Match drawn*
Trinidad: *England won by 7 wickets*
Guyana: *Match drawn*

The fact that Colin Cowdrey and not Brian Close, the unbeaten England captain in seven previous Tests, led the side to West Indies in the first three months of 1968 requires explanation. Between the second and third Tests against Pakistan the previous summer, Close had been subjected to intense Press criticism for slowing down Yorkshire's progress in the closing stages of a County Championship match against Warwickshire at Edgbaston. It was a practice which had now become standard procedure in Test cricket throughout the world and it was to get considerably worse in the future. Such was the furore in newspapers,

however, that Close was summoned to Lord's and in spite of a spirited
and logically argued defence he was severely censured for using delaying
tactics which were held to constitute unfair play. Now this was in a
county match, not a Test; as we have already seen, Test captains used
the slowing-down process as a not-infrequent tactical weapon. But just
before the closing ceremonies at The Oval to mark England's series win
over Pakistan, Close was officially told he would not be leading the
side in the West Indies. The news shattered him and it damningly
confirmed the long-held Yorkshire view that M C C did not like their
teams to be led by blunt north countrymen who were not afraid to
stick to their principles or to speak their minds.

So it was Michael Colin Cowdrey who was appointed to head the
party on the winter tour. Cowdrey seemed destined for an always-
the-bridesmaid-and-never-the-bride role because of the frequency with
which he was appointed as England's *vice*-captain. Of his cricketing
pedigree there had never been the slightest doubt. He was a brilliant
batsman of the highest class; he was a superb slip fieldsman as 638
catches testify (120 of them in Tests); he was, and remains, one of the
most charming men in the game. His background, in captaincy terms,
was impeccable (Tonbridge and Oxford) and he was never involved in
public controversies, while Close was rarely free of them. Yet in the
last analysis there was always something enigmatic about his Test captaincy. It was difficult to identify with absolute precision but it seemed
that at moments of decision he could be found wanting. There was
nothing dynamic about his leadership . . . no hint of flamboyance, no
touch of flair, no professional intensity. Cowdrey gave the impression
of reliable solidity. One felt that while nothing dramatic would occur
to swing a game England's way from a touch-and-go situation, nothing
would go spectacularly wrong, either.

So, in the potentially volatile atmosphere of the West Indies, he
probably seemed in selectorial eyes to be the safe bet. At least he would
provoke no drama in the Caribbean and if a situation arose where tact
and diplomacy were called for, these were qualities he possessed in
abundance. Close, on the other hand, if confronted by a riot would
without hesitation be prepared to take on 30,000 enraged Trinidadians
single-handed. And the selectors – entirely unwittingly, I am sure – had
found the perfect way to counter the instinctive, natural genius of the
home captain, Sobers. After three drawn Tests, West Indies led England
by 122 on the first innings in the high-charged atmosphere of the
Queen's Park Oval in Port of Spain. To the utter astonishment of his
own side and the fury of the home crowd, Sobers then declared his
second innings closed at 92 for 2. It left England to score 215 in 165
minutes against an attack in which Gary's main strike bowler, Griffith,
was out of action with a pulled thigh muscle! And Wes Hall was not

even playing in the match. It has to rank as one of the most generous, or foolhardy, declarations in cricket history and probably no captain but Sobers would have made it. England won by seven wickets with a little more than an over to spare and there was a certain bitter irony in the fact that Close was there to see it, providing expert comments for a newspaper. With a grim smile he reported: 'A captain only declares to suit his own purposes. He doesn't do it if it gives the other side a chance to win.'

But what must he have thought when Sobers (a West Indian captain being given a police escort from the ground for his own safety while his effigy was being hanged, then burned, in the streets of the city) finally explained his quixotic declaration. He had been fed up, he said, with England's negative tactics and slow over-rates in the series and was determined to get a result in at least one match!

And so, with the final Test drawn (England hanging on by the skin of their teeth), Cowdrey was a winning captain on tour and it has to be said that he did his part nobly with the bat, particularly in that win in Port of Spain where he scored 148 and 71; he retained the captaincy for the home series against Australia. If he does not rate the very highest place as a Test captain there is no doubt that he had his moments and in any case his place in cricket history is assured by his magnificent batsmanship from the earliest schooldays through 114 Tests and for his eminently courteous stance, consistently maintained.

For his personal example in the winning of the fourth Test in Trindad in 1968, this is Cowdrey's match.

WEST INDIES v. ENGLAND

Trinidad, 1968

WEST INDIES

First Innings		*Second Innings*	
Camacho c Knott b Brown	87	c Graveney b Snow	31
Carew c Lock b Brown	36	not out	40
Nurse c Edrich b Barrington	136	run out	9
Kanhai c Barrington b Lock	153	not out	2
Lloyd b Jones	43		
Sobers c Jones b Brown	48		
Butcher not out	7		
Rodriguez b Jones	0		
Murray not out	5		
Griffith ⎱ did not bat			
Gibbs ⎰			
Extras (lb6 nb5)	11	*Extras* (bl lb7 nb2)	10
Total (7 wkts declared)	526	Total (2 wkts declared)	92

Bowling: Brown 27–2–107–3; Snow 20–3–68–0; Jones 29–1–108–2; D'Oliveira 15–2–62–0; Lock 32–3–129–1; Barrington 10–2–41–1

Bowling: Brown 10–2–33–0; Snow 9–0–29–1; Jones 11–2–20–0

ENGLAND

First Innings		Second Innings	
Edrich c Lloyd b Carew	32	b Rodriguez	29
Boycott c Nurse b Rodriguez	62	not out	80
Cowdrey c Murray b Butcher	148	c Sobers b Gibbs	71
Barrington lbw b Gibbs	48		
Graveney c Murray b Rodriguez	8	(4) b Gibbs	2
D'Oliveira b Rodriguez	0	(5) not out	12
Knott not out	69		
Snow b Butcher	0		
Brown c Murray b Butcher	0		
Lock lbw b Butcher	3		
Jones b Butcher	1		
Extras (b13 lb11 w2 nb7)	33	Extras (b11 lb6 nb4)	21
Total	404	Total (for 3 wkts)	215

Bowling: Sobers 36–8–87–0; Griffith 3–1–7–0; Gibbs 57–24–68–1; Rodriguez 35–4–145–3; Carew 25–18–23–1; Butcher 13.4–2–34–5; Lloyd 4–2–7–0; Nurse 2–2–0–0

Bowling: Sobers 14–0–48–0; Gibbs 16.4–1–76–2; Rodriguez 10–1–34–1; Carew 7–2–19–0; Butcher 5–1–17–0.

India to Australia
1967–8

Tour captain: The Nawab of Pataudi jun.

Adelaide: *Australia won by 146 runs*
Melbourne: *Australia won by an innings and 4 runs*
Brisbane: *Australia won by 39 runs*
Sydney: *Australia won by 144 runs*

After three defeats in England, this meant seven in a row for the Nawab of Pataudi but he did not lose either his sense of humour or the captaincy. He missed the first Test because of injury and the leadership passed, for the first and only time, to Chandu Borde, then India's most experienced international cricketer. Borde, a genuine all-rounder (leg-spin bowler), was a popular league professional in England and also played Minor Counties cricket for Northumberland. Pataudi, back in action for the second Test, immediately struck form with the bat but Indian bowling – as ever – was weak in the pace department although Abid Ali, the new boy from Hyderabad, made a big impression in his first Test appearance (6 for 55 in Adelaide). After that, however, Simpson's very strong batting line-up worked him out and there were only two more Test wickets for Ali on the tour.

Pataudi, who was playing 'down under' for the first time, nevertheless enjoyed the Australian way of life and was a popular touring captain, not least of all for his philosophy: 'I want to win just as badly as anyone

– within the written laws of the game and the unwritten laws of sportsmanship. A game isn't worth playing unless you are trying to win. But if, having tried your hardest, you still lose, it is not the end of the world.' That endeared him to Australians, who enjoy winning a little more than most and they loved the stories which circulated about this young Indian nobleman who had been brought up in a palace with 150 rooms and 100 servants, seven or eight of whom were his personal attendants. Most of all they loved stories like that of 'The Noob', skippering Sussex in 1966 and attending a mayoral reception with his team during the Cheltenham Festival. He responded to the civic welcome in Hindi, with a translation provided by his senior pro, Ken Suttle! It goes without saying that Ken did *not* speak Hindi.

Pataudi had just one fixation as a captain – he would not tolerate sloppy fielding. Anyone who let the side down in that department, he warned, was 'for the chop'. Just how did this gifted young man manage to bat so well with such a fearful handicap? His version, told with the inevitable self-deprecating humour, is that after being given a year's leave of absence from Oxford he played down the effects of his disability to the Indian selectors who invited him to captain the President's team against Ted Dexter's 1961–2 tourists. Pataudi batted with a contact lens in the damaged eye which gave him double vision. 'I could see two balls, about six inches apart, and after a bit of experimenting I played the "inner" one of the two, and got 35!' He was selected for the second Test and was sure he would never have been picked if the extent of his handicap had been known. He then had to cry off because of a sprained ankle! He did, however, make his Test debut in the third match of 1961–2, scoring 13; but in the fourth Test he made 64 and 32 and in the fifth he hit his first Test century, with two sixes and sixteen fours. By that time he had worked out the way to play. He pulled his cap down over the right eye to eliminate the effect of its blurred vision.

He captained India at a rather low ebb in the country's cricketing fortunes, although he did oversee the development of that brilliant trio of bowlers – Bedi, Chandrasekhar and Prasanna.

India to New Zealand
1968

Tour captain: The Nawab of Pataudi jun.

Dunedin: *India won by 5 wickets*
Christchurch: *New Zealand won by 6 wickets*
Wellington: *India won by 8 wickets*

New Zealand's win at Lancaster Park was their first against India and only their fourth Test win in all, but Pataudi's men won the rubber in Wellington where the captain owed much to the man who was to succeed him, Wadekar, whose first innings 143 set up the winning position. For his miraculous comeback after a crippling injury and for scoring 103 when he could literally see out of only one eye, Pataudi's Test must be the one at Madras in 1962.

INDIA v. ENGLAND

Madras, 1962

INDIA

First Innings

Jaisimha b Knight	12
Contractor b Barber	86
Manjrekar c Lock b Parfitt	13
Nawab of Pataudi c Lock b Knight	103
Umrigar c Millman b Allen	2
Borde b Lock	31
Durani b Allen	21
Nadkarni b Allen	63
Engineer b Dexter	65
Desai lbw b Barber	13
Prasanna not out	9
Extras (b4 lb6)	10
Total	428

Second Innings

c Millman b Lock	10
c Parfitt b D. Smith	3
run out	85
c M. Smith b Lock	10
c and b Allen	11
(7) c Dexter b Parfitt	7
(8) c Millman b Lock	9
(9) c Parfitt b Lock	1
(10) not out	15
(6) c Parfitt b Lock	12
c Dexter b Lock	17
Extras (b6 lb4)	10
Total	190

Bowling: D. Smith 9–1–20–0; Knight 14–2–62–2; Lock 40–13–106–1; Allen 51.3–20–116–3; Parfitt 11–2–22–1; Barber 14–0–70–2; Dexter 5–0–22–1

Bowling: D. Smith 7–0–15–1; Knight 4–0–12–0; Lock 39.3–16–65–6; Allen 33–11–64–1; Parfitt 11–3–24–1

ENGLAND

First Innings

Richardson c Contractor b Desai	13
Barber lbw b Borde	16
Barrington c Manjrekar b Durani	20
Dexter b Borde	2
M. J. K. Smith c Umrigar b Durani	73
Parfitt c Prasanna b Durani	25
Knight c Nadkarni b Durani	19
Allen b Durani	34
Millman not out	32
Lock c Borde b Durani	0
D. R. Smith b Nadkarni	34
Extras (b1 lb12)	13
Total	281

Second Innings

c Jaisimha b Desai	2
b Durani	21
lbw b Nadkarni	48
c Nadkarni b Borde	3
c Borde b Durani	15
c Contractor b Durani	33
c Engineer b Durani	33
c Umrigar b Borde	21
c Contractor b Prasanna	14
c Nadkarni b Borde	11
not out	2
Extras (b2 lb4)	6
Total	209

Bowling: Desai 12–1–56–1; Jaisimha 5–0–18–0; Durani 36–9–105–6; Borde 30–9–58–2; Prasanna 9–2–20–0; Umrigar 12–6–11–0; Nadkarni 6.1–6–0–1

Bowling: Desai 4–0–16–1; Durani 34–12–72–4; Borde 25.3–8–59–3; Prasanna 11–3–19–1; Umrigar 6–1–12–0; Nadkarni 12–3–25–1

Australia to England
1968

Tour captain: W. M. Lawry (B. Jarman)

Old Trafford: *Australia won by 159 runs*
Lord's: *Match drawn*
Edgbaston: *Match drawn*
Headingley: *Match drawn*
The Oval: *England won by 226 runs*

It is a fair bet that anyone who saw William Morris Lawry bat on any of his three tours of England (1961, 1964, 1968) and who had no personal acquaintance with the man would form an entirely wrong impression of his character. They would see him doing a very sound job indeed as a Test opener, blunting the edge of the opposition attack, softening it up to pave the way for the gifted stroke-makers who followed. Almost certainly the impression would be gained of a dour and unsmiling personality. Nothing could have been further from the truth.

Humour had (and has) a major place in the Lawry make-up. He reminisces about cricket with superb whimsicality, specializing in the dry throw-away line. His years in the Australian dressing-room were marked by a long series of practical jokes, often with his captain as the target. Richie Benaud, in 1962, was fond of a pair of slip-on shoes which he stepped into when the day's labour was over, not bothering to sit down and pull the shoes on to his feet. This had been observed over a period of time by Lawry who, once he was satisfied that the habit was a regular one, nailed Richie's shoes to the floor. As the captain tried to hurry to a reception at close of play he found himself rooted to the spot . . . with Lawry holding on to the door for support, helpless with laughter.

Lawry it was who caused a man to approach Benaud with a handgun, reproach him for not protecting Meckiff during the throwing controversy and then fire the gun! It was, of course, not a gun loaded with live ammunition but it did produce a flash and a report which almost caused the Australian captain to have a heart attack. It took Benaud several days to appreciate the humour of that one.

Lawry was known throughout his playing career as 'The Phantom' (abbreviated to 'Phanto', or simply 'Phant'), not through any physical shortcomings – indeed, he was a strapping, broad-shouldered 6ft 2ins – but because in his boyhood he was an admirer of a comic-strip character of that name. At first glance, in 1961, he reminded me irresistibly of Chips Rafferty, the actor who in the immediate postwar years seemed to be in every film about Australia and about everywhere else as well.

Lawry was an admirer of Morris and Harvey, his two great predecessors as Australian left-handers, but in no way followed their style or technique. He was one of the most difficult of batsmen to dislodge, once entrenched, and it seemed in 1961 that he spent most of the tour at the crease. In 1968, however, leading abroad for the first time, he was troubled for much of the time by a broken finger which caused him to miss the fourth Test and gave Barry Jarman his only taste of captaincy at that level (along with Tom Graveney, similarly, taking over from Cowdrey in that match). England left it late to square the series, winning at The Oval with five minutes to spare, but Lawry had successfully defended the Ashes.

As a captain, Lawry followed the Australian tradition of being one of the boys – whose orders had to be obeyed when it mattered. He rated it as essential on tour to have a strong manager with the ability to control team, *and captain*, if necessary, amicably. He followed the Brian Close concept ('captaincy is all about giving . . . giving something of yourself to every individual player and to the side collectively') in that he tried throughout 1968 to give every member of his party the opportunity to improve his skills and to play a full part. Who was the best captain he played against? 'I would have to say Ray Illingworth though it causes a lot of pain because we lost the 1970–1 series against him. He was probably not the best all-rounder who ever played but he had a thoroughly professional approach to captaincy and moulded his side into a very professional unit. They were all behind him.' And a favourite Test memory? The second Test against the West Indies in 1968–9.

AUSTRALIA v. WEST INDIES

Melbourne, 1968–9

WEST INDIES

First Innings		Second Innings	
Camacho c Chappell b McKenzie	0	lbw b Gleeson	11
Fredericks c Redpath b McKenzie	76	c Freeman b Gleeson	47
Carew c Gleeson b McKenzie	7	(8) b Stackpole	33
Nurse c Jarman b Freeman	22	(5) c Stackpole b Gleeson	74
Butcher lbw b Gleeson	42	(7) c Jarman b McKenzie	0
Sobers b McKenzie	19	lbw b McKenzie	67
Kanhai c Sheahan b McKenzie	5	(4) c Redpath b Freeman	4
Davis b McKenzie	18	(9) c Redpath b Gleeson	10
Hendrick c Chappell b McKenzie	0	(10) c Redpath b Gleeson	3
Edwards not out	9	(3) run out	21
Gibbs b McKenzie	0	not out	0
Extras (b1 lb1)	2	Extras (b7 lb3)	10
Total	200	Total	280

Bowling: McKenzie 28–5–71–8; Connolly 12–2–34–0; Freeman 7–0–32–1; Gleeson 25–8–49–1; Stackpole 1–0–12–0

Bowling: McKenzie 20–2–88–2; Connolly 19–7–35–0; Freeman 11–1–31–1; Gleeson 26.4–9–61–5; Stackpole 13–9–19–1; Chappell 9–1–36–1

AUSTRALIA

First Innings

Redpath c Hendrick b Edwards	7
Lawry c Carew b Davis	205
I. Chappell b Sobers	165
Walters c Camacho b Sobers	76
Stackpole b Gibbs	15
Sheahan c and b Sobers	18
Jarman c Butcher b Gibbs	12
Freeman c Carew b Gibbs	2
McKenzie b Sobers	1
Gleeson b Gibbs	0
Connolly not out	3
Extras (lb4 nb2)	6
Total	510

Bowling: Sobers 33.3–4–97–4; Edwards 26–1–128–1; Davis 24–0–94–1; Gibbs 43–8–139–4; Carew 10–2–46–0

West Indies to Australia
1968–9
Tour captain: G. St. A. Sobers

Brisbane: *West Indies won by 125 runs*
Melbourne: *Australia won by an innings and 30 runs*
Sydney: *Australia won by 10 wickets*
Adelaide: *Match drawn*
Sydney: *Australia won by 382 runs*

The effigy-burning in Trinidad might have indicated local disapproval of Sobers-type captaincy but the West Indies selectors were not yet anxious to condemn his highly individual style of leadership. He was now the best cricketer in the world and he took with him to Australia a side which was stronger in batting than bowling but which included the best off-spinner around in Lance Gibbs. Hall and Griffith were both the wrong side of 30 but Sobers himself was ready, willing and extremely able to plug any gaps which might arise in any section of his attack. It would never occur to Gary that, multi-talented though he was, he had to have a considerable degree of support. He was delighted to win the opening Test but then found Australia making four successive totals of more than 500 and no captain could expect to win Tests when faced with such scores. It was still possible for the West Indies to square the series when they went to Sydney for the final Test and Sobers, equipped with his front-line attack for the first time, gambled by putting Australia in to bat. It turned out to be one of the more disastrous gambles of his life because with Lawry and Walters in tremendous form (as indeed they had been throughout the five Tests), he saw them total 619 and win by a massive 382 runs. It still didn't cost Sobers the captaincy which must cause some leaders of the 1980s – especially English captains – to sigh heavily.

England to Pakistan
1968–9
Tour captain: M. C. Cowdrey

Lahore: *Match drawn*
Dacca: *Match drawn*
Karachi: *Match abandoned as a draw because of rioting*

This tour was hastily arranged because of a disaster and it ended in disaster. England had been due to tour South Africa and had chosen a tour party which was entirely acceptable to the authorities in that country with Tom Cartwright, of Warwickshire, as the all-rounder.

When Cartwright withdrew from the side because of injury the obvious man to replace him was Basil D'Oliveira, the Worcestershire player, not only on his record but also for his magnificent 158 against Australia in the final Test of the previous summer. Indeed, there was some criticism of his non-selection in the first place and when Cartwright was unavailable the selectors, rightly ignoring political considerations in choosing their tour party under Cowdrey's captaincy, really had no choice. D'Oliveira, therefore, a Cape Coloured, was drafted into the 15-man squad.

The South African Government then announced that the tour party was unacceptable and M C C had no alternative to cancelling the tour. It was a move which was shortly to cast the country into sporting isolation and one which horrified sportsmen throughout South Africa. A tour by England was then proposed to India, Pakistan and Ceylon but there were financial problems with India, so a ten-match tour of Pakistan and Ceylon was hastily substituted. From the early tranquillity of this trip – four matches in Ceylon – the party ran into political problems of a different nature (from South Africa) in Pakistan. In Lahore, captain Cowdrey scored his 22nd century for England which was a considerable achievement in view of the number of interruptions of play by various demonstrations. With a stronger attack, England might well have won this game.

The second match was played in what was still East Pakistan, before the establishment of the independent state of Bangladesh, and this was trouble-free because the match was 'policed' by student leaders with a complete absence of official police or army. There must be a moral here somewhere!

The final game, in Karachi, was due to be played without a rest day but it had to be abandoned on the third morning when a mob waving banners burst through the gates and invaded the pitch. The England party hurriedly and gratefully left for home. It had been a thoroughly unpleasant experience which no one had enjoyed and the tourists were grateful for the reasoned and responsible leadership of Leslie Ames, as manager, and Cowdrey as captain.

West Indies to New Zealand
1969
Tour captain: G. St. A. Sobers

Auckland: *West Indies won by 5 wickets*
Wellington: *New Zealand won by 6 wickets*
Christchurch: *Match drawn*

Again with Sobers as captain, West Indies shared a series which involved New Zealand's fifth victory in Tests and saw the debut in Auckland of Glenn Turner, the country's greatest-ever batsman, who was out without scoring in his first Test innings. Sobers had his most modest tour with the bat, accumulating no more than 70 runs in five innings, but he had to do a lot of bowling and, as ever, held a series of catches close to the wicket. He was re-appointed to skipper West Indies in England in three months' time in the first part of another double-headed series.

West Indies to England
1969
Tour captain: G. St. A. Sobers

Old Trafford: *England won by 10 wickets*
Lord's: *Match drawn*
Headingley: *England won by 30 runs*

Sobers was by now the most experienced Test player in any I C C country and still he led by example, taking enormous burdens upon his own shoulders. The second Test was Gary's 75th and after scoring 50 not out with Camacho as his runner, because of a strained thigh, he then bowled 29 overs in England's second innings which left them 37 runs short of a win.

New Zealand to England
1969
Tour captain: G. T. Dowling

Lord's: *England won by 230 runs*
Trent Bridge: *Match drawn*
The Oval: *England won by 8 wickets*

Graham Dowling was an experienced opening batsman with sound technique who had visited all Test-playing countries and was making his second trip to England when he led New Zealand in the second half of 1969. A most pleasant and likeable man, he later became Secretary of the New Zealand Board of Control. His party was not strong enough either in batting or bowling to mount a serious challenge to England but he was able to observe at close quarters the maturing of his partner, Turner, who, in the second-innings rout at Lord's, carried his bat for 43, aged only 22.

Although the matter is entirely irrelevant in the context of this book, statisticians may find one aspect of the second Test of bizarre interest. On the morning of 11 August, Miss Susan Malone, a B O A C stewardess, returned to London from a flight and found her mail included a bank statement showing a credit balance of £111.11s 11d. She then took a train to Trent Bridge to see her husband-to-be, Philip Sharpe, score his only Test century (111) before he was caught and bowled by Hedley Howarth – number 11 in the New Zealand batting order.

New Zealand to India and Pakistan
1969
Tour captain: G. T. Dowling

Bombay: *India won by 60 runs*
Nagpur: *New Zealand won by 167 runs*
Hyderabad: *Match drawn*

Karachi: *Match drawn*
Lahore: *New Zealand won by 5 wickets*
Dacca: *Match drawn*

Dowling had the great satisfaction, after his party had flown from England at the end of their summer tour, to lead New Zealand to their first Test win in India in the first match to be played in Nagpur and then to their first victory over Pakistan. The captain encountered more than the usual share of sub-continental problems, ranging from an under-prepared pitch in Bombay to the inevitable rioting – this time in Hyderabad – and a disinclination on the part of the umpires to restart the match after rain on the final afternoon with New Zealand just three wickets short of winning the rubber (India 76 for 7). Howarth, the country's best-ever slow left-arm bowler, who had made his Test debut barely three months previously, played a notable part in both series and New Zealand Test cricket was given a great filip by one shared rubber and a first-ever series win in the other.

Australia to India
1969
Tour captain: W. M. Lawry

Bombay: *Australia won by 8 wickets*
Kanpur: *Match drawn*
Delhi: *India won by 7 wickets*
Calcutta: *Australia won by 10 wickets*
Madras: *Australia won by 77 runs*

There was only one riot, described as 'minor', as Lawry's tourists scored a 3–1 win in the rubber but no visit to India would be complete without at least one major eccentricity. In this case there was a public outcry (newspapers) against the selection of a modestly gifted medium-pacer, Guha, over the Madrassi off-spinner Venkataraghavan.

Guha then sportingly (and diplomatically) announced to the selectors that he would stand down from the side to play in Bombay!

Although India scored a rare victory in Delhi, Lawry fought every inch of the way, carrying his bat through the second innings for 49 out of 107.

5
END OF TEST CRICKET IN SOUTH AFRICA

Australia to South Africa

1970

Tour captain: W. M. Lawry

Cape Town: *South Africa won by 170 runs*
Durban: *South Africa won by an innings and 129 runs*
Johannesburg: *South Africa won by 307 runs*
Port Elizabeth: *South Africa won by 323 runs*

This was the end of the line for South Africa as a Test-playing country and Bill Lawry's tourists were on the receiving end of that country's finest effort in 81 years and over 172 matches.

All four Tests were won by the home country and by massive margins. It is difficult to explain this total eclipse of an Australian side which was virtually identical to the one which had beaten West Indies at home and India away; so we have to look more closely at the South African performance. At Newlands, Cape Town, they introduced for the first time one of the most brilliant opening batsmen of all time in Barry Anderson Richards. Alongside him were ranged the superb batting talents of Graeme Pollock, the bowling of his brother Peter and the outstanding all-round ability of Mike Procter, together with the experience of Goddard and the reliability of Barlow. Leading the side was Dr Aron (Ali) Bacher who was later to head South Africa's long and so-far unavailing fight to be readmitted to the I C C. Lawry's own form on tour was indifferent and his attack seemed to have lost its edge with the result that South Africa scored prolifically.

Richards was able later to put his prodigious talent on show in the English County Championship with Hampshire and Procter to air his with Gloucs, but Graeme Pollock, at 26, was lost to cricket outside his own country. South Africa, in their finest hour and with their greatest players available, played their final Test at St George's Park, Port Elizabeth, on 10 March 1970. So comprehensive was their demolition of Australia that we have no reports of Lawry's practical joking on this tour.

There was a disposition at Lord's for the planned 1970 tour to England by South Africa to go ahead and there was great support amongst the cricketing public. However, cricket is the most vulnerable of games if any faction is bent on disruption (as generations of tourists to India, Pakistan and West Indies can testify). With political anti-South African feeling reaching a high point, M C C were left with no alternative to cancelling the tour after a formal request on behalf of the Government by Jim Callaghan, then Home Secretary. I remember a sad discussion with John Arlott during the previous summer in which John shuddered at the thought of his beloved game being staged behind barbed-wire entanglements to keep out the demonstrators and with overnight guards posted to repel those who would damage the pitches.

England to Australia
1970–1
Tour captain: R. Illingworth

Brisbane: *Match drawn*
Perth: *Match drawn* (first Test to be played there)
Melbourne: *Abandoned without a ball bowled*
Sydney: *England won by 299 runs*
Melbourne: *Match drawn*
Adelaide: *Match drawn*
Sydney: *England won by 62 runs*

This was a very long tour indeed even in an age of jet-plane travel, beginning on 18 October and the party did not return home (from New Zealand) until the second week in March. It was led by Raymond Illingworth who had succeeded to the captaincy in the summer of 1969 when Cowdrey, the likely captain, sustained a leg injury before the Tests began. Illingworth was successful enough against West Indies and New Zealand to retain the captaincy of the England XI which played a World XI in place of the cancelled Test series of 1970 and now led his party to Australia with the same professional determination to win that Len Hutton had shown in 1954–5.

In his native Yorkshire, Illingworth was very much a genuine all-rounder, but up to his appointment as England captain (after he had moved to skipper Leicestershire) his spasmodic Test career had seen him cast in the role of an off-spinner who could also bat. Thus he had to compete for selection with men like Tattersall, Allen, Mortimore and Titmus. He was 37 years old when he took England to Australia and had been playing first-class cricket since he was 19. He was widely respected as a give-nothing-away opponent in the playing sense and as a shrewdly calculating captain of Leics with whom he was in the process of working a minor miracle. He knew every man in the game and had a fair idea of their individual strengths and weaknesses. His philosophy of Test captaincy was devastatingly simple: he expected every man who was selected to turn up fit for five days of hard cricket and he expected every man to give 100 per cent for every minute of those five days. It was an attitude not unknown to Australian captains and he knew it was not going to be any sort of picnic there, notwithstanding the strange Aussie collapse in South Africa.

Illingworth was endowed with a generous helping of Yorkshire characteristics: he didn't mince his words, he didn't suffer fools gladly, he didn't give an inch without a fight and he would not tolerate humbug. Consequently, he did not expect to be entirely on the same wavelength as two important members of his party – David Clark, the manager, and Colin Cowdrey, his vice-captain. And he knew, too, that he might possibly have problems of a temperamental nature with his main strike bowler, John Snow, whose rather selective attitude to what was and was not important in a day's play was not always the same as his captain's. Mr Clark offended Illingworth's sense of professionalism early in the tour by saying, in a Press interview, that he would rather see Australia win the series than have every Test drawn. Cowdrey offended the captain by his failure to organise net practice and reluctance to 'muck in' with the other members of the tour party in off-duty activities. And Snow was brought smartly to heel after a lethargic performance in the field during the first match against South Australia.

After sauntering gently round the boundary, turning singles into threes and causing dark mutterings among the other fieldsmen, Snow was summoned by the captain. Illingworth said to 'Snowy':

If you weren't an intelligent bloke you'd be on your way home by now. Because you *are* intelligent, I hope you will understand what I am going to say now. When they see you wandering about giving runs away the other bowlers are entitled to say, 'Why am I slogging my guts out when Snowy is treating it like a benefit match?' They are going to stop trying and before long I'm going to have no one trying. D'you see that? I am talking to you as an intelligent man. D'you see what I am getting at?

Snow saw. He bowled brilliantly in the Tests and was a major force in bringing home the Ashes. This was not easily accomplished. One fast bowler, Alan Ward of Derbyshire, returned home after injury and a young Bob Willis was flown out as his replacement. Not one lbw appeal by their bowlers was given in England's favour during six Tests. A run-out appeal which went against them cost nearly 200 runs. And in the final Test in Sydney, Illingworth felt it necessary to lead his team off the field when 'a drunken mob' (description by Ron Saw, Australian columnist) pelted beer cans and bottles on to the field.

It was Ian Chappell's first Test as Australian captain after Lawry had been deposed in circumstances graphically described by Richie Benaud: 'They gave him the selectorial axe right at the base of the skull in one of the most unfeeling acts I have ever seen from any group of selectors.' We may, perhaps, compare that with the end of Illingworth's reign, later.

Ray Illingworth was the best captain Chappell played against, the best Lawry played against and the best Intikhab Alam, of Pakistan, played against (jointly with Chappell) according to their own testimony. He was a player's player, a professional's professional, arguably the most *complete* captain on the field that England have ever had. From being a bowler who batted a bit, Illingworth turned himself into a worthy batsman at this level and scored his first century in only his second Test as captain; he did it without promoting himself up the order and throughout his 31 Tests as captain he notably got runs when they were badly required. He has a major part to play in this story but for the moment let us turn to his own favourite Test as leader – against West Indies at Headingley in 1969 where he thought he captained his side as well as he ever did in any of his Tests, after losing the toss.

'It was a green wicket,' he recalls, 'and after we had been put in it got better and better. In their second innings, needing 303 to win, they reached 200-odd for 3 but my bowling changes and field-placings worked and it gave me a great sense of professional pride when we won by 30 runs. D'Oliveira said afterwards that he never thought at any time that we were going to lose. That has got to be the ultimate tribute from a seasoned professional to his captain.'

ENGLAND v. WEST INDIES

Headingley, 1969

ENGLAND

First Innings		*Second Innings*	
Boycott lbw b Sobers	12	c Findlay b Sobers	0
Edrich lbw b Shepherd	79	lbw b Sobers	15
Sharpe c Findlay b Holder	6	lbw b Sobers	15
Hampshire c Findlay b Holder	1	lbw b Shillingford	22
D'Oliveira c Sobers b Shepherd	48	c Sobers b Davis	39
Knott c Findlay b Sobers	44	c Findlay b Sobers	31
Illingworth b Shepherd	1	c Lloyd b Holder	19
Knight c Fredericks b Gibbs	7	c Holder b Gibbs	27
Underwood c Findlay b Holder	4	b Sobers	16
Brown b Holder	12	b Shillingford	34
Snow not out	1	not out	15
Extras (b4 lb3 nb1)	8	*Extras* (lb5 w1 nb 1)	7
Total	223	Total	240

Bowling: Sobers 21–1–68–2; Holder 26–7–48–4; Shillingford 7–0–21–0; Gibbs 19–6–33–1; Shepherd 24–8–43–3; Davis 1–0–2–0

Bowling: Sobers 40–18–42–5; Holder 33–13–66–1; Shillingford 20.4–4–56–2; Gibbs 21–6–42–1; Davis 17–8–27–1

WEST INDIES

First Innings		Second Innings	
Fredericks lbw b Knight	11	c Sharpe b Snow	6
Camacho c Knott b Knight	4	c Hampshire b Underwood	71
Davis c Underwood b Knight	18	c and b Underwood	29
Butcher b Snow	35	c Knott b Underwood	91
Sobers c Sharpe b Knight	13	(6) b Knight	0
Lloyd c Snow b Brown	27	(5) c Knott b Illingworth	23
Findlay lbw b D'Oliveira	1	lbw b Knight	16
Holder b Snow	35	(9) c Sharpe b Brown	13
Gibbs not out	6	(10) c Knott b Brown	4
Shillingford c Knott b Brown	3	(11) not out	5
Shepherd absent hurt	–	(8) c Knott b Underwood	0
Extras (lb7 nb1)	8	Extras (lb11 nb3)	14
Total	161	Total	272

Bowling: Snow 20–4–50–2; Brown 7.3–2–13–2; Knight 22–5–63–4; D'Oliveira 15–8–27–1

Bowling: Snow 21–7–43–1; Brown 21–8–53–2; Knight 18.2–4–47–2; D'Oliveira 10–3–22–0; Illingworth 14–5–38–1; Underwood 22–12–55–4

It is interesting to note Illingworth's views on the two Australian captains who regarded him with respect. Ian Chappell: had natural flair and was a good captain to compete against because he was always looking to win, which opened up a game. Bill Lawry: preferred to keep it tight and wait for you to make a mistake.

England to New Zealand
1971
Tour captain: R. Illingworth

Christchurch: *England won by 8 wickets*
Auckland: *Match drawn*

Often touring teams arrived in New Zealand jaded from a long stay in Australia and this had been longer than most with 28 games played on the other side of the Tasman Sea. After understudying Knott so patiently in Australia, Bob Taylor got his first Test cap in Christchurch. One final note about this tour: the washed-out Test in Melbourne resulted in the staging, on what would have been the last day of the Test, of a limited-overs match which Australia won by five wickets. Thus began the one-day internationals which are now a feature of every tour and a major source of income.

India to West Indies
1971

Tour captain: A. L. Wadekar

Jamaica: *Match drawn*
Trinidad: *India won by 7 wickets*
Guyana: *Match drawn*
Barbados: *Match drawn*
Trinidad: *Match drawn*

Ajit Laxman Wadekar owed his appointment to the captaincy on this tour to one of those periodical shifts in the power-structure within the Indian Board of Control from Delhi to Bombay. It has always intrigued me that Madras and Calcutta are never involved though both have produced their share of Test cricketers. But it is usually either Delhi or Bombay in control – to this day – and this is generally reflected by the captaincy. Pataudi had had a good run as captain with scant success and the time had come for a change. Wadekar, representing Bombay, took over with dramatic results on his first and second tours, winning series in both West Indies and England. He was, perhaps, fortunate in that he had a better side than Pataudi had ever been given though this was to some extent accidental due to the arrival on the Test scene of Sunil Gavaskar and the development of all-rounders like Abid Ali and Solkar.

A tall, slim left-hander, Wadekar was not a particularly graceful batsman because of his stance which was distinctly open and it was at a relatively advanced stage of his college life (Elphinstone, then Ruia) that he showed any sign of talent as a cricketer. Clearly he made rapid progress because in his second year at Ruia he scored 324 against Delhi! And he was tipped as a future captain of India by one of his mentors, Vijay Merchant. Nevertheless, he was surprised to find a crowd on his doorstep when he returned home from shopping with his wife in December 1970, waiting to greet the newly-appointed captain of India. A journalist gave him the news, together with the inevitable floral garland.

Wadekar had been playing Test cricket for the previous four years under Pataudi's captaincy. He liked the Nawab as a man and respected him as a captain though he was not entirely sure of Pataudi's relaxed attitude to captaincy . . . 'he let everybody do his own thing.'

Wadekar was clearly going to be his own man as he led his first tour and he had the great advantage of being a keen student of human nature. He might well have made a good doctor as his mother wanted but for the fact that he couldn't stand the sight of blood! He took the trouble to get to know his men as few Indian captains have done and observed them all keenly, not only during leisure hours but on the field as well: Abid Ali, who muttered his Muslim 'Ins'Allah' before bowling or taking up a close-fielding position ... Sardesai, who touched his amulet early in an innings and invoked divine blessings on his performance ... Gavaskar, who didn't like instructions being relayed to him when he was deeply concentrating in mid-innings ... Venkata-raghavan (his vice-captain), hard and abrasive on the surface, modest and understanding underneath. Sardesai, who started the tour by hitting the first double century by an Indian against West Indies in the first Test, must have given the manager a few problems, too; he was deeply superstitious and refused ever to occupy a room where the number added up to a total of eight!

The only positive result in the series came in the second Test, first of the traditional two in Port of Spain, where Sobers inevitably came under fire again. A radio commentator made a public demand for his sacking and another wanted the pitch to be dug up. It was India's first victory over the West Indies in 25 Tests and Wadekar's personal contribution was a duck, no catches and, of course, he did not bowl. But he handled his side well, made his bowling changes shrewdly and viewed with satisfaction the debut of the 21-year-old Gavaskar who made 65 and 67 not out, followed it with 116 and 64 not out in Georgetown, 1 and 117 not out in Bridgetown and saved his best shot for the final Test – 124 and 220. Ajit Wadekar came home a very happy captain indeed to rapturous welcomes throughout the country. Indian cricket was entering a new era.

Pakistan to England
1971

Tour captain: Intikhab Alam

Edgbaston: *Match drawn*
Lord's: *Match drawn*
Headingley: *England won by 25 runs*

Recalling the relatively comfortable passage his friend and former colleague Brian Close had enjoyed in the double-header of 1967, Illing-worth was given the nastiest of shocks by opposition from the same two countries. Both Pakistan and India, however, were better equipped and better led than their predecessors: Intikhab had three years' experience of English conditions, playing with Surrey; Mushtaq Mohammad was a Northants player, Asif Iqbal was with Kent and Majid Khan was at Cambridge. At Edgbaston a young man named Imran Khan made his debut and another called Zaheer Abbas played his second Test. Imran was run out for 5 and took no wickets in either England innings; Zaheer scored 274 magnificent runs and was promptly signed for the following season by Gloucs.

So Intikhab had plenty of experience and talent at his disposal and he was a wily bird of a captain, as befitted an extremely good leg-break and googly bowler. 'Inty' was another nominee as captain of A. H. Kardar, the power behind the Pakistan cricket throne and a veteran of Test cricket since 1959 when he took the wicket of Australia's Colin McDonald with his first ball in Tests. So there wasn't much anyone could teach Intikhab about the tricks of the trade. He had England in a lot of trouble at Edgbaston, saw the Lord's match utterly ruined by rain and pushed the opposition very close to defeat at Headingley where a fascinating battle of wits took place between the two captains. If Illingworth had chosen this as his favourite Test it would not have surprised me at all though the manœuvring of the two captains produced much cricket that was, to outward appearances, dull in the extreme. But a tactical battle between 'Illy' and 'Inty' resulted in, to my eyes at any rate, a quite absorbing spectacle.

Intikhab had seen many managers on tour who were simply there for the ride, to bask in reflected glory, to enjoy themselves as visiting dignitaries, leaving all the hard work to the captain. That is why he lists 'having a good manager' as one of the prime requirements of a successful tour captain and why he was, in due course, to become the best tour manager Pakistan have ever had.

We shall look at this side of Intikhab in due course. In 1971 he returned from tour not dissatisfied at all with a moral victory and a narrow defeat to show for the trip, as well as a profound respect for Illingworth as a captain.

India to England
1971
Tour captain: A. L. Wadekar

Lord's: *Match drawn*
Old Trafford: *Match drawn*
The Oval: *India won by 4 wickets*

India under Wadekar made the second half of the summer even harder for England than the Pakistanis had done. The weather throughout the English season was miserable with spin bowlers dominating the first-class averages so that the Indians' brilliant trio were likely to be particularly effective – Bedi, orthodox slow left-arm; Venkataraghavan, off-spin; and Chandrasekhar, leg-breaks and top-spinners bowled at almost medium pace. Scoreboards throughout the country struggled to accommodate the polysyllabic names of the southern Indians and commentators had their problems, too. Faced with the virtually impossible task of enunciating Srinivasaraghavan Venkataraghavan, we consulted the genial Farokh Engineer, now well-established as Lancashire's wicket-keeper, who advised: 'Forget the first name and make the second rhyme, and scan, like "rent a caravan".' It worked perfectly.

Rain interfered with a beautifully poised finish at Lord's, rescued India from almost certain defeat at Old Trafford and although it washed out the second day at The Oval it could not prevent India's first victory in 22 Tests in England. It was the first defeat for Illingworth in 20 Tests and it would not have pleased him to learn later that while it was being accomplished his opposite number was sleeping peacefully on a dressing-room settee. Considering the nationwide rejoicing which the result evoked at home, there was a fine touch of Sir Francis Drake about Wadekar's slumbers. Chandrasekhar and Venkataraghavan had bowled out England for 101, leaving India needing 173 to write a new page of history. Gavaskar went for 0, Ashok Mankad (son of Vinoo) for 11 and the captain himself for 45 (at 76 for 3). But when the winning run had been struck, an hour after lunch, it was an astonished Ken Barrington who woke up the sleeping Wadekar: 'It's all over. They'll want you up on the balcony now.'

From this it may be deduced that Wadekar was a phlegmatic individual but that is certainly not the case. He was, in fact, a sentimental – romantic, even – type, deeply devoted to his wife and his mother and quite passionately involved with his side. Passing over his own sound innings which had steadied the ship and laid the foundations of the win, he gave all the credit to his bowlers for having dismissed England for 101, especially Chandrasekhar whose figures, he declared in a delightful Malapropism, 'deserved to be engraved in letters of gold'.

In that England second innings we can see a tactical brain at work in a way not too many Indian captains had shown in the field up to that point. Chandra and Venkat bowled 39 of the 46 overs and Bedi only one. The little Sikh was at that time acknowledged as the best slow left-armer in the world, the very type a captain would normally employ to restrict scoring (in those days) when faced with a first-innings deficit of 71. But Wadekar did not like Bedi because he did not trust him to follow instruction: 'The praise he received in England on his first tour [1967] went to his head. He always wanted to bowl but he did it in his own way, not to the captain's instructions.'

In English annals, Ajit Wadekar does not rank in the forefront of Indian Test players but he most certainly should not be under-rated, either as batsman or captain. He played a major part in the arrival of Indian Test cricket at full international stature and he did it by shrewd and thoughtful leadership, by care and respect for his players, and for that he deserves the highest credit. It is fair to say that India never looked back after Wadekar's reign as captain. His Test has to be that at The Oval on 19–24 August 1971.

ENGLAND v. INDIA

The Oval, 1971

ENGLAND

First Innings		*Second Innings*	
Luckhurst c Gavaskar b Solkar	1	c Venkataraghavan b Chandrasekhar	33
Jameson run out	82	run out	16
Edrich c Engineer b Bedi	41	b Chandrasekhar	0
Fletcher c Gavaskar b Bedi	1	c Solkar b Chandrasekhar	0
D'Oliveira c Mankad b Chandrsekhar	2	c sub b Venkataraghavan	17
Knott c and b Solkar	90	c Solkar b Venkataraghavan	1
Illingworth b Chandrasekhar	11	c and b Chandrasekhar	4
R. Hutton b Venkataraghavan	81	not out	13
Snow c Engineer b Solkar	3	c and b Chandrasekhar	0
Underwood c Wadekar b		c Mankad b Bedi	11
Venkataraghavan	22	lbw b Chandrasekhar	3
Price not out	1	*Extras* (lb3)	3
Extras (b4 lb15 w1)	20		
Total	355	Total	101

Bowling: Abid Ali 12–2–47–0; Solkar 15–4–28–3; Gavaskar 1–0–1–0; Bedi 36–5–120–2; Chandrasekhar 24–6–76–2; Venkataraghavan 20.4–3–63–2

Bowling: Abid Ali 3–1–5–0; Solkar 3–1–10–0; Chandrasekhar 18.1–3–38–6; Bedi 1–0–1–1; Venkataraghavan 20–4–44–2

INDIA

First Innings		*Second Innings*	
Gavaskar b Snow	6	lbw b Snow	0
Mankad b Price	10	c Hutton b Underwood	11
Wadekar c Hutton b Illingworth	48	run out	45
Sardesai b Illingworth	54	c Knott b Underwood	40
Viswanath b Illingworth	0	c Knott b Luckhurst	33
Solkar c Fletcher b D'Oliveira	44	c and b Underwood	1
Engineer c Illingworth b Snow	59	not out	28
Abid Ali b Illingworth	26	not out	4
Venkataraghavan lbw b Underwood	24		
Bedi c D'Oliveira b Illingworth	2		
Chandrasekhar not out	0		
Extras (b6 lb4 nb1)	11	*Extras* (b6 lb5 nb1)	12
Total	284	Total (for 6 wkts)	174

Bowling: Snow 24–5–68–2; Price 15–2–51–1; Hutton 12–2–30–0; D'Oliveira 7–5–5–1; Illingworth 34.3–12–70–5; Underwood 25–6–49–1

Bowling: Snow 11–7–14–1; Price 5–0–10–0; D'Oliveira 9–3–17–0; Illingworth 36–15–40–0; Underwood 38–14–72–3; Luckhurst 2–0–9–1

New Zealand to West Indies
1972

Tour captain: G. T. Dowling (B. E. Congdon)

Jamaica: *Match drawn*
Trinidad: *Match drawn*
Barbados: *Match drawn*
Guyana: *Match drawn*
Trinidad: *Match drawn*

Graham Dowling's achievement in leading his side unbeaten through a series in the West Indies was a considerable one, particularly as Sobers won the toss five times in a row. His decision to put the tourists in to bat in the first match in Trinidad almost misfired when Dowling was the one to set the target – 296 in 170 minutes. It was not entirely a generous one but we see the sage and experienced New Zealand captain dangling a carrot before the mercurial Sobers who was ever unable to resist temptation. Fortunately for West Indies there was enough depth of batting to ensure salvation after five wickets had gone for 95. New Zealand were now stronger in batting than at any stage in their history so far, with Turner developing into a very sound opener indeed, Bevan Congdon scoring well at number 3 and Bruce Taylor performing usefully as an all-rounder. Lawrence Rowe and Alvin Kallicharran made centuries on their Test debuts, Rowe actually scoring 214 and 100 not out at Sabina Park, while Turner made two double hundreds. When he made 259 in Georgetown he passed his captain's record score for New Zealand (239 made four years earlier).

Dowling had to miss the final Test and Congdon took over at Port of Spain but it had been an immensely satisfactory tour from New Zealand's point of view. They had scored more heavily and more consistently than ever before and Dowling handed over the captaincy to Congdon with the knowledge that he had seen significant developments taking place during his reign. In fact, a general levelling of standards was now taking place all over the world.

Australia to England
1972

Tour captain: I. M. Chappell

Old Trafford: *England won by 89 runs*
Lord's: *Australia won by 8 wickets*
Trent Bridge: *Match drawn*
Headingley: *England won by 9 wickets*
The Oval: *Australia won by 5 wickets*

It is difficult to believe that at any stage of his career – indeed, of his life – Ian Michael Chappell was any less tough or rugged a character than when he led Australia in this magnificent series which produced cricket to stand with any in the long history of Ashes Tests. Chappell ranks, with Bradman and Benaud, in the very highest echelons of Aussie captaincy and while in character he differed from the other two he most certainly shared their qualities of profound knowledge of the game and the keenest edge of competitiveness. He felt that he came to England (with the defeat in Sydney in February 1971 in mind) 'a tougher and more experienced skipper', and his contest against Illingworth's England team was an epic affair.

Chappell was born to be a cricketer and as he was (and is) archetypally Australian, he was born to be an outstandingly good one. Grandson of a captain of Australia, elder brother of another one, he not only led from the front as an excellent batsman, more-than-useful leg-break bowler (with a bit of medium pace thrown in, if necessary) and fine slip fieldsman, but he also brought to his captaincy the bonus of a fine cricket brain and the greatest reluctance to accept that any adverse tactical situation could not be rectified.

As a naturally aggressive character, he collected a fair amount of folklore about him in his playing days and there is no doubt that there was a strong strain of abrasiveness in his make-up. Benaud's mailed fist was disguised by his velvet glove; Chappell affected no such camouflage. Illingworth enjoyed pitting his wits against the man, and his determination to win; Chappell reciprocated warmly. His philosophy of Test captaincy was exactly what one would expect:

First of all you must have the respect of your players. You can not ask it, or demand it; you can only gain it, by showing your worth as a player and winning their confidence by your tactical approach. Then you have to have the players' respect as a human being. I think you reap the rewards on the field for the way you get on with the players when you are off it. Sitting down over dinner to discuss problems is only part of it. You have to be aware of the problems, to anticipate them if you can, and to be prepared to tackle them no matter what form they take.

I think the most important thing I learned from Illingworth was setting a field to save runs yet still letting the opposition know you are trying to take wickets. Take one and then – bang! – back to all-out attack.

This was reflected through the whole of a series which I found as fascinating as any in more than half a century of Test-watching. Setting aside for a moment the reputations that some of the protagonists were to build for themselves in the future, both sides were short of really great players and yet the intensity of competitive spirit more than compensated. It was a fairly young Australian side in which many of the tourists had yet to win their spurs and a wet summer ensured conditions they did not really like. Lillee, 22 years old at the start of the tour, gave us a glimpse of the greatness to come but it was the 25-year-old Western Australian, Bob Massie, who shocked England to the core. Two years earlier he had tried his luck with an English county but after two second-team games with Northants he failed to make any impression at all. This time, on his Test debut at Lord's when he took 8 for 84 followed by 8 for 58, he startled the England batsmen in a way that few novice bowlers had ever done. He achieved those figures by swinging the ball prodigiously both ways and bowling both over and round the wicket, and it has to be said that at Lord's, on 22, 23, 24 and 26 June he found atmospheric conditions which suited him more than any others at any time in his life. He played in only five more Tests for Australia and only 28 first-class games in all for Western Australia and faded quietly out of the picture.

England went into the final Test with the Ashes secure; they were 2–1 up in the series. But Chappell and his tourists played that match at The Oval as if their very lives depended on the outcome and what a truly superb game of cricket it was. England, rescued by Knott's 92 batting at number 8, made a first-innings 284. Australia replied with 399 after centuries by the captain and his brother, Greg. England made a solid 356 in their second innings, leaving Australia needing 242 with plenty of time but with the pitch showing a few signs of wear which caused a little, normal dusting.

England's second innings provided Chappell with the classic situation to apply the experience he had learned from Illingworth in Sydney – to contain the run-scoring while remaining very much aware of the need to take wickets. Illingworth, on the other hand, was concerned with the accumulation of runs in concert with the consumption of time . . . a perfect confrontation of two master-tacticians.

'I think,' says Chappell, 'it was the best match I have ever played in. It was a good cricket wicket, good weather, terrific match – everything you expect an England versus Australia match to be – no quarter asked, none given . . . both sides at one time or another in with a chance of winning.' This is Ian Chappell's choice of a favourite Test.

ENGLAND v. AUSTRALIA

The Oval, 1972

ENGLAND

First Innings			*Second Innings*	
Wood c Marsh b Watson	26		lbw b Massie	90
Edrich lbw b Lillee	8		b Lillee	18
Parfitt b Lillee	51		b Lillee	18
Hampshire c Inverarity b Mallett	42		c I. Chappell b Watson	20
D'Oliveira c G. Chappell b Mallett	4		c I. Chappell b Massie	43
Greig c Stackpole b Mallett	16		c Marsh b Lillee	29
Illingworth c G. Chappell b Lillee	0		lbw b Lillee	31
Knott c Marsh b Lillee	92		b Lillee	63
Snow c Marsh b Lillee	3		c Stackpole b Mallett	14
Arnold b Inverarity	22		lbw b Mallett	4
Underwood not out	3		not out	0
Extras (lb8 w1 nb8)	17		*Extras* (b11 lb8 nb7)	26
Total	284		Total	356

Bowling: Lillee 24.2–7–58–5; Massie 27–5–69–0; Watson 12–4–23–1; Mallett 23–4–80–3; Inverarity 4–0–19–1; G. Chappell 2–0–18–0

Bowling: Lillee 32.2–8–123–5; Massie 32–10–77–2; Watson 19–8–32–1; Mallett 23–7–66–2; Inverarity 15–4–32–0

AUSTRALIA

First Innings			*Second Innings*	
Watson c Knott b Arnold	13		lbw b Arnold	6
Stackpole b Snow	18		c Knott b Greig	79
I. Chappell c Snow b Arnold	118		c sub b Underwood	37
G. Chappell c Greig b Illingworth	113		lbw b Underwood	16
Edwards b Underwood	79		lbw b Greig	1
Sheahan c Hampshire b Underwood	5		not out	44
Marsh b Underwood	0		not out	43
Inverarity c Greig b Underwood	28			
Mallett run out	5			
Massie b Arnold	4			
Lillee not out	0			
Extras (lb8 w1 nb7)	16		*Extras* (lb6 nb10)	16
Total	399		Total (for 5 wkts)	242

Bowling: Arnold 35–11–87–3; Snow 34.5–5–111–1; Greig 18–9–25–0; D'Oliveira 9–4–17–0; Underwood 38–16–90–4; Illingworth 17–4–53–1

Bowling: Arnold 15–5–26–1; Snow 6–1–21–0; Greig 25.3–10–49–2; Underwood 35–11–94–2; Illingworth 8.5–2–26–0; Parfitt 2–0–10–0 (Illingworth sprained his ankle in his ninth over)

That win squared the series and although England retained the Ashes, Chappell went home reasonably well satisfied with his progress as a captain. He had not been short of confidence when he was handed the job (rather to his surprise) either in terms of ability to play, or to lead. Indeed, he had invited England to bat in his first Test as captain (Sydney, 1971) for good and carefully thought-out reasons. After bowling out England for 184, his decision seemed abundantly justified and he did a lot of thinking about the reasons for the ultimate defeat in that match. He felt he had learned a few lessons and at The Oval had put them successfully into practice. He was on his way to becoming one of the great captains.

Tours were now being played thick and fast during what in England were the winter months but which formed the cricket season in all other Test-playing countries. The winter of 1972–3 saw series between India and England, Australia and Pakistan, New Zealand and Pakistan, West Indies and Australia, Pakistan and England. We shall take them in chronological order of starting.

England to India and Pakistan
1972–3

Tour captain: A. R. Lewis

Delhi: *England won by 6 wickets*
Calcutta: *India won by 28 runs*
Madras: *India won by 4 wickets*
Kanpur: *Match drawn*
Bombay: *Match drawn*

Lahore: *Match drawn*
Hyderabad: *Match drawn*
Karachi: *Match drawn*

If there were a Long Service and Good Conduct medal for touring, then it was earned on this trip by Anthony Robert Lewis who set out with his party in November and did not return until the end of March. By the time they reached their first venue (the Indian Hyderabad as distinct from the city of the same name in Pakistan), three players were already out of action with stomach trouble. The distances travelled were immense: up and down, to and fro *across* India for 11 matches, then south to the island of Ceylon (now renamed Sri Lanka) for two and finally back north for five in Pakistan. All the usual problems were encountered, ranging from internal disorders amongst his troops to the odd stand-burning by crowds; yet in all the years I have known and worked with Tony Lewis I have never heard him utter one serious complaint about the trip . . . a wry smile here and there, a self-deprecating comment occasionally . . . but never a heartfelt snarl of the type which usually marks the reaction of those who have spent long months on the sub-continent. This marks Lewis as a man of uncommon resilience.

Illingworth, never a gambling man in any way, took a calculated risk in turning down M C C's invitation to lead the tour. While he shared the belief common amongst fellow Northerners that M C C would seize any opportunity to remove him from the captaincy of his country as soon as possible, he reasoned that he was now well established and would be needed the following summer to skipper England against the West Indies. M. J. K. Smith was approached next and when he, too, declined, the choice was between Lewis and Mike Brearley. Seniority in his leadership of Glamorgan over Brearley's in Middlesex finally resulted in Lewis's appointment. He was a popular leader with his men and proved a first-class choice in terms of dealing with potentially sensitive Asian officials and situations. He was also able to establish a healthy rapport with opposition teams which included a number of players with whom he was personally familiar through university and county cricket in England – men like Mushtaq Mohammad, Farokh Engineer, Majid Khan, Intikhab Alam and Pataudi (now playing as Mansur Ali Khan since this was one of the periods when the Indian Government had decided to abolish princely titles).

Both India and Pakistan were now strong teams, able to compete on equal terms with most other international sides. Lewis's was not a full-strength England party and his batsmen had problems with the Indian spinners in particular, but the captain (after joining the ranks of those who failed to score in a first Test innings) achieved a win in his first outing as England skipper and his second innings 70 not out played a major part.

Pakistan to Australia and New Zealand
1972–3
Tour captain: Intikhab Alam

Adelaide: *Australia won by an innings and 114 runs*
Melbourne: *Australia won by 92 runs*
Sydney: *Australia won by 52 runs*

Wellington: *Match drawn*
Dunedin: *Pakistan won by an innings and 166 runs*
Auckland: *Match drawn*

Intikhab, who had just time to celebrate his 31st birthday between the first and second Tests in Australia, now had 13 years' experience of Test cricket, four seasons with Surrey and knew as much as anyone about international players. He found Australia, under Ian Chappell, in something of a transitional stage but still too strong for the tourists though they required a remarkable bowling performance by Max Walker (16–8–15–6) in only his second Test to complete a 3–0 rubber victory in Sydney. The first Test in New Zealand saw the debut of Richard Hadlee and the second, selected by Intikhab as his most satisfying Test memory, gave Pakistan their first win in that country.

Eighteen of the home country's wickets fell to leg-spin bowling by Mushtaq and Intikhab himself, while Mushtaq also hit 201 runs. This is Intikhab's view of the desirable qualities in a tour captain: 'To get 17 or 18 different personalities to merge together, to keep them all happy and working as an integrated unit.' That cannot have been easy for him at all times in his career for there have usually been one or two strong characters in teams from that country and he had with him in the Antipodes on this occasion the highly individual temperament of Sarfraz Nawaz, the fast bowler who, in his day, was to take on not only captains he did not entirely respect but the whole Pakistan Board of Control as well.

Intikhab was, of course, a tough nut in his own right and did not tolerate any nonsense from relative newcomers to the side. In his later, managerial years he developed some highly interesting views of one or two of the more controversial aspects of international cricket. On umpires, for instance, he feels strongly that serious efforts have to be made to achieve increased expertise and more uniformity and (during the New Zealand v. Pakistan series of 1989) he put forward four suggestions: (1) greater use of electronic aids, as in tennis; (2) a panel of experts sitting in front of TV monitors, as in American football, to give a decisive ruling on hairline decisions; (3) umpires standing for only half a day to help concentration; (4) frequent seminars to exchange information and experience.

Intikhab particularly liked touring Australia where he relished the involvement with, and of, the crowds. He cannot remember ever having trouble with Aussie spectators and, one suspects, he liked playing there a little more than playing at home. And so, the Intikhab Test:

NEW ZEALAND v. PAKISTAN

Dunedin, 1973

PAKISTAN

First Innings

Sadiq Mohammad b D. Hadlee	61
Zaheer Abbas c Wadsworth b Hadlee	15
Majid Khan c and b Taylor	26
Mushtaq Mohammad c Wadsworth b Congdon	201
Asif Iqbal c Hastings b Taylor	175
Wasim Raja not out	8
Intikhab Alam c Pollard b Howarth	3
Wasim Bari not out	2
Salim Altaf	
Sarfraz Nawaz did not bat	
Pervez Sajjad	
Extras (lb13 nb3)	16
Total (6 wkts declared)	507

*Bowling:*D. Hadlee 24–3–100–2; Taylor 22–3–91–2; Congdon 17–1–72–1; H. Howarth 29–6–83–1; Pollard 13–2–64–0; O'Sullivan 18–2–81–0

NEW ZEALAND

First Innings		Second Innings	
Turner c Mushtaq b Intikhab	37	c Mushtaq b Intikhab	24
Jarvis c Mushtaq b Sarfraz	7	c Wasim Bari b Mushtaq	39
Congdon c Wasim Bari b Intikhab	35	c Majid b Mushtaq	7
Hastings c Sarfraz b Intikhab	4	b Mushtaq	9
Burgess b Intikhab	10	c Pervez b Intikhab	4
Pollard c Sarfraz b Intikhab	3	b Intikhab	61
Taylor c Sarfraz b Intikhab	0	(8) run out	3
Wadsworth b Mushtaq	45	(7) c Majid b Intikhab	17
D. Hadlee st Wasim Bari b Intikhab	1	c Majid b Mushtaq	0
O'Sullivan c Wasim Raja b Mushtaq	4	b Mushtaq	1
H. Howarth not out	4	not out	7
Extras (b1 lb2 nb3)	6	*Extras* (b5 lb7 nb1)	13
Total	156	Total	185

Bowling: Salim 5–0–23–0; Sarfraz 5–0–20–1; Intikhab 21–3–52–7; Mushtaq 3.5–1–15–2; Pervez 17–5–40–0

Bowling: Salim 4–2–11–0; Sarfraz 4–0–16–0; Intikhab 18.4–2–78–4; Mushtaq 18–2–49–5; Pervez 3–0–10–0; Wasim Raja 2–0–8–0

Australia to West Indies
1973
Tour captain: I. M. Chappell

Jamaica: *Match drawn*
Barbados: *Match drawn*
Trinidad: *Australia won by 44 runs*
Guyana: *Australia won by 10 wickets*
Trinidad: *Match drawn*

Ian Chappell was felt by some of his players to have been seen at his best on this tour, though it is difficult to think of Chappell in terms of ever being much *below* his best. But he had to overcome seemingly insuperable problems when first Lillee, then Massie broke down; drawn games had become the norm in West Indies Tests and Rohan Kanhai, who had taken over from Gary Sobers, was regarded as a defensive-minded captain. Everything was against Chappell but he was not a man who gave up any fight. One of his players (Richie Benaud's brother John, in fact) afterwards recalled lunchtime on the last day of the third Test, with West Indies needing 60 to win with four wickets in hand. Chappell lay on a bench without saying a word until it was time to take the field. Then he looked at every man and quietly remarked, 'It'd be a good one to win.' Australia won by 44 runs.

Outside his own dressing-room Chappell achieved a reputation for aggressiveness; inside it he was ever regarded as a man who could be relied upon, who would never surrender, who would ask nothing less than the utmost from every player and who would never give less than that himself. He was an inspirational captain, a genuine leader of men, the toughest of opponents, a shrewd and thoughtful tactician. That doesn't leave an awful lot that he lacked!

Australia won the fourth Test, drew the last and took the rubber. The 28-year-old Clive Lloyd watched, and learned, and bided his time.

New Zealand to England
1973
Tour captain: B. E. Congdon

Trent Bridge: *England won by 38 runs*
Lord's: *Match drawn*
Headingley: *England won by an innings and 1 run*

This was another double-tour summer with the eighth New Zealand tour party to England led by Bevan Ernest Congdon who was at that time their most experienced international player.

Bev Congdon, in an 18-year first-class career, played for no fewer than four of New Zealand's six first-class provincial sides and he toured all the Test-playing countries. A quietly-spoken, reflective and determined captain, he set a splendid example in 1973 (the third of his four tours to this country) with innings of 175 at Lord's and 176 at Trent Bridge – a game which has gone into New Zealand folklore for the second innings total of 440 after 'extras' had been the highest 'scorer' in the first innings. Congdon was also a useful medium-pace bowler, able to get a bit of movement in the air and off the pitch in the Shackleton-Cartwright style, if he did not quite reach the quality of those two English bowlers. Richard Hadlee was noted as 'showing promise' as a bowler but the tourists were sorely disappointed by the failure of their opening batsmen, Turner and Parker, who at that time were both playing for Worcestershire.

West Indies to England
1973
Tour captain: R. B. Kanhai

The Oval: *West Indies won by 158 runs*
Edgbaston: *Match drawn*
Lord's: *West Indies won by an innings and 226 runs*

Rohan Babulal Kanhai was one of the finest of all West Indian batsmen, a versatile player who could also bowl medium pace and who kept wicket in the earlier stages of his career. He was such a prolific scorer with a dazzling array of strokes that it is little short of tragic that his career was highlighted to such an extent by one controversial incident in the middle of this tour. In the second Test at Edgbaston (Kanhai's 'home' ground, incidentally – he had been a Warwicks player since 1968), he was furious when an appeal for a catch behind the stumps against Geoff Boycott was turned down. His displeasure was not only apparent; it was ostentatiously displayed to the crowd and he audibly referred to it at some length during the remainder of that session. Arthur Fagg, the umpire who had given the decision, a most experienced former player with Kent and standing in his 14th Test, was seriously offended and, following much speculation in the morning newspapers, did not appear when play resumed. His place was taken by Alan Oakman (Warwickshire's coach and a former umpire) so that play could resume on time, while vigorous debate took place in the pavilion. After an apology had been offered while the first over of the day was being bowled, Fagg resumed his umpiring duties.

Kanhai's quick temper and the earnestness of his desire to win were well known in the game. On this tour he was particularly anxious to do well as captain because Sobers, who had skippered him for so long, was in the team simply as a player, and because so many of the 'touring' party were in fact contracted players with English counties – ten of the team in the first Test, all eleven at Edgbaston. This could, and probably should, have improved relationships between the two sides; the incident at Edgbaston caused them to deteriorate.

The 'atmosphere' plus a certain feeling within the West Indies camp that their captain had not done them any favours by his attitude at Edgbaston, perversely inspired Kanhai in the final Test at Lord's where he scored 157, passing 6,000 Test runs in the process and West Indies won massively after scoring 652 for 8 declared. It was an occasion which caused England's captain, Illingworth, much bitterness because his determination to square the series was wrecked when one fast bowler (Chris Old) announced he had an injured ankle on the eve of the match, another (Tony Greig) had lost a stone-and-a-half in weight and was 'shattered', and a third (Geoff Arnold) told his captain after his first few overs, 'I don't feel as though I have anything left in me at all.' It was a devastating blow to a captain who asked simply of his players that they went into a Test fully fit and gave him everything they had got. That Lord's defeat cost Illingworth the England captaincy; Kanhai led the West Indies in the next home series . . . against England.

During England's 1981 tour to the West Indies, I worked with Kanhai on commentary and found him a pleasant, as well as a knowledgeable, colleague. I also saw a good deal of him when, his first-class career over, he played league cricket in the north of England, and got on well with him. These instances, however, are a long way removed from the fever-pitch which is reached at times in Test cricket and an assessment of an international captain cannot be based on personal experiences off the field. Rohan Kanhai contributed much to the glory of West Indies cricket as a batsman and perhaps something less than that as a captain. He was not so much an astute tactician as a grinder-down of the opposition by the steamroller approach he was able to adopt because of his own ability and that of a hugely talented team.

Nevertheless, he led his side to a two-nil victory in 1973 and for the sheer dimensions of the win at Lord's, and his own contribution, that match is Kanhai's monument.

ENGLAND v. WEST INDIES

Lord's, 1973

WEST INDIES

First Innings

Fredericks c Underwood b Willis	51
D. L. Murray b Willis	4
Kanhai c Greig b Willis	157
Lloyd c and b Willis	63
Kallicharran c Arnold b Illingworth	14
Sobers not out	150
Foster c Willis b Greig	9
Julien c and b Greig	121
Boyce c Amiss b Greig	36
Holder not out	23
Gibbs did not bat	
Extras (b1 lb14 w1 nb8)	24
Total (8 wkts declared)	652

Bowling: Arnold 35–6–111–0; Willis 35–3–118–4; Greig 33–2–180–3; Underwood 34–6–105–0; Illingworth 31.4–3–114–1

ENGLAND

First Innings		*Second Innings*	
Boycott c Kanhai b Holder	4	c Kallicharran b Boyce	15
Amiss c Sobers b Holder	35	c Sobers b Boyce	10
Luckhurst c Murray b Boyce	1	(4) c Sobers b Julien	12
Hayes c Fredericks b Holder	8	(5) c Holder b Boyce	0
Fletcher c Sobers b Gibbs	68	(6) not out	86
Greig c Sobers b Boyce	44	(7) lbw b Julien	13
Illingworth c Sobers b Gibbs	0	(8) c Kanhai b Gibbs	13
Knott c Murray b Boyce	21	(3) c Murray b Boyce	5
Arnold c Murray b Boyce	5	c Fredericks b Gibbs	1
Willis not out	5	c Fredericks b Julien	0
Underwood c Gibbs b Holder	12	b Gibbs	14
Extras (b6 lb4 w3 nb17)	30	Extras (b9 w1 nb14)	24
Total	233	Total	193

Bowling: Holder 15–3–56–4; Boyce 20–7–50–4; Julien 11–4–26–0; Gibbs 18–3–39–2; Sobers 8–0–30–0; Foster 1–0–2–0

Bowling: Holder 14–4–18–0; Boyce 16–5–49–4; Julien 18–2–69–3; Gibbs 13.3–3–26–3; Sobers 4–1–7–0

New Zealand to Australia
1973–4
Tour captain: B. E. Congdon

Melbourne: *Australia won by an innings and 25 runs*
Sydney: *Match drawn*
Adelaide: *Australia won by an innings and 57 runs*

Bev Congdon was again the captain of New Zealand on what was the first official Test series between the two countries in Australia. In view of the number of Tests which had now been played since the Second World War it seems remarkable that the first match, in Melbourne, was only the second game between the two countries on either side of the Tasman Sea, and the first – in Wellington in 1946 – had not been 'upgraded' to official Test status until two years later. Australia took the opportunity to introduce five players new to international cricket of whom Gary Gilmour, the left-handed all-rounder, was destined to make the biggest impact. An injury to Turner gave a first opportunity in Sydney to Jeremy Coney who was to become one of New Zealand's most successful captains.

England to West Indies
1974
Tour captain: M. H. Denness

Trinidad: *West Indies won by 7 wickets*
Jamaica: *Match drawn*
Barbados: *Match drawn*
Guyana: *Match drawn*
Trinidad: *England won by 26 runs*

Less than six months after their hammering at Lord's, England were in action against the West Indies again and their new captain, Mike Denness, the softly-spoken Scot who had skippered Kent in the two previous English seasons, walked straight into a major controversy. At the end of the second day's play in the first Test – in Trinidad of all places! – Bernard Julien played the last ball of the day defensively in front of him and as the non-striker, Alvin Kallicharran, started to walk to the pavilion, Tony Greig, at silly point, picked up the ball and threw down the bowler's wicket with Kallicharran out of his ground. Greig's appeal could only be answered in the affirmative by the umpire, Douglas Sang Hue. If many of the crowd had not been concerned with their departure from the ground, if more had noticed the appeal and its answer, the consequences could have been serious.

As it was, embarrassment in the England camp was exceeded only by apprehension about the future of the game when the dismissal was publicised. Greig already had a reputation as an aggressive competitor within the Laws of the game in England where he had just completed his first season as captain of Sussex. It was feared that his action, and the fact that he was a white South African, might lead to a disastrous reaction from the crowd at that and future Tests in the series.

A meeting in the pavilion by managers and captains went on for nearly three hours before a statement was issued announcing that the England captain had *withdrawn the appeal* which was the only legal way that Kallicharran's innings could be allowed to continue the following day. Whether it was *strictly* legal in that the day's play had long since ended when the appeal was withdrawn was a matter of considerable public debate but the important thing was that the otherwise inevitable riot was avoided. Kallicharran was 142 when he was 'out'. The following morning he added 16 runs before being caught by Underwood off Pocock and thus the compromise reached now seemed a masterpiece of diplomacy. Donald Carr was the England manager.

Whether this furore less than 36 hours after the series started unnerved Denness is difficult to say. In his 19 Tests as England's captain he rarely seemed totally at ease and never looked a confident and dynamic leader, while his worries undoubtedly affected his form as a batsman. I had known Mike since his earliest days as a Kent player and always found him a pleasant and likeable companion who loved his cricket. If one compared him with his predecessor, however, it seemed that some spark of determination was absent. It was, perhaps, an unfortunate time for him to have been chosen as captain in that he came up against Kanhai's uncompromising captaincy in the potentially hot-headed atmosphere of the West Indies on his first tour, and the ruthless leadership of Ian Chappell (backed by the menace of Lillee and Thomson) in Australia on his second. At least he was able to enjoy a more peaceful, and personally successful, summer at home between these traumas. And at the end of the West Indies trip he led England to victory in the final Test (and a squared rubber) after heroic performances by Boycott (99 and 112) and Greig (13 wickets for 156).

Australia to New Zealand
1974
Tour captain: I. M. Chappell

Wellington: *Match drawn*
Christchurch: *New Zealand won by 5 wickets*
Auckland: *Australia won by 297 runs*

Ian Chappell has always had mixed feelings about this short tour, with three Tests played within the month of March. The first saw an achievement to adorn the pages of any family scrapbook where in the unlovely (until its facelift in 1979) setting of the Basin Reserve Ian scored 145 and 121 while his brother Greg hit 247 not out and 133. The match yielded 1,455 runs for only 24 wickets. In the second Test, however, New Zealand scored their first win over Australia and that is a blot on the escutcheon that the eldest Chappell certainly does not like, even though the rubber was squared at Eden Park.

India to England
1974
Tour captain: A. L. Wadekar

Old Trafford: *England won by 113 runs*
Lord's: *England won by an innings and 285 runs*
Edgbaston: *England won by an innings and 78 runs*

Wadekar's second tour to England as captain was nothing like as successful as the previous one had been, largely because of the solid batting of the home side. Boycott voluntarily opted out of Test cricket for a spell after a series of failures (for Yorkshire, M C C and England) to cope with the opening medium-pace attack of Abid Ali and Solkar – problems which left him bewildered – but his successor, David Lloyd of Lancashire, scored heavily, along with Denness, Edrich, Amiss and Fletcher. On paper, Wadekar had what was, arguably, the best Indian attack of all time with four excellent spinners – Chandrasekhar, Bedi, Prasanna and Venkataraghavan – and that useful pairing of Abid Ali and Solkar as openers, backed up by Madan Lal. The latter, however, had a poor summer and it was only on later confrontations with England, at home and in this country (after experience in northern league cricket), that he looked a much better bowler.

Pakistan to England
1974

Tour captain: Intikhab Alam

Headingley: *Match drawn*
Lord's: *Match drawn*
The Oval: *Match drawn*

Intikhab's party, like the West Indians of the previous year, consisted largely of players with experience in English conditions and in between the showers – frequent and heavy in a very poor summer – he enjoyed himself a great deal in pitting his wits against Denness in a number of interesting tactical situations. His side was notably stronger in batting than bowling where he had no fewer than three leg-spinners but no off-break bowler.

An unpleasant note was struck during the Lord's Test when a heavy overnight storm caused seepage, down the slope and under the covers, to create a wicket on which Underwood was unplayable, but the complaints (in intemperate terms) were voiced by the undiplomatic manager, Omar Qureshi, rather than the captain. Intikhab completed his tour with a side unbeaten in any match and scored a win in both one-day internationals.

6

THE LLOYD ERA

West Indies to India and Pakistan

1974–5

Tour captain: C. H. Lloyd

Bangalore: *West Indies won by 267 runs*
Delhi: *West Indies won by an innings and 17 runs*
Calcutta: *India won by 85 runs*
Madras: *India won by 100 runs*
Bombay: *West Indies won by 201 runs*

Lahore: *Match drawn*
Karachi: *Match drawn*

The long reign of Clive Hubert Lloyd, the most significant figure in West Indies cricket history because of the effect his policies have had on the game worldwide, began with a win in the first Test ever to be played in Bangalore, starting on 27 November 1974. It was a game which saw the debuts of Vivian Richards and Gordon Greenidge. A new era of international cricket was dawning but few could have foreseen the impact these men were to have upon the game.

There are many anachronistic features in the character of Clive Lloyd and we shall examine these in a gradual process as we look at various stages of his career; but first, let us consider his basic philosophy as a captain: 'I wanted to win. I had to develop the killer instinct. That doesn't necessarily mean that sportsmanship has to suffer. You can still play fairly while playing in a tough professional manner. I wanted most of all to get the loyalty of the players, for them to have belief in my leadership so that they would all *try* all the way.'

In the years since he took over the captaincy, Lloyd has become a revered figure in the West Indies and also in Lancashire for whom he played from 1968, with a couple of breaks, to 1986. His personality was rarely, if ever, known to be less than genial; few have ever heard him raise his voice; the image he has always projected has been one of courtesy and quiet good humour. When, in 1980, his team was criticised heavily for gross misbehaviour on the field in New Zealand, I made a personal, incredulous check to make sure that Clive Hubert Lloyd had actually been skippering the side.

Of his world-class ability as a player there can never be any doubt. He was a more powerful, though perhaps less graceful, striker of the ball than Sobers; he could bowl usefully at medium pace or as a leg-spinner in his younger days; he was a miraculous fielder in the covers and later an excellent one in the slips. He had at his disposal, certainly during the second half of his 74 Tests as captain, the most powerful cricketing force in the world and it became fashionable for his critics to say that the team was so good it ran itself without any great requirement of tactical direction. This is to overlook completely the respect – perhaps even awe – he engendered in his players. He changed the whole course of world cricket by his deliberate and calculated use of four fast bowlers, operating in various permutations all day long and often indulging in sustained spells of short-pitched deliveries. This is not universally regarded as the most attractive turn the game has taken but it provided the West Indies with the winning sequences which were, and are, so important to them. Yet such is the affection in which Lloyd has been held by so many admirers over so long a period that, somehow, many find it possible to dissociate him from the unpleasantness this form of attack has brought into the game. He alone created it, yet rarely does one hear him (outside the actual playing ranks) condemned for its consequences. It is the most remarkable phenomenon and at the same time the most remarkable tribute to the man's personality.

It is almost as much as one's life is worth to criticise Clive Lloyd to a Lancastrian yet it was one of his team-mates, Graeme Fowler, who returned to the England dressing-room during the 1984 series to remark bitterly that 'the stumps never came into play' by the West Indies attack under Lloyd's direction.

But all this was still to come when Lloyd led out his side for the first time in Bangalore and saw Greenidge begin his Test career with 93 (run out) and 107 while the captain himself celebrated with a second innings 163. After the second win, in Delhi, there were shock defeats in Calcutta and Madras, where Lloyd noted with interest the supremacy of the Indian spinners over his own (including his cousin, Lance Gibbs). Honour was restored by a decisive win in the deciding Test in Bombay where Lloyd hit a marvellous 242 not out. It had been an eventful and energetic tour with a remarkable five clear results and the captain felt he had learned something about the task that lay ahead for he saw his future in the long term rather than as a stop-gap incumbency; he was 30 years of age.

The tour moved on to Pakistan where the two Tests were drawn and

Andy Roberts bowled brilliantly, as he had done in India. There were the now usual riots during games in both countries.

England to Australia and New Zealand
1974–5

Tour captain: M. H. Denness (J. H. Edrich)

Brisbane: *Australia won by 166 runs*
Perth: *Australia won by 9 wickets*
Melbourne: *Match drawn*
Sydney: *Australia won by 171 runs*
Adelaide: *Australia won by 163 runs*
Melbourne: *England won by an innings and 4 runs*

Auckland: *England won by an innings and 83 runs*
Christchurch: *Match drawn*

Denness's second tour as captain could not really have had a more unpromising start. When the party was announced, Ray Illingworth publicly criticised Denness's captaincy qualities and also the non-selection of the 33-year-old John Snow. Greig, too, was critical of selection matters when he was interviewed; while Boycott – undoubtedly the soundest Test opening batsman – decided not to tour.

That was all before England boarded their plane! Once in Australia, they were ill-equipped to deal with Lillee at his brilliant best and the relative newcomer, Jeff Thomson, backed up by Max Walker – the power harnessed intelligently and unrelentingly by Chappell. Thomson, big and powerful and extremely fast, blasted England into submission in the opening Test in which Amiss sustained a fractured thumb and Edrich a broken hand. Greig, standing 6ft 7½ins tall, scored a defiant century in Brisbane but most of his team mates from that point onwards appeared to be, in varying degrees, depressed and demoralised. Denness found it doubly difficult to 'lift' his side when he could manage only 65 runs in his first six Test innings. Greig found his natural combative qualities, allied to his height and reach, useful in playing a series of defiant innings; but his hundred at The Gabba was the only three-figure innings by an England batsman in the first four Tests. In Sydney, Denness showed great character by insisting on dropping himself from the side; Edrich, his vice-captain, took over – and sustained fractured ribs from the first ball he received from Lillee.

Denness returned in Adelaide to make top score of 51 but it couldn't prevent another defeat and when England finally won the sixth Test there was a clear indication of the part Lillee and Thomson had played in regaining the Ashes. Thomson had injured a shoulder during the fifth Test and was unable to play in the sixth, in which Lillee was able to bowl only six overs before bruising a foot. In the absence of the pair of them, England scored 529 of which Denness made 188. Sadly, and a little cruelly, the achievement was obscured by the claims of those who had maintained he was always suspect against genuinely fast bowling and that his captaincy was too timorous to contend with an opponent like Chappell. The arrival of Lillee and Thomson, skippered by Chappell, was awaited with more than usual interest by English fans the following summer.

First, though, Denness made another big hundred (181) in Auckland in a match marred by a blow on the head to Ewen Chatfield which caused his heart to stop beating for seconds. Only prompt and expert attention by the England physiotherapist, Bernard Thomas, saved the life of the Wellington bowler.

Mike Denness's tours had provided more than his fair share of traumatic moments and from his 19 Tests as captain the one in Melbourne, 8–13 February 1975, ranks as his best. Even with Thomson and Lillee (for the most part) out of the way, a depressed touring side still had to be coaxed to a victory.

AUSTRALIA v. ENGLAND

Melbourne, 1975

AUSTRALIA

First Innings		*Second Innings*	
Redpath c Greig b Lever	1	c Amiss b Greig	83
McCosker c Greig b Lever	0	c Cowdrey b Arnold	76
I. Chappell c Knott b Old	65	c Knott b Greig	50
G. Chappell c Denness b Lever	1	b Lever	102
Edwards c Amiss b Lever	0	c Knott b Arnold	18
Walters c Edrich b Old	12	b Arnold	3
Marsh b Old	29	c Denness b Lever	1
Walker not out	20	c and b Greig	17
Lillee c Knott b Lever	12	(11) not out	0
Mallett b Lever	7	(9) c Edrich b Greig	0
Dymock c Knott b Greig	0	(10) c Knott b Lever	0
Extras (b2 lb1 nb2)	5	Extras (b9 lb5 w4 nb5)	23
Total	152	Total	373

Bowling: Arnold 6–2–24–0; Lever 11–2–38–6; Old 11–0–50–3; Greig 8.7–1–35–1

Bowling: Arnold 23–6–83–3; Lever 16–1–65–3; Old 18–1–75–0; Greig 31.7–7–88–4; Underwood 18–5–39–0

ENGLAND

First Innings

Amiss lbw b Lillee	0
Cowdrey c Marsh b Walker	7
Edrich c I. Chappell b Walker	70
Denness c and b Walker	188
Fletcher c Redpath b Walker	146
Greig c sub b Walker	89
Knott c Marsh b Walker	5
Old b Dymock	0
Underwood b Walker	11
Arnold c Marsh b Walker	0
Lever not out	6
Extras (b4 lb2 nbl)	7
Total	529

Bowling: Lillee 6–2–17–1; Walker
42.2–7–143–8; Dymock 39–6–130–1; Walters
23–3–86–0; Mallett 29–8–96–0; I. Chappell
12–1–50–0

Australia to England
1975

Tour captain: I. M. Chappell

Edgbaston: *Australia won by an innings and 85 runs*
Lord's: *Match drawn*
Headingley: *Match drawn*
The Oval: *Match drawn*

This was a four-Test series, led by Ian Chappell, because the earlier part of the summer was occupied by the first Prudential World Cup, won by West Indies who beat Australia by 17 runs in a wonderfully exciting final. Perhaps in a last desperate throw of the dice Denness, who realised his days as captain were numbered unless he could win, and do so imaginatively, put Australia in to bat on a reputedly placid pitch with unsettled weather about, a move which was critically condemned. Denness now *had* to win. In the event, Australia were never knocked off course in scoring 359 and the weather broke just as England were starting their first innings. On a rain-affected pitch Lillee, Thomson and Walker bowled out England twice and Denness surrendered the captaincy to Greig, a very different sort of character.

Chappell now found himself pitted against a skipper who believed in fighting fire with fire. Although Greig had nothing like the same pace at his disposal, he showed himself quickly to be a naturally aggressive leader. He was a sound, and sometimes inspired, middle-order batsman and a bowler who could operate at medium-fast pace, seam up, or with off-cutters at medium pace, as well as orthodox off-spinners. His height enabled him to get bounce and when he took over the captaincy he was the leading all-rounder in the country. He had also plenty of Test experience since his first game against the Australians in 1972 and he knew Chappell's style well.

Nevertheless – with Lillee and Thomson in full cry – the Australian captain had an edge, until Greig sought advice about how to stiffen the middle-order batting. The name suggested to him was that of David Steele, of Northants, who had rarely been considered by any of the professional (or amateur) critics. With a stubborn front-foot defence, Steele defied the tourists' pace attack for hour after hour, scoring 50 and 45 at Lord's, 73 and 92 at Headingley, 39 and 66 at The Oval, batting in the problem spot of number 3. Both sides regarded themselves as in with a chance of winning at Leeds when the pitch was damaged early on the final day by relatives campaigning for the release of a convicted criminal.

Chappell hit a splendid 192 at The Oval, forced England to follow-on 341 runs in arrears but was thwarted by England's new-found determination for which Greig must be given a lot of credit. Nevertheless, Chappell had retained the Ashes with only one 'result' Test. He had also led his side to the final of the World Cup, a game which the Aussies might well have won but for a remarkable innings of 102 off 82 balls by his opposite number, Clive Lloyd.

Ian Chappell had, as ever, handled his party well, never more so than when ensuring that Thomson kept a full head of steam despite being no-balled frequently and bowling a high proportion of wides. Thomson caused Graham Gooch to bag a pair at Edgbaston in his first Test appearance, and his second-innings dismissal is very clear indeed in my mind as resulting from the most unplayable single delivery I have ever seen.

West Indies to Australia
1975–6
Tour captain: C. H. Lloyd

Brisbane: *Australia won by 8 wickets*
Perth: *West Indies won by an innings and 87 runs*
Melbourne: *Australia won by 8 wickets*
Sydney: *Australia won by 7 wickets*
Adelaide: *Australia won by 190 runs*
Melbourne: *Australia won by 165 runs*

This was probably the most significant series of Test Matches since Jardine's 'bodyline' tour to Australia in 1932–3 because it was now that Clive Lloyd first began to think seriously about the value of a top-class pace attack. His ideas actually germinated a few months later, during India's visit to the West Indies, as we shall see, but the seeds were sown in Australia where he was impressed by the way Lillee (who hit him a painful blow on his chin) and Thomson played such a major part in a 4–1 defeat of West Indies which their captain regarded as a humiliation. It was not a happy tour for the relatively new, and highly ambitious skipper. He had been a Test player for eight years when he became captain; he had strong, and often critical, views on the administration of the game at home and he had observed with concern some of the errors made by captains under whom he had served.

He had regarded the leadership of Sobers on occasions as 'appalling' but he was discreet enough not to air his views publicly at the time. He knew only too well that criticism from the ranks was not welcome in West Indian cricket. But he came to the job with many well-formulated ideas about how it should be done and in Australia, in 1975–6, they did not seem to be working.

Both Gordon Greenidge and Vivian Richards were later – *much* later – to express themselves strongly on Lloyd's leadership during that tour when morale sagged and finally disintegrated. The dressing-room, according to Richards, was 'a shambles' and Lloyd himself conceded that he was unable to motivate the players. He was bitter about a number of umpiring decisions, some of which outraged Lloyd as much as any he experienced in his long career but he was realistic enough to accept that some of his batsmen contributed to their own downfall by their liking for the hook shot. It seemed a natural counter (for players with keen eyes and lightning reflexes) to the bowling of Lillee and Thomson, Walker and Gilmour. The only snag, as their captain was quick to appreciate, was that they were not used to playing the shot against bowlers of such quality. It was discussed at length in team meetings but Lloyd was unable to dissuade his impetuous tourists that it was not, in all the circumstances, the most effective means of dealing with fast, short-pitched deliveries from bowlers of real class. He returned home angry, disappointed – and thoughtful.

India to New Zealand
1976

Tour captain: B.S. Bedi

Auckland: *India won by 8 wickets*
Christchurch: *Match drawn*
Wellington: *New Zealand won by an innings and 33 runs*

After the retirement of Wadekar, following the tour to England in 1974, Indian cricket went through one of its regular periods of turmoil with the balance of power shifting from Bombay (represented by Wadekar) to Delhi, with Pataudi recalled to lead the national side against Lloyd's West Indians – though he missed the second Test of that series because of injury and, remarkably, the leadership passed temporarily to Venkataraghavan, a Madrassi. The tangled web was woven a little more intricately by the suspension of Bishen Singh Bedi, the brilliant slow left-armer, by the President of the Indian Board of Control, for giving an unauthorised television interview in England during the previous summer.

Bedi was a prominent member of the Delhi power-group and a candidate for the captaincy. Instead, he missed the first Test against the West Indies of 1974–5 but played in the remaining four under Pataudi and Venkataraghavan. Now read on . . .

For the trip to New Zealand in January and February 1976, Bedi was appointed captain and promptly missed the first Test because of a leg injury, giving a first taste of leadership to Sunil Gavaskar – a Bombay man! There was a considerable rivalry between the two men and when Bedi returned to steer the ship in the second and third matches, he was not too happy to find pitches which did not suit his bowling while Gavaskar scored runs freely. Nevertheless, Bedi was confirmed as captain for the trip to West Indies which began less than a month later and thus became the first skipper to face Lloyd's heavy artillery barrage which, however, did not happen immediately . . .

India to West Indies
1976
Tour captain: B. S. Bedi

Barbados: *West Indies won by an innings and 97 runs*
Trinidad (24–29 March): *Match drawn*
Trinidad (7–12 April): *India won by 6 wickets*
Jamaica: *West Indies won by 10 wickets*

The rubber began on orthodox and, one might say, expected lines with an easy win for the host country for whom the leg-spinner, Holford, and the slow left-armer, Jumadeen, played a not inconsiderable part in bowling out India twice. The second Test went very much India's way because of the batting of Gavaskar (156) – Lloyd and his men knew all about that little fellow from 1971 – and Brijesh Patel (115 not out). If play had not been wiped out on the opening day, India might well have won although it can be argued that it was a rain-affected wicket which put the skids under West Indies, 16 of the 18 wickets they lost falling to Bedi, Chandrasekhar and Venkataraghavan. Bedi was adept at handling a slow-bowling attack, regarding his medium-pacers simply as an agency for taking the shine off the ball. Lloyd was not so good with spinners, notwithstanding the success of Holford and Jumadeen in Barbados.

Those critics who for so long have voiced their doubts about Lloyd's tactical skill in the field base their argument to a great extent on the paucity of evidence of his ability to use slow bowling and it is a valid one. From this point in his career onwards he very rarely placed trust or reliance on spin as an attacking weapon; suspicions about its value or efficacy became a certainty in his mind after the next Test, also played at the Queen's Park Oval in Port of Spain because the Bourda ground in Georgetown, Guyana, was waterlogged.

Lloyd set Bedi a target of 403 to win, one which seemed well beyond the reach of the tourists since only Bradman's Australians in 1948 had ever made more than 400 in a fourth innings to win a Test. Very much more to the point, he gave his bowlers just under ten hours to dismiss the opposition – and they failed. They not only failed but India serenely scored 406 for 4 to win, taking their time over the task, but never looking in trouble. Three slow bowlers returned figures which almost reduced their captain to tears . . . of rage: Padmore 47–10–98–0, Jumadeen 41–13–70–2, Ali 17–3–52–0. Two of the four Indian wickets to fall were run outs. Lloyd was furious and his faith in spin bowling – if, indeed, he had ever had any – was utterly destroyed. He swore a solemn oath never again to put his trust in spinners, and he kept it.

For the fourth and final Test at Kingston, Jamaica, Lloyd insisted on dispensing with the services of Imtiaz Ali and Padmore and calling up Wayne Daniel, the formidably built Barbadian, to join Michael Holding, Bernard Julien and Vanburn Holder. Holding had arrived on the scene during the recent tour of Australia; Julien and Holder were the experienced pair; Daniel looked the fastest, although the wildest, of the lot. To complete the disastrous scene set for the unfortunate tourists, the Sabina Park pitch had recently been relaid and offered unpredictable bounce. Indian batting had taken a long time to recover from the shock of meeting F. S. Trueman at Old Trafford in 1952. The clock was now put back 24 years . . . perhaps even further.

Slowly and – quite literally – painfully, India inched their way to 306 for six wickets at which point Bedi, who was never slow to voice an opinion or to make the dramatic gesture, threw in the towel to save his men from further punishment and declared the innings closed. Three of his batsmen had been taken to hospital and Bedi himself, without facing the barrage in the first innings, announced that he was unfit to bat in the second. It is worth looking at the Indian card in that terrible, utterly demoralised second innings:

Gavaskar c Julien b Holding	2
Vengsarkar lbw b Jumadeen	21
Amarnath st Murray b Jumadeen	60
Madan Lal b Holding	8
Venkataraghavan b Holding	0
Kirmani not out	0
Gaekwad absent hurt	
Viswanath absent hurt	
Bedi absent hurt	
Chandrasekhar absent hurt	
Patel absent hurt	6
Extras (nb 6)	97
Total	

The casualty list read: Viswanath (broken and dislocated finger), Patel (cut mouth), Gaekwad (cut ear which kept him in hospital for two days). The injuries to Bedi and Chandrasekhar were not specified. Gavaskar described the West Indies policy of short-pitched, ultra-fast bowling as 'barbarism', claiming that it was accompanied by chants from the crowd of, 'Kill him, maaan!' Years later, the man who has scored more Test runs than anyone else wrote: 'These people belong to the jungles and forest instead of to a civilised country.'

Clive Lloyd had proved his point to himself and, as things were to turn out, to the rest of the world as well. But the fact is that the game has never been the same since those four bloodthirsty days in Kingston in April 1976. England were next to feel the backlash . . .

West Indies to England
1976
Tour captain: C. H. Lloyd

Trent Bridge: *Match drawn*
Lord's: *Match drawn*
Old Trafford: *West Indies won by 425 runs*
Headingley: *West Indies won by 55 runs*
The Oval: *West Indies won by 231 runs*

This tremendously successful tour for Lloyd and his men probably saw the West Indies at the full height of their powers because England at this point were still capable of at least attempting to stage some sort of resistance. It was swept almost contemptuously aside by a brilliant team which performed superbly. Richards, despite missing one Test altogether, scored 832 runs at an average of 118.42, Greenidge and Fredericks made big scores and Lloyd's batting was rarely required. Two specialist slow bowlers were included in the party, Jumadeen and Padmore, but between them they bowled just 31 overs (1 wicket) in the five Tests.

England knew exactly what to expect, in the light of the Indians' experience, when five fast bowlers were chosen by the West Indian selectors, plus Collis King who combined brisk medium pace with aggressive middle-order batting. Greig, the home captain, decided that the best way of establishing the morale of his troops was to adopt a bellicose stance and did so in terms which must rank amongst the most monumentally unfortunate ever uttered by a captain. In a TV interview before the series he announced that England would 'make the West Indies grovel'. The verb was spectacularly tactless, conjuring up visions of slave labour in the sugar plantations of the Caribbean and Lloyd, after recovering from the shock of this frontal verbal assault, growled grimly that 'the days of grovelling are over'. The scene was set.

Mike Brearley, now 34 and making his first Test appearance 12 years after touring South Africa, was the first to reap the whirlwind of Greig's indiscretion and at Trent Bridge joined the list – it is a distinguished one – of those who made no score in a first Test innings. England managed a draw, due in the main to resolute batting by Steele, Edrich and Woolmer. Richards started his personal tour with 232 and 63. The second Test was also drawn with England having, if anything, slightly the better of the game, but the tourists' fast bowlers came into their own at Old Trafford where the ball went through the top of the pitch – bone dry in a very hot summer – on the first day. Brian Close (aged 45) and John Edrich, six years younger, were asked by Greig to open the innings because, he told Close, he didn't want Bob Woolmer, who *was* an opening batsman for Kent, 'killing off'.

The two veterans, both of whom would rather have died before flinching or backing away, were battered badly by Roberts, Holding and Daniel and England were bowled out for 71 and 126. Close's 'box' was actually splintered by a delivery from Roberts. In these circumstances, and on such a pitch, Greenidge's two hundreds represented wonderful batting, and West Indies won by a massive margin. At Headingley, Lloyd once again simply unleashed his fast bowlers and let them wreak havoc in their various permutations. At The Oval we finally saw the real quality of Michael Holding (after another double hundred from Richards). On a flat, completely unresponsive wicket, where short-pitch bowling – even by the most formidable quartet in the game – seemed futile, Holding put the ball up to the bat and beat batsman after batsman by sheer pace. Chris Balderstone, now an umpire but at that time 35 years old with 15 years' experience of county cricket behind him, was clean bowled in each innings by Holding without scoring and counts it as one of the most interesting experiences of his life!

The West Indies who, remember, were playing their third consecutive Test series without a break, had taken a little time to get into their stride but now there was no looking back. They remain today the most potent force in world cricket as a result of Clive Hubert Lloyd's decision largely to dispense with spinners taken in Trinidad on 12 April 1976. As for Greig, not only had he failed to make the tourists 'grovel' (or anything remotely like it) but his captaincy came under fire at The Oval when, in an attempt to frustrate Lloyd's progress towards a second innings declaration, he spread his fieldsmen round the boundary edge. He still could not prevent Greenidge and Fredericks streaking to 182 without loss. When he was bowled by Holding on the Saturday evening, he left the field with an escort of West Indies supporters offering their views on the subject of grovelling.

There were further duels to come between these two captains of contrasting styles, but Clive Lloyd had clearly won the first round. He played in 110 Tests and skippered West Indies in a record 74 of them and in that time lost only two series out of 18. One of these, as we have seen, was in Australia and the consequences of that have long been felt by the rest of the cricketing world. The other, incredibly, was in New Zealand which we shall look at in due course. To most of us it would probably present some difficulty to choose one outstanding Test memory from 110 but without hesitation Clive answers that question with: 'Lord's, 1984, I don't think we got enough praise for that.' It was a notable occasion since it marked the centenary of Test cricket at Lord's and during the game the West Indian captain celebrated his 7,000th Test run.

ENGLAND v. WEST INDIES

Lord's, 1984

ENGLAND

First Innings			*Second Innings*	
Fowler c Harper b Baptiste	106		lbw b Small	11
Broad c Dujon b Marshall	55		c Harper b Garner	0
Gower lbw b Marshall	3		c Lloyd b Small	21
Lamb lbw b Marshall	23		c Dujon b Marshall	110
Gatting lbw b Marshall	1		lbw b Marshall	29
Botham c Richards b Baptiste	30		lbw b Garner	81
Downton not out	23		lbw b Small	4
Miller run out	0		b Harper	9
Pringle lbw b Garner	2		lbw b Garner	8
Foster c Harper b Marshall	6		not out	9
Willis b Marshall	2			
Extras (b4 lb14 w2 nb15)	35		*Extras* (b4 lb7 w1 nb6)	18
Total	286		Total (9 wkts declared)	300

Bowling: Garner 32–10–67–1; Small 9–0–38–0; Marshall 36.5–10–85–6; Baptiste 2–6–36–2; Harper 8–0–25–0

Bowling: Garner 39.3–3–91–3; Small 12–2–40–3; Marshall 22–6–85–2; Baptiste 26–8–48–0; Harper 8–1–18–1

WEST INDIES

First Innings			*Second Innings*	
Greenidge c Miller b Botham	1		not out	214
Haynes lbw b Botham	12		run out	17
Gomes c Gatting b Botham	10		not out	92
Richards lbw b Botham	72			
Lloyd lbw b Botham	39			
Dujon c Fowler b Botham	8			
Marshall c Pringle b Willis	29			
Baptiste c Gatting b Willis	44			
Harper c Gatting b Botham	8			
Garner c Downton b Botham	6			
M. Small not out	3			
Extras (lb5 w1 nb7)	13		*Extras* (b4 lb4 nb13)	21
Total	245		Total (for 1 wkt)	344

Bowling: Willis 19–5–48–2; Botham 27.4–6–103–8; Pringle 11–0–54–0; Foster 6–2–13–0; Miller 2–0–14–0

Bowling: Willis 15–5–48–0; Botham 20.1–2–117–0; Pringle 8–0–44–0; Foster 12–0–69–0; Miller 11–0–45–0

Greenidge's double century, the first by a West Indian at Lord's, came from 241 balls, with two sixes and 29 fours, and ranks as one of the greatest – perhaps the greatest – innings ever seen at Headquarters. It made the tourists' task, which had started as an even-money bet after Gower's declaration, seem astonishingly easy.

New Zealand to Pakistan and India
1976

Tour captain: G. M. Turner (J. M. Parker)

Lahore: *Pakistan won by 6 wickets*
Hyderabad: *Pakistan won by 10 wickets*
Karachi: *Match drawn*

Bombay: *India won by 162 runs*
Kanpur: *Match drawn*
Madras: *India won by 216 runs*

In the light of his great experience and the fact that he was New Zealand's most 'professional' captain since John Reid, it seems astonishing that Glen Maitland Turner led his country no more than 10 times. He had 10 seasons of English county cricket behind him with Worcestershire and had been a Test player for eight years when he took his tour party to Pakistan and India. From his earlier concentration on defence, Turner had now developed into one of the most accomplished batsmen in the world, with all the strokes and the truly great batsman's ability to dominate attacks once he was 'in'.

He might well have skippered as many sides as Reid had it not been for a series of personality clashes between Turner and some senior members of the New Zealand Board. He was ever a man of strong character and, in the eyes of some of his countrymen, too keen to have things his way. There is no doubt that he knew a great deal more about the game, and the way it had developed worldwide during his playing career, than some of those who held the power and greater efforts to achieve compromise – on both sides – would almost certainly have been of distinct benefit to New Zealand cricket. As it was, we saw the real strength of the man at its best when he became cricket manager of the national side in the 1980s when some notable successes were achieved. Perhaps New Zealand cricket was not (quite) ready for such a forceful personality during the previous decade.

Of his ability as a batsman there was never any doubt. He averaged just under 50 in his career (44.64 in Tests) with 103 centuries, a top score of 311 not out and nine other innings of over 200. He staged-managed the climax of his 15 years at Worcester with breathtaking brilliance when, on 29 May 1982, he opened the innings with Alan Ormerod needing one three-figure innings to complete 100 first-class hundreds. When the Worcs innings was declared closed at about a quarter to six he was 311 not out.

Turner was a protégé of my good friend Khalid ('Billy') Ibadulla who, after 18 seasons with Warwickshire and four Tests for Pakistan, settled in Dunedin where he built up a considerable reputation as a coach. It was Billy who recommended the young Turner to Worcs and he was at New Road to drink a glass of champagne with him to celebrate the century of centuries.

That was four and a half years in the future when Turner, aged 30, led his country for the first time abroad (he had already been captain in the home series against India at the beginning of the year). It was not a successful tour for the party, with no victory in any of the six Tests, but something of Turner's steely professionalism was absorbed by at least one of his men who was to be a successful captain of the future – Geoff Howarth. Turner missed the third Test in Pakistan where his duties were taken over by John Parker in a match in which a future Pakistan captain, Imran Khan, was first warned, then banished, by the umpires for bowling too many short-pitched deliveries.

England to India
1976–7
Tour captain: A. W. Greig

Delhi: *England won by an innings and 25 runs*
Calcutta: *England won by 10 wickets*
Madras: *England won by 200 runs*
Bangalore: *India won by 140 runs*
Bombay: *Match drawn*

Hard on the heels of Turner's New Zealanders came Greig's highly successful tour as England's captain with the series decided in England's favour after the first three Tests. Greig's mixture of stern ruthlessness and colourful derring-do was too much for Bedi's Indians, even though the tour party was some way below full strength and the series was not without its share of controversy. Bedi, never one to take defeat lightly and searching round desperately for an excuse for three consecutive defeats which gave England their best result for more than 40 years, suddenly accused them of cheating.

The burden of his complaint was that John Lever, the Essex left-arm quick bowler, had used an artificial aid to get the ball to swing in achieving figures of 7 for 46 and 3 for 24 on his debut and more particularly his match figures of 7 for 77 in Madras. The allegations were denied angrily and Lever, writing an autobiography a dozen years later, returned to the subject once again with renewed vehemence. When the subject (using lip-salve to enhance the shine on the ball) was touched upon obliquely by one of my 'Test Match Special' commentary colleagues in the summer of 1989, an Essex listener wrote to me recalling the first County Championship encounter between Lever and Bedi (then with Northants) after that tour. 'Lever greeted Bedi with a bouncer,' he recalled. 'It was the most vicious delivery to a batsman I ever saw him bowl.' Lever was indeed a genial and amiable, though highly accomplished, bowler who did not include attempted intimidation in his repertoire.

Greig, after his traumas in the home summer of 1976, was hugely delighted by the success of his team which culminated in the captain being chaired from the field in Madras. He looked, at the age of 30, set for a considerable reign as captain as the party flew off to Melbourne for the Centenary Match to mark 100 years of official Australia–England Tests. The reign, however, ended prematurely only a few months later for reasons far removed from Greig's handling of the side, so his outstanding Test becomes the one – Calcutta, 1–6 January 1977 – in which he led England to a second successive victory in India for the first time, hit the only hundred of the match and became the first England player to score 3,000 runs and take 100 wickets.

INDIA v. ENGLAND

Calcutta, 1977

INDIA

First Innings			*Second Innings*	
Gavaskar c Old b Willis	0		b Underwood	18
A. Gaekwad b Lever	32		c Tolchard b Greig	8
P. Sharma c Greig b Lever	9		c Knott b Willis	20
Viswanath c Tolchard b Underwood	35		c Lever b Greig	3
Patel hit wkt b Willis	21		lbw b Old	56
Solkar c Greig b Willis	2		c Knott b Willis	3
Madan Lal c Knott b Underwood	17		c Brearley b Old	16
Kirmani not out	25		b Old	0
Prasanna b Willis	2		c Brearley b Underwood	13
Bedi c Lever b Old	1		b Underwood	18
Chandrasekhar b Willis	1		not out	4
Extras (lb2 nb8)	10		*Extras* (b2 lb4 nb16)	22
	Total	155	Total	181

Bowling: Willis 20–3–27–5; Lever 22–2–57–2; Underwood 13–5–24–1; Old 20–5–37–2

Bowling: Willis 13–1–32–2; Lever 3–0–12–0; Underwood 32.5–18–50–3; Old 12–4–38–3; Greig 10–0–27–2

ENGLAND

First Innings		*Second Innings*	
Amiss c Kirmani b Prasanna	35	not out	7
Barlow c Kirmani b Madan Lal	4	not out	7
Brearley c Solkar b Bedi	5		
Randall lbw b Prasanna	37		
Tolchard b Bedi	67		
Greig lbw b Prasanna	103		
Knott c Gavaskar b Bedi	2		
Old c Madan Lal b Prasanna	52		
Lever c Gavaskar b Bedi	2		
Underwood c Gavaskar b Bedi	4		
Willis not out	0		
Extras (b5 lb5)	10	*Extras* (lb1 nb1)	2
Total	321	Total (no wicket)	16

Bowling: Madan Lal 17–4–25–1; Solkar 6–1–15–0; Bedi 64–25–110–5; Chandrasekhar 33–9–66–0; Prasanna 57.4–16–93–4; Sharma 1–0–2–0

Bowling: Madan Lal 1–0–3–0; Bedi 1.4–0–6–0; Prasanna 1–0–5–0

Pakistan to Australia
1976–7
Tour captain: Mushtaq Mohammad

Adelaide: *Match drawn*
Melbourne: *Australia won by 348 runs*
Sydney: *Pakistan won by 8 wickets*

Mushtaq Mohammad, though still only 34 years of age at the start of this tour as captain of Pakistan, was the most experienced Test player in the world since his international career had begun during the West Indies tour to his country in 1958–9. At first his appearances were intermittent – not surprisingly since he was only 15 years old when he first appeared – but gradually he established himself as a regular member of the Test side. While he was a genuine all-rounder, he played most of his international matches primarily as a batsman which again is unsurprising since he played so much alongside Intikhab who had a certain seniority as the number one leg-spinner and later came Wasim Raja and Javed Miandad, both useful practitioners of that particular art.

Since 1964, Mushtaq had been a professional with Northants and when he retired from county cricket (1977) he went into league cricket in the Midlands with outstanding success while making his home in Birmingham as an employee of Pakistan International Airlines. Thus, over a lengthy period, Mushtaq had become thoroughly anglicised and accumulated a great deal of professional experience. Later still he joined our 'Test Match Special' commentary team when Pakistan toured England (and on World Cup occasions) where his expertise was highly respected and his good fellowship much appreciated.

He took with him to Australia in December 1976 a powerful party which was very strong in batting, as well-equipped in fast bowling (Sarfraz Nawaz and Imran Khan) as any previous team had been and included a formidable number of all-rounders. It was the fast bowling pair, plus the all-round talent of Asif Iqbal and Javed Miandad which enabled Mushtaq to lead Pakistan to their first win in Australia and to share the three-match rubber. While he was a cheerful and sociable character off the field, 'Mushy' was a tough and uncompromising cricketer out in the middle, tactically aware to a pronounced degree and acutely knowledgeable in most, if not all, the tricks of the trade. He was a very good batsman indeed, as his 31,044 career runs (average 42.17) show, a good bowler and a fine close catcher.

Australia to New Zealand
1977

Tour captain: G. S. Chappell

Christchurch: *Match drawn*
Auckland: *Australia won by 10 wickets*

Australia squeezed in this short trip to New Zealand to provide a bit of extra practice for the forthcoming Centenary Test against Greig's England side and now Gregory Stephen Chappell had taken over the captaincy from his elder brother.

Greg Chappell was one of the outstanding Test batsmen of his generation, stylish and handsome as a stroke-player, polished to a higher degree than his more vigorous and aggressive brother. He had had two fairly formative seasons with Somerset and had more than six years' experience of Test cricket since making his debut with a century against Illingworth's 1970–1 tourists, playing almost the whole of his international cricket under his brother's leadership. It was inevitable, therefore, that many of Ian's characteristics should be adopted by Greg. The fact that, as a batsman, he *stroked* the ball rather than smashing it gave rise to an impression – misleading, but perhaps understandable – that he was a less uncompromising captain than his brother and this was probably reinforced by the fact that he had the Lillee–Thomson duo at his disposal on fewer occasions than Ian had enjoyed. Thomson, in the second half of his spectacular career, was becoming more injury-prone and thus less regularly available.

Greg at all times worked closely in conjunction with two men whose careers paralleled his own – Dennis Lillee and Rodney Marsh. It is possible to look at the Australian leadership in this period as a kind of triumvirate, formed by the three of them – as tough, talented and unyielding a trio as ever performed together for Australia. Their time together as Test players was interrupted by Kerry Packer's World Series cricket (now shortly to make its shattering impact) and though they resumed as Australian players afterwards, their country's Test cricket was slower to recover than most. Nevertheless, Greg Chappell skippered his country on a record 48 occasions and so impressive was his ability as batsman, captain and fielder that it is an enormous pity that a couple of incidents in one-day internationals have sullied a fine record, as we shall see.

Pakistan to West Indies
1977
Tour captain: Mushtaq Mohammad

Barbados: *Match drawn*
Trinidad: *West Indies won by 6 wickets*
Guyana: *Match drawn*
Trinidad: *Pakistan won by 266 runs*
Jamaica: *West Indies won by 140 runs*

Mushtaq Mohammad knew all about Clive Lloyd's fast bowling policy and was prepared for an ordeal by short-pitched deliveries but what came as an extra surprise was the introduction of Joel Garner, a daunting 6ft 8ins figure who had not yet appeared in English county cricket, and Colin Croft, four inches shorter than Garner but posing problems of an entirely different nature. With Garner, it was his steep bounce which caused major difficulties; Croft, who could bowl a vicious back-break, had a disconcerting habit of adopting a round-the-wicket attack from very wide of the crease which made that particular delivery extremely difficult indeed to counter. And there were Roberts, Holder and Julien around too, though no Holding in this series.

Nevertheless, Mushtaq's instructions to his troops were mandatory: 'No retreat. We must not be dominated by their fast bowlers.' And his batsmen resisted well until the last, and decisive, Test, despite Croft's shattering 8 for 29 return in the second Test which was won by the West Indies. Revenge was exceedingly sweet, therefore, for the Pakistan captain when he played a leading part in Pakistan's victory on their second visit to the Queen's Park Oval – a spinner's pitch – and that is Mushtaq Mohammad's outstanding Test as Pakistan's skipper in 19 international matches.

WEST INDIES v. PAKISTAN
Trinidad, 1977

PAKISTAN

First Innings

Majid Khan c Murray b Croft	92
Sadiq Mohammed c Lloyd b Roberts	0
Zaheer Abbas b Roberts	14
Haroon Rashid c Kallicharran b Ali	11
Mushtaq Mohammad c Greenidge b Richards	121
Asif Iqbal c Ali b Roberts	11
Wasim Raja c and b Ali	28
Imran Khan c Greenidge b Ali	1
Sarfraz Nawaz c Richards b Croft	29
Wasim Bari not out	5
Iqbal Qasim b Richards	2
Extras (b4 lb8 nb15)	27
Total	341

Bowling: Roberts 25–2–83–2; Croft 21–4–56–2; Garner 24–6–55–0; Ali 32–9–86–3; Richards 18.3–6–34–2; Fredericks 1–0–1–0

Second Innings

c Murray b Croft	16
b Ali	24
lbw b Garner	9
lbw b Garner	11
c Fredericks b Roberts	56
c and b Ali	10
b Garner	70
c and b Croft	30
c Lloyd b Croft	51
not out	2
Extras (b8 lb11 nb3)	22
Total (9 wkts declared)	301

Bowling: Roberts 20–2–56–1; Croft 22.5–6–79–3; Garner 23–4–71–3; Ali 20–2–73–2

WEST INDIES

First Innings

Fredericks b Imran	41
Greenidge b Qasim	32
Richards b Imran	4
Kallicharran c Srafraz b Mushtaq	11
I. Shillingford st Wasim Bari b Mushtaq	15
Garner c Qasim b Mushtaq	0
Lloyd lbw b Imran	22
Murray lbw b Imran	0
Roberts c Qasim b Mushtaq	6
Inshan Ali c Qasim b Mushtaq	4
Croft not out	0
Extras (b11 lb2 nb6)	19
Total	154

Bowling: Imran 21–6–64–4: Sarfraz 10–4–17–0; Qasim 13–6–26–1; Mushtaq 10.5–3–28–5; Wasim Raja 1–1–0–0

Second Innings

c Majid b Qasim	17
c Majid b Sarfraz	11
st Wasim Bari b Mushtaq	33
c Asif b Mushtaq	45
c Qasim b Mushtaq	23
(8) b Sarfraz	0
(6) b Sarfraz	17
(7) c Sadiq b Wasim Raja	30
c Majid b Wasim Raja	35
c Sadiq b Wasim Raja	0
not out	0
Extras (b7 lb1 nb3)	11
Total	222

Bowling: Imran 21–5–46–0; Sarfraz 19–10–21–3; Qasim 20–6–50–1; Mushtaq 31–9–69–3; Wasim Raja 3.5–1–22–3; Majid 10–8–3–0

7

THE PACKER CIRCUS

Centenary Test
1977
Tour captain: A. W. Greig

Melbourne: *Australia beat England by 45 runs*

Australia to England
1977
Tour captain: G. S. Chappell

Lord's: *Match drawn*
Old Trafford: *England won by 9 wickets*
Trent Bridge: *England won by 7 wickets*
Headingley: *England won by an innings and 85 runs*
The Oval: *Match drawn*

Before this series began it was known that Kerry Packer, an Australian multi-millionaire and owner of newspapers and TV and radio stations, would stage during the following Australian summer (English winter) a series of games between teams representing Australia, West Indies and the Rest of the World. To do this he had signed up many of the best players in Australia and West Indies with a smattering from Pakistan, England and South Africa. The English players had been recruited by Tony Greig. As soon as the project became known in England (the story 'broken', if I remember correctly, by the *Daily Mail*'s prize-winning columnist, Ian Wooldridge), Greig was deposed as England's captain and replaced by Mike Brearley, although Greig remained an England player and took part in all five Tests.

The Packer 'Circus' was not a matter of public knowledge when the Australian party was picked and set off to Europe and it was only during the rain-soaked month of May that it was announced. It was then learned that of the Australian party no fewer than 13 had signed contracts to play in the World Series. The Aussies after that seemed to be divided into two camps – the Packer men and the others – with

Chappell seemingly making no effort to cultivate any togetherness. There were occasions when the party arrived for off-the-field functions in two obviously discernible groups, some formally dressed, the others not. In these circumstances it was clearly impossible to generate any sort of team spirit and the Australians gave a rather poor account of themselves. In fact there was an unreal atmosphere with much splitting-up into groups and whispering in corners, not just amongst the Australians but amongst the English players, too.

Consequently, Brearley had a less difficult introduction to Test captaincy than might have been the case, helped by the return of Boycott (after a self-imposed exile of three years) at Trent Bridge where he scored a century, followed by another at Headingley which was his 100th first-class hundred.

Notwithstanding the fact that the first Test had been designated a Jubilee Test to mark the 25th anniversary of Queen Elizabeth II's reign and produced the then record receipts of £220,384, it was not a pleasant or happy series in which England won back the Ashes. There was much suspicion and disharmony on the field, particularly at Headingley, and one was left wondering if cricket would ever be quite the same again – after Packer. At Trent Bridge, Ian Botham made his first appearance for England.

India to Australia
1977–8

Tour captain: B. S. Bedi

Brisbane: *Australia won by 16 runs*
Perth: *Australia won by 2 wickets*
Melbourne: *India won by 222 runs*
Sydney: *India won by an innings and 2 runs*
Adelaide: *Australia won by 47 runs*

With so many of their experienced players in Packer's ranks, the Australian Board were forced to call Bobby Simpson out of retirement to skipper a Test side against Bishen Singh Bedi's tourists that introduced six men new to Test cricket in the first match, two more in the second and another four for the last (which had to be won to take the series). After winning the first two Tests, Simpson's gallant band of rookies were spun to defeat in Melbourne and Sydney by Bedi and Chandrasekhar. Notwithstanding Simpson's heroic leadership, Bedi should have achieved better results than he did. He bowled well, taking 31 wickets in the rubber, but on the excellent batting wicket in Adelaide he could not conjure a match-winning performance from his tourists, though his batsmen backed him nobly in scoring 445 in the fourth innings of that game. As a tactician he was not Simpson's equal; as a leader of men he was left far, far behind by the veteran Australian. But the powers in Delhi were still dictating the course of Indian cricket and he retained the captaincy until the pendulum swung back to Bombay with Gavaskar's appointment, but that was some time ahead.

All the same, Bedi was arguably the best slow left-armer in the world in his day and of his 22 Tests as captain (out of 67 he played) the one in Melbourne over the New Year holiday of 1978 stands out as his greatest achievement. To win a Test in Australia after losing his fine opening pair of Gavaskar and Chauhan in the first nine balls of the innings and without a run scored was indeed a notable success – even if some of the Australian names are a little unfamiliar!

AUSTRALIA v. INDIA

Melbourne, 1978

INDIA

First Innings		Second Innings	
Gavaskar c Rixon b Thomson	0	c Serjeant b Gannon	118
Chauhan c Mann b Clark	0	run out	20
Amarnath c Simpson b Clark	72	(7) b Cosier	41
Viswanath c Rixon b Thomson	59	lbw b Clark	54
Vengsarkar c Simpson b Thomson	37	c Cosier b Clark	6
Mankad c Clark b Gannon	44	b Clark	38
Kirmani lbw b Simpson	29	(3) c Thomson b Mann	29
Ghavri c Rixon b Gannon	6	c Simpson b Clark	6
Prasanna b Clark	0	c Rixon b Gannon	11
Bedi not out	2	not out	12
Chandrasekhar b Clark	0	lbw b Cosier	0
Extras (lb3 nb4)	7	Extras (lb1 nb7)	8
Total	256	Total	343

Bowling: Thomson 16–2–78–3; Clark 19.2–2–73–4; Gannon 14–2–47–2; Cosier 12–3–25–0; Simpson 3–1–11–1; Mann 5–1–15–0

Bowling:Thomson 18–4–47–0; Clark 29–3–96–4; Gannon 22–4–88–2; Cosier 12.7–2–58–2; Simpson 3–0–22–0; Mann 4–0–24–1

AUSTRALIA

First Innings		Second Innings	
Dyson b Ghavri	0	lbw b Bedi	12
Cosier c Chauhan b Chandrasekhar	67	b Chandrasekhar	34
Ogilvie lbw b Ghavri	6	c Chauhan b Bedi	0
Serjeant b Chandrasekhar	85	b Chandrasekhar	17
Simpson c Mankad b Chandrasekhar	2	lbw b Chandrasekhar	4
Toohey c Viswanath b Bedi	14	c Chauhan b Chandrasekhar	14
Mann c Gavaskar b Bedi	11	c Gavaskar b Chandrasekhar	18
Rixon lbw b Chandrasekhar	11	c and b Chandrasekhar	12
Clark lbw b Chandrasekhar	3	c Ghavri b Bedi	33
Thomson c Ghavri b Chandrasekhar	0	c and b Bedi	7
Gannon not out	0	not out	3
Extras (b6 lb7 nb1)	14	Extras (b6 lb4)	10
Total	213	Total	164

Bowling: Ghavri 9–0–37–2; Gavaskar 2–0–7–0; Bedi 15–2–71–2; Chandrasekhar 14.1–2–56–6; Prasanna 10–1–32–0

Bowling: Ghavri 4–0–29–0; Bedi 16.1–5–58–4; Chandrasekhar 20–3–52–6; Prasanna 8–4–5–0; Amarnath 3–0–10–0

England to New Zealand and Pakistan
1977–8

Tour captain: J. M. Brearley/G. Boycott

Lahore: *Match drawn*
Hyderabad: *Match drawn*
Karachi: *Match drawn*

Wellington: *New Zealand won by 72 runs*
Christchurch: *England won by 174 runs*
Auckland: *Match drawn*

Brearley's first tour as captain was brief but eventful – in terms of off-the-field matters rather than those happening on it. He set out purposefully, putting Boycott, his second-in-command, in charge of net practice and since the Yorkshireman was probably the most industrious practiser in the history of the game this made good sense, in theory. In practice, however, it partly misfired when in Lahore Boycott arranged a full-scale practice match against a local side and spent most of the time accumulating a century himself! The first Test was ruined by two days of rioting, on the second of which I became a tear-gas casualty which was of no great help to broadcasting. Mudassar Nazar scored a century of record length (9 hours 17 minutes) while Boycott laboured for 290 minutes over 50 runs. The overall scoring rate was 31 runs an hour.

In a meaningless one-day friendly between the second and third Tests, Brearley was struck on the left forearm and had to return home to England for treatment to a fractured ulna. We shall look at his captaincy in more detail, therefore, at a later stage. Boycott took over leadership of the party for the final match in Karachi and the three Tests in New Zealand. There was further rioting in Karachi and a threatened strike by the England players when a story appeared in local newspapers that a group of Packer players (who would otherwise have been in the Pakistan side) were flying back to take part in the third Test. A group, including Zaheer Abbas and Asif Iqbal, was reported to have flown as far as Singapore at which point the England manager, Ken Barrington, asked for a meeting with B C C P officials.

At the end of this meeting, an assurance was given that the Packer players had not been recalled at the behest of the Pakistan Board and that they would not be playing in the Test! Six hours earlier, the Pakistan Press had been proclaiming a right to choose *anyone* to play in their Test side and there is no doubt at all that if Zaheer, Javed and Asif had turned out the England team would have refused to play the match. Kerry Packer had induced strong and bitter feelings in English cricket.

After the sterile cricket and unsavoury by-products in Pakistan, the party moved on to New Zealand with a feeling of overwhelming relief but not before one incident, seemingly minor at the time, had occurred which would be recalled ten years hence. In the England first-innings scorecard there appears 'Gatting lbw b Abdul Qadir 5'. The umpire was Shakoor Rana. In December 1987, I had occasion to look up my notebook for that tour and against Gatting's dismissal in his first Test innings appear four words and a punctuation mark: 'Pitched outside leg stump?' We may, perhaps, recall that when we reach England's tour to Pakistan in 1987.

New Zealand cricket history was made on the morning of 15 February 1978, when England suffered their first-ever defeat at the hands of the country with the most modest Test history. Although New Zealand had scored at least one win over all the other Test-playing countries, never before in 48 matches and nearly 50 years had England been beaten. It was a devastating blow to Boycott with his burning ambition to be confirmed in the captaincy of his country and his deep-rooted belief that he merited that honour. No one, in fact, could have fought harder than Boycott himself to avoid that defeat at the Basin Reserve where he batted for over seven hours in difficult conditions in scoring 77 runs – by some way the biggest individual total in the game – but there was little resolution amongst the other batsmen.

In terms of long experience and technical expertise, Boycott was handsomely qualified; he was the best defensive batsman in the world, the most difficult man to dislodge, the opener whose every dismissal evoked unbridled rejoicing in the opposition ranks, the most-prized scalp for bowlers everywhere. Sadly for his hopes and ambitions, he fell down in exactly the area where Brearley most excelled – understanding, management and leadership of men.

Brearley was a brilliant psychologist; Boycott, in stark contrast, has ever been a subjective thinker. He was known throughout the game for his preoccupation with amassing personal records of scoring and his players on tour in New Zealand were not willing to give him the benefit of any doubt about his desire to lead a winning *team*. When the time came for a declaration – needed to ensure a rubber-squaring win in Christchurch – it was to Bob Willis that the team looked. Willis and the other players wanted to declare before play started on the final morning; Boycott wanted to bat on for a short time. In the face of the most ostentatious opposition within his dressing-room, the captain acquiesced.

It was a chastened, but still hopeful, Boycott who returned to England but he was destined never to lead his country again.

Australia to West Indies
1978

Tour captain: R. B. Simpson

Trinidad: *West Indies won by an innings and 106 runs*
Barbados: *West Indies won by 9 wickets*
Guyana: *Australia won by 3 wickets*
Trinidad: *West Indies won by 198 runs*
Jamaica: *Match drawn*

With Australia shorn of their Packer men while the West Indies Board insisted on their right to play theirs, the result of this series seemed to be very much a foregone conclusion – at least for the first two Tests, after which an internal dispute struck deep into the ranks of the home side. While the West Indies Board, throughout all the disputes around the world which resulted from the Packer Circus in Australia, had staunchly defended the right of their players 'to make money wherever they could' (a charitable outlook not echoed when it came to the desire of English players to play in South Africa) there was a certain feeling of pique at the way Packer had been able to draw so deeply from the well of West Indian talent without a whisper of the World Series enterprise reaching the Board's collective or individual ears. They overlooked, all too obviously, the fact that it is very much easier for one man to command loyalty and secrecy than a committee of members scattered over groups of islands and the South American mainland, too, in the case of Guyana.

The Packer Series had given the West Indies players something like three times the amount they normally earned in a Test series and before the first Test they opened negotiations with their Board of Control for better pay. No conclusion had been reached by the opening day of the Test and at this point the Board relieved Deryck Murray, the players' shop steward and chief negotiator, of the vice-captaincy of the side. It was seen as a petty, spiteful and futile gesture but as Murray remained a member of the side the players took no action . . . yet.

After the second Test – easily won, like the first against the below-strength Aussies – the Board then ventured a little further and announced that three players were to be dropped for the Guyanan Test – Desmond Haynes, who in his first three Test innings as Roy Fredericks' successor had scored 61, 66 and 55, Richard Austin and Deryck Murray. Haynes and Austin, together with Colin Croft, had just signed contracts to join the second series of Packer cricket in Australia and it was clear that the Board were now playing a game of brinkmanship.

How far could they go before the players reacted? Clive Lloyd left them in no doubt at all. He asked the Board to state the principles which had governed their selection of the team for the third Test. To the somewhat feeble response that they were looking ahead to the tour of India in eight months' time, Lloyd asked, 'Why change a winning side? Why drop Haynes who is young, as well as brilliant? Why drop Murray whose batting in the second Test was invaluable?' The Board, staggered by unprecedented defiance from a player, had no answer to the questions. Within an hour of the end of the meeting, Lloyd resigned the captaincy; by the following day every other member of the side who had a Packer contract had joined him.

The Board now had to attempt to bluff it out by picking a new team for the Test at Bourda and in what might be termed a second-team match, the Australians won by three wickets. A similar side was put out by West Indies in the fourth Test and this time Simpson's tourists were beaten but the public now pronounced *their* verdict on the dispute by staying away from the ground.

Simpson must at times have reflected that there were many more pleasant ways of spending his retirement than in being given a close-up view of West Indian cricket politics but his difficulties reached their climax in the final Test in Jamaica. His declaration set West Indies 358 to win and they were still 100 runs adrift when their ninth wicket fell with 6.2 overs still to be bowled. At that point the crowd invaded the ground and no further play was possible. All attempts by the tourists to have the lost time made up by (part of) an extra day's play foundered and Simpson was denied a likely second victory with his scratch side. Nothing, however, can diminish the immense credit due to Bobby Simpson for carrying the Australian flag, at the age of 42, through a sea of troubled Caribbean waters and later, as we shall see, playing an important part in the rebuilding of Australian Test cricket in the aftermath of Packer.

In the West Indies, still refusing to bow to player-power, the selectors persevered with the second string for one more series; but with the prestige of the World Cup at stake in England in the summer of 1979, Lloyd and his men were welcomed back to the fold. The mercenary foot-soldiers had won a notable victory over their own generals.

Pakistan to England
1978

Tour captain: Wasim Bari

Edgbaston: *England won by an innings and 57 runs*
Lord's: *England won by an innings and 120 runs*
Headingley: *Match drawn*

Wasim Bari had had a tremendously long run as Pakistan's wicket-keeper (dating back to 1967) when he was appointed captain for the home series against England in the winter of 1977–8. He retained the captaincy for the tour to England the following summer which was his fourth tour to this country and there was one more to come.

There have been few wicket-keeper-captains in Test cricket which at first glance may seem strange since captains (especially batsman-captains) in the field traditionally rely heavily on the men behind the stumps for information on the pace and state of the pitch, technical chinks in the batsman's armour, and such matters. Perhaps it is that wicket-keepers make ideal first lieutenants rather than skippers. Certainly the need for a wicket-keeper's complete concentration on every delivery is absolute, especially in a side with specialist spin bowlers of a complex nature . . . Intikhab Alam, Mushtaq Mohammad, Abdul Qadir . . . and thus it is difficult to see how he can focus his attention on the many wider ranging considerations which occur in the course of a day's Test cricket. Wasim, a pleasant and likeable cricketer, had the general respect of his players in that they had all joined a side in which he was already well-established. Also, such is the tightly knit community of first-class cricket (other than Tests) in Pakistan that Wasim had a sound knowledge of the abilities, and the temperaments, of his players. Yet it often seemed to me – and I watched him perform in three different continents – that he had some difficulty in grasping the wider strategic issues and was content to put the side on automatic pilot, so to speak, for long periods. He had great patience in *waiting* for something to happen, not too much verve in *causing* something to happen.

His first tour as captain was unsuccessful in three Tests, largely because of the all-round brilliance of Botham and good bowling, too, by Old and Edmonds. Pakistan were in something of a transitional stage, particularly amongst the batsmen (because five leading players were not selected due to their involvement with Packer cricket) and they did not enjoy the wet English summer.

New Zealand to England
1978

Tour captain: M. G. Burgess

The Oval: *England won by 7 wickets*
Trent Bridge: *England won by an innings and 119 runs*
Lord's: *England won by 7 wickets*

Mark Gordon Burgess was a fine all-round sportsman from a family
with cricketing traditions. He led the New Zealanders with the confidence born of a personally successful tour as a batsman five years earlier
and captaincy of the team which had won its first-ever Test against
England only a few months previously. Burgess was a most likeable
man and captain who was probably unfortunate to run into an England
side in which Botham was now firing on all cylinders and David Gower
had emerged (during the Pakistan series) as a cultured and accomplished
left-hand batsman. It has been said in New Zealand that Burgess was
too nice a man, that he lacked the 'killer instinct'.

To the impartial observer it was a little difficult to see how Burgess
could ever get into a position on this tour to show whether he did or
did not, in fact, possess the ruthlessness to press home an advantage.
It would undoubtedly have helped if he could have enjoyed the services
of Turner to open, and anchor, the New Zealand batting, but Turner
– heavily criticized at home for it – was taking a benefit with Worcestershire and in the interests of his long-term financial future decided to
concentrate on that. Dayle Hadlee, elder brother of Richard, broke
down after one game and took no further part in the tour, and the
party had no specialist wicket-keeper. In all these circumstances, Burgess
had little chance to avoid a three-nil drubbing but he maintained his
country's tradition of sending tour parties under popular ambassadorial
captains. During this summer, Test cricket in England was sponsored,
for the first time, by the Cornhill Insurance Company.

India to Pakistan
1978

Tour captain: B. S. Bedi

Faisalabad: *Match drawn*
Lahore: *Pakistan won by 8 wickets*
Karachi: *Pakistan won by 8 wickets*

With rivalry on the cricket field taking over from border hostilities, the two neighbours resumed Test contact under the captaincy of Bedi and Mustaq Mohammad (restored to the leadership after being omitted from Pakistan's tour of England because of his involvement with Packer). It was a series in which both sides, as ever, showed themselves capable of heavy scoring but the difference was that in Sarfraz Nawaz and Imran Khan, Pakistan had a pair of opening bowlers capable of making an early breakthrough. In view of the long history of problems between the governments of the two countries, success was more important than ever. Nerves and tempers were often frayed and in the first Test the umpires (Khalid Aziz and Shakoor Rana!) refused to officiate for a time after Gavaskar had, it was claimed, used bad language. In which language he had used it is, unfortunately, not a matter of record. Bedi was frustrated to find a series of pitches which were of little use to him, or to Chandrasekhar and Prasanna. Pakistan had found their best opening attack in history and used it to good effect.

England to Australia
1978–9
Tour captain: J. M. Brearley

Brisbane: *England won by 7 wickets*
Perth: *England won by 166 runs*
Melbourne: *Australia won by 103 runs*
Sydney: *England won by 93 runs*
Adelaide: *England won by 205 runs*
Sydney: *England won by 9 wickets*

In terms simply of results achieved, John Michael Brearley was an outstandingly successful captain and this five-Tests-to-one rubber was the highlight of his career. At the same time, it has to be borne in mind that notwithstanding the experience gained in a home series against India and the tour to the West Indies, the Australians (still without the Packer men) were chronically short of players of the highest class. On the other hand, many of the men led by Graham Yallop, the Victorian left-hander, in this series went on to establish themselves as international cricketers in the years which followed.

A brilliant academic career at Cambridge established Brearley as possessing the best *brain* of any England captain and this enabled him to overcome the handicap of being regarded in severely professional eyes as not a good enough player to merit selection for his batting talents alone. He dominated his teams intellectually (though he would probably quarrel with that choice of words) and at times, it seemed, the selectors as well. As a result, cricketers who might otherwise have regarded his batting technique with suspicion, spent their years under his command in awe of the man. Of Brearley's brilliance as a leader of men there can be no doubt whatsoever, just as his tactical skill is unquestioned. He had studied captaincy in all its aspects, much as Napoleon's successful generalship was due to his analysis of the methods and strategy of other European military leaders. He undertook this tour to Australia in the face of much public questioning of his right to a place in the party at all and brought back a victory which answered most, if not all, of his critics. His finest hour was to come later when, after retirement, he returned to lead England in 1981 to three Test victories against a much stronger Australian side. For the moment his record read eight victories and one defeat in Tests against Australia, two draws each against Australia and Pakistan.

In his book *The Art of Captaincy* (Hodder and Stoughton, 1985) Brearley provides an absolutely fascinating insight into the detail in which he studied cricket leadership and the psychology of cricketers. Almost every word in the book and almost everything he did on the field and in the dressing-room stamps Mike Brearley as the most perceptive and gifted captain England have ever had. Almost? Yes indeed. The one move which has always seemed to me totally incomprehensible was his recommendation to the selectors that Ian Botham should be his successor as captain of England. It was as if the Head Boy of a good school, leaving with six 'A' grades in his A-level examinations to go up to Oxbridge on a scholarship, had proposed to his Head teacher that he should be replaced by a prop forward in the School XV who was currently struggling with his GCSE.

West Indies to India
1978–9
Tour captain: A. I. Kallicharran

Bombay: *Match drawn*
Bangalore: *Match drawn*
Madras: *India won by 3 wickets*
Calcutta: *Match drawn*
Delhi: *Match drawn*
Kanpur: *Match drawn*

Alvin Kallicharran had become the West Indies' stop-gap captain during the home series against Australia and now he continued as leader of the non-Packer players on a long tour of India. He had fast bowling strength at his disposal in Norbert Phillip, Sylvester Clarke and Vanburn Holder together with the newly capped (second Test) Malcolm Marshall who was to become one of the West Indies' greatest-ever quick men. He found, however – and not for the last time in India when Sunil Gavaskar was leading the home side – that the pitches generally were designed to favour batsmen and virtually to immobilise touring fast bowlers. 'Kally', while a superb left-hand batsman who had been a Warwickshire player for eight years, was an altogether quieter and less controversial character than some of his predecessors. He knew his performance was under critical scrutiny at home and approached his captaincy with a certain diffidence and uncertainty.

Kallicharran had toured India before and he knew it was hard work to coax victory from unresponsive pitches against stubborn opposition. He also knew only too well the partiality of India's new captain, Gavaskar, to long spells of batting. With a daring which was largely out of character he put India in to bat when he won the toss in Bombay – and saw his opposite number bat for nearly 6¾ hours! Off-the-field political troubles and a lot of rain made it a difficult series and although Kallicharran showed a strong lead with his personal batting, the rapidly improving Indian side took the series with a solitary Test victory.

Pakistan to New Zealand
1979

Tour captain: Mushtaq Mohammad

Christchurch: *Pakistan won by 128 runs*
Napier: *Match drawn*
Auckland: *Match drawn*

Mushtaq was back at the helm and Wasim Bari, free to concentrate solely on his wicket-keeping, reaped a rich harvest of victims including seven out of the first eight batsmen dismissed in Auckland. Mushtaq, however, enjoyed the first Test as both captain and bowler with the New Zealanders unable to cope with his leg-spin and that of Wasim Raja. I saw this series as a guest commentator for Radio New Zealand and for the second Test in Napier had the company of Geoffrey Saulez, Sussex and England scorer, pursuing a hobby of visiting all the Test grounds of the world – McLean Park on that occasion became the 50th to stage Test cricket. Even without four Packer players, Pakistan were

too strong for New Zealand in the first Test and, paradoxically, after
the tourists had been restored to full strength (when the World Series
finished), New Zealand performed more resolutely.

For the first time, one of the more unpleasant aspects of Packerism
manifested itself in this series. The World Series in Australia had been
backed by strong professional marketing methods and publicity
designed to give the games credibility. What all the 'hype' could not
disguise was that the cricket was meaningless in international competition terms and so an element of artificial aggression was introduced
in the form of bumper wars and excessive 'sledging' of each other by
the contestants.

Sadly, one or two of the Pakistan players, on their return to orthodox
Tests, seemed incapable of (or disinclined to) a reversion to the normal
idiom and there were one or two unsavoury episodes in the second and
third Tests. The fact that this has been repeated on such a wide scale
in the ten years which have elapsed since the World Series of 1978–9
represents, in the author's view, one of the most damning indictments
of Packer cricket. This, and the operations of West Indian all-pace
attack, must be regarded as being responsible for the vastly changed
attitudes of players to the game, a deterioration in their sense of values
and the consequent plunge of standards of behaviour, of respect for the
opposition, and for each other. It can, of course, be argued that Packer
cricket brought increased benefits to players everywhere in terms of
financial rewards and to cricket as a whole in the form of sponsorship.
Whether the one satisfactorily balances the other will remain a matter
of personal taste and opinion.

Pakistan to Australia
1979

Tour captain: Mushtaq Mohammad

Melbourne: *Pakistan won by 71runs*
Perth: *Australia won by 7 wickets*

This brace of Tests brought Mushtaq's international career to an end.
It had been a distinguished one and it ended on a high note in at least
two instances. In what seemed a remarkably short space of time, Pakistan had now been involved in 100 Test Matches and it was the 100th
which saw them win in Melbourne. Although a nasty taste had been
left in a number of New Zealand mouths the previous month, Australia
now applauded Mushtaq's chivalry in seeking to bring back Rodney
Hogg who had been dismissed, run out, for wandering out of his ground

before the ball was dead. The request was refused but the Pakistan captain received nearly as much (favourable) publicity as did Hogg for his flamboyant demolition of his stumps with a testily flourished bat. The unpredictable Sarfraz Nawaz produced a breathtaking spell of seven wickets for one run in 33 deliveries – one of the greatest pieces of Test bowling. In the second Test, Andrew Hilditch intercepted a ball returned from the field and handed it to Sarfraz who appealed for Hilditch's dismissal, handled the ball. The appeal was upheld, as was Sarfraz's reputation for bewildering changes of character. When his playing days ended he turned to politics and no one could have been surprised.

Mushtaq completed a notable career by playing his 100th innings for Pakistan. He had been a good and relatively successful captain who could be as tough as any when he chose, but he more frequently found that a softly-softly approach suited him better. It was a pity he never led his country in England where his knowledge of conditions and players would have made him a formidable opponent.

India to England
1979
Tour captain: S. Venkataraghavan

Edgbaston: *England won by an innings and 83 runs*
Lord's: *Match drawn*
Headingley: *Match drawn*
The Oval: *Match drawn*

Srinivasaraghavan Venkataraghavan was, for very obvious reasons, known simply as Venkat in English cricket where he spent three seasons (1973–5) playing for Derbyshire and made four Test-playing tours. He entered international cricket three years after India's other great off-spinner, Prasanna, and finished three years after him so that on many occasions Indian captains were able to work on the basis that if one didn't come off, the other might well do so.

Venkat was a physical fitness fanatic and a man who did not mince his words, as a number of captains found to their cost – or at least those who could understand him for his language was the machinegun-like Madrassi while most captains came either from the north or from Bombay. Indeed, after so many years of alternation between Bombay and Delhi, Venkat's appointment was viewed with more than a little surprise, especially since Gavaskar had so recently led India to a series win over the West Indies. But Gavaskar was known to tilt at windmills of authority in Indian cricket; Venkat reserved his barbs, when required, for the men he led.

His appointment made sense in at least two ways: he had a great deal of experience in England since this was his fourth tour and he had also had those three seasons with Derbyshire; he was regarded as a strong character who could command the midfield between two other big personalities and former captains in Bedi, on the one hand, and Gavaskar on the other. It was unfortunate for Venkat that his men did not perform well, departing ignominiously from the second World Cup (which occupied the first half of the season), losing the first Test and drawing the next two. There were many fine players in his side – sound openers, accomplished middle-order batsmen, Kapil Dev proving himself their finest-ever opening bowler and well-supported by Ghavri who somehow contrived to take wickets when they were least expected – but they rarely operated well as a unit. The fielding was sub-standard and the wicket-keeping something worse than that. The heroics of the tour were all crammed into the last day of the tour. Brearley had set India 438 to win in 498 minutes and Gavaskar and Chauhan took their opening partnership from the penultimate day into the final one with 213 for the first wicket. Gavaskar paced himself admirably and the odds were very much on an Indian win – no matter how unlikely this had seemed at the start of the innings – when he fell to Botham after scoring 221 in one of the most vital Test innings I have ever seen. The momentum of the Indian innings was fine so long as Gavaskar was there, in control. When he was out, it was lost, even though the tourists still had six wickets in hand with 49 needed from 46 deliveries. The later batsmen failed to cope with the pressure applied by Brearley and India had to settle for a draw but the memory of 4 September 1979 lingers in the mind as one of the best day's cricket a team from India has ever produced – and Srinivasaraghavan Venkataraghavan was the captain on that occasion.

Australia to India
1979
Tour captain: K. J. Hughes

Madras: *Match drawn*
Bangalore: *Match drawn*
Kanpur: *India won by 153 runs*
Delhi:*Match drawn*
Calcutta: *Match drawn*
Bombay: *India won by an innings and 100 runs*

On the Australians' 1977 tour to England, Kimberley John Hughes was one of the minority of players who had not signed contracts to play in the Packer Circus and as such did not have a personally happy time. He made his debut in the final Test of that tour, scoring just one run; played in two Tests during India's tour of Australia in 1977–8, again without making any impact, and he had been in the West Indies with Bobby Simpson's party without being able to gain a Test place. He had, therefore, a modest Test pedigree when, in the second of the two home Tests against Pakistan in 1979, Yallop was injured and unable to lead in Perth; thus Hughes became the first Western Australian player to skipper his country.

Hughes was a quiet and sensitive leader, in contrast to many of his predecessors. His clean-cut, boyish, almost cherubic appearance belied a strength of character which led him to play for several seasons in South Africa in the 1980s, in defence of the principle that a cricketer was entitled to ply his trade and earn a living where he wished. In 1976, before his first tour to England with Greg Chappell's party, Hughes coached and played in Scotland, scoring five hundreds for Watsonians, averaging 74.39 with an aggregate of 1,711 runs in the East Scotland League. More to the point, he was a highly popular visitor who made many friends during his summer in Edinburgh.

Hughes always seemed to me to be a one-off type of Australian captain. There was not the steely abrasiveness of a Chappell, the ruthless single-mindedness of a Bradman, the (on-the-field) grim determination of a Lawry or a Simpson and one could not see him, as Lindsay Hassett once did, taking off his trousers in the grill room of the Park Lane Hotel when ice cream had been spilled on them, handing them to the waiter with a polite request for the pants to be sponged and dried, then, trouserless, carrying on with his meal. Hughes' style was not of the Hassett variety – but then no one ever quite managed to scale the little Victorian's peaks of dead-pan humour! Hughes was a thoughtful and intelligent man who seemed to find a more-than-usual loneliness in the role of captain.

He had a notable personal success with the bat in India in 1978–9 and in Calcutta showed himself not afraid to risk defeat by going for a win, but Indian Test cricket was getting better by the day and the series was largely decided by the fast bowling of Kapil Dev, the slow left-armer Dilip Doshi and the new off-spinner, Shivlal Yadav. It was India's first winning rubber against Australia.

8

THE POST-PACKER DECADE

Pakistan to India
1979–80

Tour captain: Asif Iqbal

Bangalore: *Match drawn*
Delhi: *Match drawn*
Bombay: *India won by 131 runs*
Kanpur: *Match drawn*
Madras: *India won by 10 wickets*
Calcutta: *Match drawn*

It had been a long wait for Asif Iqbal Razvi for the honour of skippering his adopted country – he had been born in Hyderabad (India) and played his early first-class cricket there before moving to Pakistan. Now, at the end of his career and at the age of 36, he had a final fling as captain in the six-Test series which once again emphasized the growing strength of India.

Asif at this time had been playing for Kent in the English County Championship for 11 years, had figured in Packer's Australian operations and was a veteran of 52 Tests for Pakistan. He led a thoroughly experienced side and while the first Test resulted in the now-expected war of attrition with batsmen on top, there were exciting sequences in most of the remaining five – and a touch of whimsical humour in Delhi. Doshi, moving out of his ground to indicate how the shadow of a tree was distracting him, was run out! His anguished entreaty for the appeal to be withdrawn which bordered on the theatrical was addressed to Majid Khan, as Asif was off the field at the time, and Majid relented. One doubts whether Asif, an altogether tougher character, would have been as generous. He was a far-from-flamboyant character but he was quietly in control in his own rather low-key fashion. He, too, had a sense of humour (as Doshi most certainly had) but it did not usually extend to recalling a batsman who had been given out.

The six Tests of this series were his only experience in leading Pakistan, but he skippered Kent for a time. A fine middle-order batsman, he was also an extremely useful medium-pace bowler of 'little seamers'.

West Indies to Australia
1979–80

Tour captain: C. H. Lloyd (D. L. Murray)

Brisbane: *Match drawn*
Melbourne: *West Indies won by 10 wickets*
Adelaide: *West Indies won by 408 runs*

All was forgiven, if not forgotten, with the Packer schism now healed
and both sides returned to full strength. With Lloyd still recovering
from a knee injury, Deryck Murray led West Indies in the drawn game
at The Gabba where Hughes, having returned the captaincy to Greg
Chappell, scored 130 not out in Australia's second innings. West Indies
fielded four fast bowlers plus Collis King's medium pace; Australia had
three quickies plus Chappell's medium pace.

When Lloyd returned for the two remaining Tests it was to lead West
Indies to massive victories, with Croft, Holding, Roberts and Garner
sharing the wickets.

England to Australia
1979–80

Tour captain: J. M. Brearley

Perth: *Australia won by 138 runs*
Sydney: *Australia won by 6 wickets*
Melbourne: *Australia won by 8 wickets*

Australia took revenge for the humiliation of their first defeat in a home
rubber by the West Indies by achieving a 3–0 clean sweep against
England in a hastily arranged double tour in which Australia played
alternately against West Indies and England. As part of the settlement
of the breach with Packer's 'alternative' cricket, a series of 14 one-day
internationals was played as a three-cornered contest with West Indies
beating England in the final.

Brearley's second tour as captain in Australia, therefore, was in
marked contrast to the success of his first. England's refusal to regard
the Ashes as being at stake (because it was only a three-match rubber)
caused some resentment in Australia; the general view back in England
was that the series was not to be taken as seriously as traditional-type

tours. With Kerry Packer's organisation now 'packaging and marketing' Tests there was a distinct suspicion and cynicism in this country about the new concept of triangular tournaments, whether they involved Tests or one-day games. These sentiments were confirmed when Lillee went out in Perth wielding a bat made of aluminium and had to be persuaded to change it! It was all some distance from Ashes series as seen through British eyes.

West Indies to New Zealand
1980
Tour captain: C. H. Lloyd

Dunedin: *New Zealand won by 1 wicket*
Christchurch: *Match drawn*
Auckland: *Match drawn*

In this short but dramatic series, standards of player behaviour on the field plummeted to previously unknown depths and marked the beginning of the end of the concept that the umpire's decision is final. The rot set in and was destined to spread around the world over the next decade.

The tourists were dismayed and angry at their defeat in Dunedin in which a (then) record 12 lbw decisions were given – seven against West Indian batsmen, five against New Zealanders. Fred Goodall, the country's senior umpire, stood in Dunedin and again in the second Test when the tourists remained in their dressing-room after the tea interval on the third day and requested a change of umpire. This was refused and they finally resumed the game 12 minutes late. On the rest day there were heated debates during which the West Indies threatened to abandon the match and the tour but were persuaded to continue. On the fourth morning, after an appeal by Croft against Hadlee had been turned down, Croft ran in for the next ball, collided with Mr Goodall and knocked him to the ground. When the umpire sought to complain to the tourists' captain, Clive Lloyd stood his ground in the slips and Goodall had to walk the length of the pitch to state his case. From that ill-tempered tour has been bequeathed to Test cricket one of the classically disgraceful pictures of all time – Holding pirouetting like a ballet dancer to kick down the stumps after an appeal by *him* had been turned down.

Lloyd's comment on it all was: 'After the things Holding and Croft went through I had some sympathy for the way they felt although in the strictest sense what they did could never be right. There can be no excuse for bad behaviour but I would strongly say we have never been bad sportsmen.'

England in India
1980
Tour captain: J. M. Brearley

Bombay (Golden Jubilee Test): *England won by 10 wickets*

On their way home from Australia, England played this match to celebrate 50 years since the formation of the Board of Control for Cricket in India. Brearley was the captain and saw an historic perform-ance by Botham who scored 114 of England's total of 296, took 6 for 58 in India's first innings and 7 for 48 in the second, while Bob Taylor held seven catches in the first innings and three more in the second.

Australia to Pakistan
1980
Tour captain: G. S. Chappell

Karachi: *Pakistan won by 7 wickets*
Faisalabad: *Match drawn*
Lahore: *Match drawn*

Greg Chappell made his share of runs on this, one of Australia's rare visits to Pakistan but, in an age when fast bowling was beginning to be the dominant attacking force around the world, quickly discovered that on this particular trip he would have been glad of two top-class spinners. In the first Test, which produced the only clear result and thus gave the home country a first rubber victory over Australia, Bright, the slow left-armer, had a match analysis of 10 for 111, while Iqbal Qasim, a similar type, returned 11 for 118. The difference was that Bright had no spin bowling support at the other end while Qasim enjoyed the back-up of the little off-spinner, Tauseef Ahmed, whose match figures on his Test debut were 7 for 126. Runs galore came in Faisalabad (999 while only 12 wickets fell) and Chappell amused himself on the final day by keeping wicket to enable Rodney Marsh to have his first bowl in Test cricket –

all 11 Aussies turned their arm over. Javed Miandad led Pakistan, at 22 the youngest man to do so.

West Indies to England
1980
Tour captain: C. H. Lloyd

Trent Bridge: *West Indies won by 2 wickets*
Lord's: *Match drawn*
Old Trafford: *Match drawn*
The Oval: *Match drawn*
Headingley: *Match drawn*

Mike Brearley, now 38, had retired from Test cricket and his designated successor, Ian Botham, had been duly appointed by the selectors. It was a miserably wet summer for Lloyd's touring West Indians who were now the leading attraction in world cricket and working to tight schedules. They had returned from New Zealand in March, played a five-week domestic competition and were back in England by the beginning of May. At least they were not short of match-practice but towards the end of the tour the fast bowlers began to show signs of strain and Croft, Garner and Roberts all suffered injuries. That still left two more, Holding and Marshall, fully fit!

Lloyd's men won the first Test, not without their problems as England's bowlers – Willis in particular – fought hard; the second was drawn with the West Indies very much on top; the third was interestingly poised; a century by Willey saved England from probable defeat at The Oval, and more than 14 hours of play lost to rain at Headingley ruined any chance of a result there. Botham completed a double of 1,500 runs and 150 wickets in only 30 Tests.

Australia to England
1980
Tour captain: G. S. Chappell

Lord's: *Match drawn*

Rain, which had dogged cricket all summer, wrecked this one-off match to celebrate 100 years of Test cricket in England. Chappell led Australia in a match which could have reached a fascinating climax had eight hours' play not been lost. Our good friend John Arlott retired as a member of the 'Test Match Special' commentary team just after three o'clock on the final afternoon and was applauded from the box by his colleagues, the players and the crowd.

West Indies to Pakistan
1980–1
Tour captain: C. H. Lloyd

Lahore: *Match drawn*
Faisalabad: *West Indies won by 156 runs*
Karachi: *Match drawn*
Multan: *Match drawn*

West Indies now seemed to be travelling the world in an unending series of Tests and it was to continue that way for a long time. Lloyd's heavy artillery brigade on this tour had Marshall and Clarke taking the place of Holding and Roberts (Garner and Croft were there too) and the day-long barrage of fast bowling took its toll of victims: Abdul Qadir, shoulder injury (Croft), Taslim Arif, finger (Clarke), Zaheer Abbas, head (Clarke) were the main victims. In Multan – the first Test to be played there – Clarke was pelted with fruit by some spectators and retaliated by picking up a brick and hitting a local student leader. In Karachi, the start of one day's play was delayed for 23 minutes because an umpire (Shakoor Rana!) had forgotten to take his kit to the ground. Test cricket in Pakistan was rarely without a bizarre touch of some kind.

New Zealand to Australia
1980
Tour captain: G. P. Howarth

Brisbane: *Australia won by 10 wickets*
Perth: *Australia won by 8 wickets*
Melbourne: *Match drawn*

This was another triangular tournament summer in Australia with New Zealand and India as the visitors and the now-inevitable one-day international competition swollen to 19 matches. It was these matches, in their final stages, which saw one of the most unsavoury moves by a captain in the history of the game and we shall deal with that shortly; but first, an appraisal of New Zealand's captain, Geoffrey Philip Howarth, younger brother of that country's outstanding slow left-arm bowler, Hedley.

Geoff Howarth, an accomplished batsman in the number 3 position, brought the sort of professionalism to his captaincy that New Zealand had only seen from Turner and, in his own way, John Reid. Nine years with Surrey gave Howarth a competitive edge to his leadership which was complemented by Richard Hadlee's three seasons with Nottinghamshire and John Wright's four with Derbyshire. The remainder of his party consisted of amateur, part-time players in the usual New Zealand mould. Howarth's maxim as a captain was 'Advise, encourage and motivate' and as a conscientious and thoughtful professional he was well placed to do this. He confesses to having completed many days' play feeling utterly drained, opting for the nearest available meal of any kind and then trying to get as much sleep as possible. It has to be borne in mind that skippering a team of full-time professionals in the field, accustomed to competitive cricket on every day of their working lives is one thing; leading a team in which eight of the 11 are unpaid part-timers is something entirely different. The need for encouragement is more acute; criticism, if necessary, has to be tempered.

Howarth liked to take things in stages, setting goals for himself and for his men, always with Test Matches as the most urgent priority. By 1984 he was probably the best captain in the world, bearing in mind the way he achieved maximum use of his resources. Here, skippering his country abroad for the first time, he was short of fire-power in terms of top-class support for Hadlee, weak in spin bowling and not too strong in middle-order batting.

Like most of his countrymen he knew how to be phlegmatic in adversity and quietly satisfied when rare success came his way. In many years of friendship with Geoff Howarth I have never seen him lose his temper. But I was not at the Melbourne Cricket Ground on 1 February 1981 . . .

The four-match 'final' of the World Series of one-day internationals had seen New Zealand win the first by 78 runs, lose the second by six runs and in the third Australia had scored 235 for four wickets in their 50 overs. Wood and Greg Chappell added 145 for the second wicket but long before Chappell was out for 90 he had skied a ball from Cairns (when he was 58) to mid-wicket where Snedden raced 30 yards to bring off what was seen as a brilliant catch. Chappell stood his ground although Snedden indicated that he had made a clean catch and, when consulted, both umpires said they had not seen the catch because they were watching for a possible run-out!

earley, 'The Ayatollah', and his men in Melbourne, 1980

eg Chappell and Bob Willis in competition in Adelaide, 1982-83

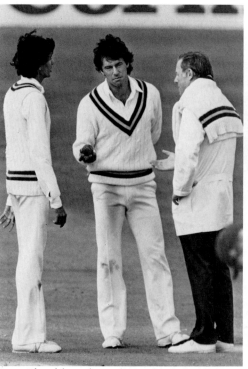

Imran Khan debates the condition of the ball with Barry
Meyer; Sikhander Bakht looks on

The new boys in Test cricket — Sri Lankan captain
Duleep Mendis

Clive Lloyd ponders on which of his fast bowlers to use next, while Don Oslear keeps his eye on the time

ivian Richards in action against Australia (David Boon at short leg)

Rival captains in Bombay: David Gower and Sunil
Gavaskar

Kapil Dev and his Cornhill Trophy — the winning
Indian side of 1986

A series win for New Zealand in 1986 and
congratulations from Mike Gatting to Jeremy Coney

Allan Border — came good as captain in 1989

Worse was to follow. New Zealand needed an improbable 15 to win from the last over of the match. Hadlee hit a four and was out lbw; Smith hit two twos and was bowled, leaving McKechnie to hit the last ball of the match for six to tie the scores. Unlikely though this was, Chappell instructed his brother Trevor (youngest of the three) to bowl underarm along the ground and so entered the darkest portals in the temple of bad sportsmanship.

Let Geoff Howarth describe the scene:

I was still cursing and swearing in the dressing-room about the lbw decision against Richard Hadlee when I noticed 'this funny thing' that was going on out in the middle. When it was clear what was going to happen I vaguely remembered, or thought I did (I was wrong as it happened) something about the T C C B making it illegal. I ran out to the umpires and 'made a blue' because I told them to look at the rules!

It was an incident which flashed like lightning round the world. I was in the West Indies and remember discussing it with Clive Lloyd and with members of the England touring party. There was a general agreement that if anyone was going to employ that particularly unpleasant piece of tactical sharp-practice first, one would not have expected it to be an Australian captain. Criticism of G. S. Chappell came from top Government level as well as the higher echelons of cricket.

It had, of course, nothing to do with Test cricket and therefore does not, strictly speaking, merit a reference in this book. Except that it was the decision of a Test captain, and one of Australia's most distinguished captains, too. Howarth reflects:

It is something which Greg will probably regret for the rest of his life, while, with hindsight, it was probably the best thing that could have happened from the point of view of stimulating interest in New Zealand cricket. When we played our next home one-day international against Australia there were 50,000 people packed into Eden Park and they let Greg know he wasn't too popular there.

India to Australia
1980–1
Tour captain: S. M. Gavaskar

Sydney: *Australia won by an innings and 4 runs*
Adelaide: *Match drawn*
Melbourne: *India won by 59 runs*

Sunil Gavaskar took his captaincy very seriously indeed, to such an extent that he came close to an international incident which would have had the most disastrous consequences for him and for Indian cricket. When he was given out lbw to Lillee in the second innings in Melbourne he disagreed so violently with the decision that he induced his partner, Chetan Chauhan, to quit the field with him. Had Chauhan actually reached the dressing-room, who can say what the consequences might have been? Mercifully the tour manager, S. K. Durrani, met the pair at the gate and ordered Chauhan to resume his innings. And India won the Test! That in itself, however, is not as important as the fact that the game continued on normal lines.

As a man destined to become the heaviest-scoring Test batsman of all time (10,122 runs, average 51.12, with 34 centuries), Gavaskar at this time still had much to contribute to the game. Had he succeeded in halting that game in Melbourne by taking Chauhan back to the pavilion with him we might well have missed the second half of a marvellous career. From the outset, he was a man who believed strongly in principles and if he felt he was right he would defend his position vigorously. Off the field, I found him a charming and companionable person, a shrewd businessman, a proud and affectionate family-man.

On the cricket field he was not too happy if things were not going his, or India's, way and fortunately for his peace of mind he was a good enough player to be able to turn a game. His strength of character was established from the first moment he set foot on a Test ground in the West Indies in 1970–1 and proceeded to perform prodigious and precocious feats of batsmanship – 65 and 67 not out in his first Test, 116 and 64 not out in his second, 1 and 117 not out in his third, 124 and 220 in the fourth.

It is interesting to recall his first innings in the first-ever World Cup when at Lord's, on 7 June 1975, he carried his bat for 36 in India's bewildered reply (132 for 3) to England's 334 for 4, for all the world as though he was batting to save a game. 'Sunny' bitterly resented some of the sardonic reporting of that game and nothing pleased him more than to be a member of India's World Cup-winning team on that same ground eight years later, even though his batting on that occasion made no major impact. He was a proud and patriotic Indian cricketer who found expression for the resentment he felt at criticism of Indian umpires by attacking, when he felt it justified, the officials in other countries. Nevertheless, tourists in India felt on many occasions that Gavaskar, through his brilliance as a player or perhaps sheer weight of his cricketing personality, achieved a certain dominance over Indian umpires.

The Bombay–Delhi rivalry in Indian cricket affairs found its most public expression in violent and extremely public disagreements between Gavaskar and Kapil Dev in Sunny's later years and he was not a man who found it easy to compromise. He had become, by this time, a cosmopolitan and highly knowledgeable member of cricket's aristocracy and, as his country's greatest-ever batsman, felt strongly that his opinions deserved respect. It is difficult to see how anyone who listened for any length of time to Sunny's views on cricket in his time could fail to respect them.

England to West Indies
1981
Tour captain: I. T. Botham

Trinidad: *West Indies won by an innings and 79 runs*
Guyana: *Match did not start*
Barbados: *West Indies won by 298 runs*
Antigua: *Match drawn*
Jamaica: *Match drawn*

Ian Botham's captaincy of England abroad for the first time had the most far-reaching effect upon relations between a touring party and the British cricketing Press, a situation which was to worsen steadily in the following years. His appointment was a split decision by the selectors, with Alec Bedser (the chairman), Charlie Elliott and Ken Barrington voting for Botham as captain, and Brian Close determinedly against it. Of the four, Close knew Botham by far the best, even though Barrington had managed the 1977–8 tour on which Ian had been a player. Close had captained Somerset when Botham first came into county cricket, had watched (and played a mentor's part in) his development and was, moreover, a personal friend. He now urged Botham to turn down the leadership of the party because, he said, (a) Botham's personal form would suffer from the cares of captaincy with the consequence that (b) results would be bad and he would be publicly criticized for them.

It was the best possible advice but Botham decided not to follow it on the essentially simplistic grounds that 'You don't turn down the captaincy of England, do you?' He was strongly influenced by a tabloid newspaper headline which had proclaimed him 'The People's Choice' and Ian was a young man (25) who enjoyed favourable publicity as much as he disliked unfavourable comment. He still is. The headline was probably quite accurate. Botham was undoubtedly the most popular cricketer in the country – a fast bowler who was a prolific wicket-taker and a big-hitting batsman who loved to smash sixes, as well as a slip fielder with Sobers-like reactions and reflexes. What he never understood on that tour (and still doesn't) is that no one, however popular with the general public, can be totally exempt from critical appraisal from those whose duty it is to look at cricket objectively, irrespective of personal feelings.

It is true to say that Botham went on that tour with the liking and support of the large media party representing the national daily and Sunday newspapers of Britain and radio and television journalists. To a man, everyone wanted him to do well. He did not do well as a tour captain and this proved utterly disastrous for player-media relations because he simply could not and would not accept that he ever did *anything* wrong.

His style of leadership was – like his view of publicity – naively simplistic: he wanted to be 'one of the boys', only more so. He had to be manifestly and ostentatiously more one of the boys than anyone else in the group. That was his off-the-field approach. On it he hoped to lead by example as the best all-rounder England had produced and found he couldn't do it: 0 and 16, 2 for 113 in the first Test; 26 and 1, 7 for 179 in Barbados; 1 run and 4 for 127 in Antigua; 13 and 16, 2 for 73 in Jamaica. Yet to all suggestions that his personal form suffered because of his involvement in tactical and strategic consider-ations he defiantly insisted that his performances were generally better than those of other members of his side.

He strayed into off-duty indiscretion and although the newspapermen covered up loyally for him, he developed an increasing resentment to perfectly legitimate criticism of his on-the-field direction and form. The depths were finally plumbed when, on the way home, he physically manhandled one journalist who had criticized him in terms which were, it must be admitted, a little over the top. Tragically, that tour caused Ian Botham to develop the absurdly ingenuous view that those who flattered and fawned were 'all right' while those who offered any differ-ent view were idiots who didn't know what they were talking about. It wasn't the end of him as an all-round cricketer by any means, as we shall see, but it was the beginning of the end of him as a captain whose views he could expect journalists to respect.

It was a tragic tour in many ways . . . Ken Barrington's untimely death in Barbados shattering everyone in the party . . . and high-level idiocy in Guyana causing the cancellation of the Test Match there because Robin Jackman, married to a South African girl and thus spending much of his winter in that country, had been flown in as a replacement for the injured Bob Willis. This was petty political points-scoring at its most pathetic.

India to New Zealand
1981

Tour captain: S. M. Gavaskar

Wellington: *New Zealand won by 62 runs*
Christchurch: *Match drawn*
Auckland: *Match drawn*

Gavaskar had three Test debutants in his side in Wellington but defeat was still something of a shock to him, coming in the same month as India's notable win in Melbourne. It was the first Test to be played on the Basin Reserve ground since it had been cosmetically revolutionized during the previous three years. Alone amongst the major grounds of New Zealand, it stages association football in winter, as opposed to rugby, and it had previously been amongst the dreariest and most uncomfortable grounds in the world. A handsome new stand and extensive landscaping had transformed the Reserve into a most attractive stadium though there was (and is) still something a little strange about playing a cricket match on a ground where traffic whirls by on all sides! One of Gavaskar's new boys was the tall, elegant left-hander from Bombay, Ravi Shastri, at that time only 18 years old. As he had been flown in as a replacement for the injured Doshi he was played purely as a slow left-arm bowler (with great success, taking 3 for 54 and 3 for 9) but from the start of his career he was a genuine all-rounder of high class and destined to become a considerable force in Indian Test cricket. Even when Doshi had recovered, Shastri retained his place in the side in a short tour which proved a disappointment for Gavaskar since it was the first defeat in a rubber against New Zealand.

Australia to England
1981

Tour captain: K. J. Hughes

Trent Bridge: *Australia won by 4 wickets*
Lord's: *Match drawn*
Headingley: *England won by 18 runs*
Edgbaston: *England won by 29 runs*
Old Trafford: *England won by 103 runs*
The Oval: *Match drawn*

No more dramatic or spectacular Ashes series has ever been seen in England than this one which had virtually everything . . . a sensational change of captaincy, great batting, record-breaking bowling, controversy, colour, heart-break, tension, heroics, incisive captaincy and even a touch of churlishness. People stopped each other in the street to inquire what was the latest news from Headingley, from Edgbaston, from Old Trafford; crowds gathered around television shop-windows to watch the cricket.

Although the men who had played in the Packer series were now eligible and available to play for Australia, Greg Chappell declined to tour and his elder brother had now retired once again. It was left to the youngest of the three, Trevor, to represent the family in 1981 and while he was a goodish cricketer he did not reach the same high class as the other two. With a man as aggressive and resolute as either Ian or Greg as captain the result of the rubber might well have been different – certainly one cannot see a side under Chappell direction surrendering the initiative as at Headingley or Edgbaston – but that would have been to deny England their brief (as it turned out) hour of glory which had the whole country talking cricket again, as in the heady days of the 1930s, or 1948.

Botham, still smarting from what he regarded as media persecution in the West Indies, led England at Trent Bridge where Terry Alderman, on his Test debut, took 9 wickets in the match for 130. At Lord's, batting in the lower regions of the order, Botham bagged a pair and as he left the field he forestalled the selectors' decision to replace him as captain by resigning. Brearley was persuaded to return as captain and played a memorable part in what seemed (after the first three days) a wildly improbable victory at Headingley, though the individual glory was Botham's, with 50 in the first innings and 149 not out in the second after England had followed on. His batting, together with that of Dilley and Old, had given England the barest glimpse of possible victory on the last morning when Australia needed 130 to win.

It seems inconceivable that an Australian Test captain could not rouse his players to score those runs and to eradicate the jitters which now so obviously afflicted the entire Australian camp. But Kim Hughes lacked the killer instinct which has been a staple factor in so many Aussie captains. Brearley, on the other hand, juggled brilliantly with his fast bowling resources bearing in mind that he had so few runs to play with; he read accurately the Australian state of mind; he took risks, but they were calculated risks; he stimulated Willis into bowling faster and more aggressively than most of us had ever seen; and above all, by convincing his side that he was in control of the situation, however precarious it seemed, he positively inspired the team to an outstanding performance in the field.

If Botham's batting had been astonishing, Willis's bowling down the hill from the Kirkstall Lane end was staggering. The pronounced slope, levelling out on reaching the square, is difficult for most fast bowlers; to a man of Willis's size, charging in at full gallop, it is almost impossible to avoid the occasional no-ball. Brearley urged him to forget all about that probability and to bowl fast and straight. He watched every delivery like a hawk, brought all his knowledge of the opposition batsmen to bear on advising his bowlers and adjusting the field.

Hughes, poor Hughes, was out-thought and out-generalled by a superb piece of captaincy. There have been other occasions when one has admired tactical leadership, often when it has involved delicate handling of spin bowling and the even greater subtlety of field placing required in such circumstances but none, I think, which had fired the imagination or fuelled the admiration more than on that occasion. Botham – *still* proclaiming that it was nonsense to suggest that captaincy had impaired his personal performances in his 12 Tests as skipper – bowled magnificently at Edgbaston and played one of the most brilliant innings I have seen anywhere at Old Trafford; the shell-shocked Hughes and his tourists fought back well to an honourable draw at The Oval; but for on-the-field direction bordering on genius, Brearley's captaincy at Headingley provides one of my cherished Test memories. Very well – England could not have been in a position to win without Botham's century; they could not have accomplished it on the last day without Willis's bowling; but the mastermind dictating the course of events was that of John Michael Brearley. It has to be his match:

ENGLAND v. AUSTRALIA

Headingley, 1981

AUSTRALIA

First Innings		*Second Innings*	
Dyson b Dilley	102	c Taylor b Willis	34
Wood lbw b Botham	34	c Taylor b Botham	10
T. Chappell c Taylor b Willey	27	c Taylor b Willis	8
Hughes c and b Botham	89	c Botham b Willis	0
Bright b Dilley	7	(8) b Willis	19
Yallop c Taylor b Botham	58	(5) c Gatting b Willis	0
Border lbw b Botham	8	(6) b Old	0
Marsh b Botham	28	(7) c Dilley b Willis	4
Lawson c Taylor b Botham	13	c Taylor b Willis	1
Lillee not out	3	c Gatting b Willis	17
Alderman not out	0	not out	0
Extras (b4 lb13 w3 nb12)	32	*Extras* (lb3 w1 nb14)	18
Total (9 wkts declared)	401	Total	111

Bowling: Willis 30–8–72–0; Old 43–14–91–0; Dilley 27–4–78–2; Botham 39.2–11–95–6; Willey 13–2–31–1; Boycott 3–2–2–0

Bowling: Willis 15.1–3–43–8; Old 9–1–21–1; Dilley 2–0–11–0; Botham 7–3–14–1; Willey 3–1–4–0

ENGLAND

First Innings

Gooch lbw b Alderman	2
Boycott b Lawson	12
Brearley c Marsh b Alderman	10
Gower c Marsh b Lawson	24
Gatting lbw b Lillee	15
Willey b Lawson	8
Botham c Marsh b Lillee	50
Taylor c Marsh b Lillee	5
Dilley c and b Lillee	13
Old c Border b Alderman	0
Willis not out	1
Extras (b6 lb11 w6 nb11)	34
Total	174

Bowling: Lillee 18.5–7–49–4; Lawson 13–3–32–3; Alderman 19–4–59–3

Second Innings

c Alderman b Lillee	0
lbw b Alderman	46
c Alderman b Lillee	14
c Border b Alderman	9
lbw b Alderman	1
c Dyson b Lillee	33
not out	149
c Bright b Alderman	1
b Alderman	56
b Lawson	29
c Border b Alderman	2
Extras (b5 lb3 w3 nb5)	16
Total	356

Bowling: Lillee 25–6–94–3; Alderman 35.3–6–135–6; Lawson 23–4–96–1; Bright 4–0–15–0

Pakistan to Australia
1981
Tour captain: Javed Miandad

Perth: *Australia won by 286 runs*
Brisbane: *Australia won by 10 wickets*
Melbourne: *Pakistan won by an innings and 82 runs*

Still only 24 years old, Javed Miandad was now in his fifth year as a Test cricketer but experience had not at this stage calmed a naturally aggressive and combative temperament, nor have later years. As early as the 1979 tour of New Zealand, Javed had been building a reputation for carrying aggression to verbal extremes on the field and in the first Test in Perth he took matters a stage further when Lillee claimed he had been provoked into an actual physical confrontation with the touring captain. Lillee, one of the finest fast bowlers of all time, was no stranger to controversy as we have seen and this was a potentially combustible pairing in any event.

Javed has developed into one of the best batsmen in the world but his temper has not sweetened over the years and any on-the-field controversy usually finds him involved to some extent. This is an enormous pity since he has undoubtedly become a world-class player in any company but his volatile nature has made him an unwise choice as captain, particularly on overseas tours.

West Indies to Australia
1981–2
Tour captain: C. H. Lloyd

Melbourne: *Australia won by 58 runs*
Sydney: *Match drawn*
Adelaide: *West Indies won by 5 wickets*

The next opposition in another double-header in that Australian summer were Lloyd's all-conquering West Indians whose sequence of 15 Tests without defeat came to an end in Melbourne where they were without Greenidge and both innings started disastrously. Hughes, having handed the captaincy back to Greg Chappell, scored 100 not out in Australia's first innings total of 198; Lillee overtook the records of Trueman and Lance Gibbs as Test wicket-takers; and even with four of the fastest bowlers in the world (Holding, Roberts, Croft and Garner), Lloyd could not avoid defeat. Yardley's off-spin proved vital in the fourth innings of the game. Nevertheless, Lloyd led from the front with his batting in Adelaide to square the series and retain the Frank Worrell Trophy for matches between the two countries.

England to India and Sri Lanka
1981–2
Tour captain: K. W. R. Fletcher

Bombay: *India won by 138 runs*
Bangalore: *Match drawn*
Delhi: *Match drawn*
Calcutta: *Match drawn*
Madras: *Match drawn*
Kanpur: *Match drawn*

Colombo: *England won by 7 wickets*

With Brearley declining to tour – a decision he had reached 18 months previously – the selectors' choice of Keith Fletcher as captain was a fairly obvious one. A thoroughly professional captain, he had led Essex with considerable success since 1974, been on two previous tours of India and four to Sri Lanka, and was a good player of spin bowling.

234   *The Wisden Book of Captains on Tour*

His personal record commanded instant respect from his tourists and his pleasant and helpful attitude made him popular with the media party (who outnumbered the players) after their traumas in the West Indies seven months previously.

There were times when he was glad of the support of a good manager in Raman Subba Row, particularly when, in Calcutta, the difficult decision had to be made that Boycott's 'attitude was not right' and he returned home to England – not, however, before Boycott had passed Gary Sobers' record of 8,032 Test runs. There were problems, too, with umpiring decisions when a number of verdicts went against batsmen playing the sweep shot and after defeat in Bombay there was a certain danger of paranoia developing about umpiring. With a less level-headed management team this could have been a major problem. After the opening defeat, the tourists found pitches in the remaining Tests utterly lifeless and whenever England looked like making progress, Gavaskar brought the slowing down of the over-rate to an unprecedented nine an hour – with two slow bowlers operating! It was a longish (111 days) tour, made more difficult by an itinerary which took the party up and down and across the country in a bewildering progress exacerbated by uncertain airline schedules and some sub-standard accommodation.

In spite of the all these frustrations, players and media united in a good spirit which was a tribute to captain and manager. Fletcher was, therefore, disappointed when he was overlooked for the captaincy the following winter in Australia. He had the complete sympathy and support of those who had toured with him.

Political problems – because Boycott and Geoff Cook were known to have sporting links with South Africa – threatened the tour before it even began but after a posturing display of brinkmanship the Indian Government finally consented to let it take place. Ambassadorial work in Sri Lanka, which had been accorded full I C C membership and thus was staging the first official Test in that country, was carried out in a pleasant atmosphere with many British supporters watching play on the world's newest, and 53rd, Test ground.

Four days after the party returned from tour, another 'political' turmoil began with the departure for an unofficial series in South Africa of a rather strong side made up of Gooch (captain), Emburey, Lever, Underwood, Boycott, Amiss, Knott, Hendrick, Larkins, Willey, Old and Les Taylor (Leics), who were joined by three others – Woolmer, Humpage and Sidebottom – already wintering in South Africa. The Indian tourists, expected for the English summer, threatened to cancel the trip if any of the 'rebels' was selected. In the event, the men who had been in South Africa were not only banished for the Indian series but banned from Test cricket for three years.

Australia to New Zealand
1982

Tour captain: G. S. Chappell

Wellington: *Match drawn*
Auckland: *New Zealand won by 5 wickets*
Christchurch: *Australia won by 8 wickets*

This was Greg Chappell's first visit to New Zealand since the underarm incident of the previous year and it naturally caused major attention to be focused on the three one-day internationals. There was nationwide rejoicing when New Zealand won the first of these games before a full house at Eden Park, Auckland, but Chappell, never one to concern himself unduly about the sentiments of a crowd, cocked a personal snook by scoring 108 in a total of 194 and made sure New Zealand were crushed comprehensively in the remaining two matches.

Auckland, too, was the scene of a Test defeat for the tourists but Chappell, with 176, steered his men comfortably home in the final Test. In leadership by example he had few peers as a Test average of 53.11 indicates.

Sri Lanka to Pakistan
1982

Tour captain: B. Warnapura (L. R. D. Mendis)

Karachi: *Pakistan won by 204 runs*
Faisalabad: *Match drawn*
Lahore: *Pakistan won by an innings and 102 runs*

Bandula Warnapura, a neat and dogged opening batsman who led his national side in the inaugural Test (at home to England) and two of the three Tests of this first overseas tour, had an extremely short career of four matches. He was banned for 25 years after joining an unofficial Sri Lankan visit to South Africa which caused an almost complete re-building of the side representing a small country which had only the slenderest of resources in the first place. His team in Pakistan acquitted themselves well enough in their first Test innings abroad, totalling 344 in Karachi, and went one better in Faisalabad with a total of 454. But, as expected, the bowling was neither penetrative enough, nor experienced enough to dismiss Pakistan cheaply. Their visit, however, was notable because the Pakistan players who had been in Australia under Javed Miandad refused to play again under his leadership. Refusing to accept player-power, the Pakistan Board confirmed Javed's captaincy and took the opportunity to 'blood' a number of younger players of whom Salim Malik was to prove the outstanding discovery. Still not 19, he scored 100 not out in his second Test innings.

India to England
1982
Tour captain: S. M. Gavaskar

Lord's: *England won by 7 wickets*
Old Trafford: *Match drawn*
The Oval: *Match drawn*

Gavaskar led his men in England in determined mood and carried the battle to the enemy by objecting to the inclusion on the panel of Test umpires of David Constant, veteran of 22 Tests and widely regarded with respect by the cricketing world. As I saw it, this was no more and no less than a tit-for-tat move in retaliation to English criticism of Indian umpiring during the previous winter. That is, however, easy enough to say. The wider implications were more serious . . . the questioning of umpiring integrity (as opposed to competence – no one could seriously question Constant's competence) and a lack of respect for established authority which was spreading through the world of cricket.

This controversial start to the domestic season followed the upheaval of the so-called 'rebel' tour to South Africa by a team of English players. For taking part the whole group was banned from Test cricket for three years, so it was doubly ironical that in the first of the summer's Tests we saw the debut for England of the South African-born Allan Lamb. Gavaskar's hopes of success against a weakened England side foundered partly because of an unbalanced attack and partly because he had no experienced opener to partner him and when Botham, in the course of a whirlwind innings of 208 off 220 balls at The Oval, fractured the Indian captain's shinbone (when he was misguided enough to go in very close at silly point), he was unable either to bat or field after the first afternoon . . . not one of Gavaskar's happier tours.

Pakistan to England
1982

Tour captain: Imran Khan

Edgbaston: *England won by 113 runs*
Lord's: *Pakistan won by 10 wickets*
Headingley: *England won by 3 wickets*

The second visitors of the summer, Pakistan, were led by Imran Khan, one of the most significant figures in his country's relatively short cricketing history. He was perhaps better known at this time to spectators in England than to those at home after being educated at Worcester Royal Grammar School and Oxford University and playing for Worcs (1971–6) and Sussex since 1977. Imran has consistently proved himself one of the outstanding fast bowlers in the world as well as an excellent middle-order batsman. He has 'retired' a number of times, then returned to world-class cricket either by popular demand in Pakistan or personal inclination and sometimes because of a combination of both.

It all represents a remarkable career which could never have been possible but for his patrician – almost regal – status in the country of his birth because he has been violently critical of the administrative structure of cricket in Pakistan, whose function, he has claimed, has been to 'assert mindless authority and blunder through'. No one else has dared to be so outspoken against the BCCP, not even Sarfraz Nawaz.

Imran's fiercely independent character was clearly inherited to a great extent from his father who was actively involved in the struggle for the establishment of the state of Pakistan and who was apt to reprimand waiters in the stately Lahore Gymkhana Club who addressed him in English, rather than Urdu. His mother's family, the Burkis, nurtured a similar tribal pride to his father's (the Niazi) and this mixture of aristocratic Pakistan blood, followed by English public school and Oxbridge influences have, over his most distinguished cricketing years, fused to produce a rather complex character. Not surprisingly, consistency of argumentative line has not always been Imran's strong suit. He has sometimes been quick to condemn, through his columns in the *Daily Telegraph* and elsewhere, faults which he has been seen to display himself. His criticisms of Mike Gatting's brush with umpiring authority in 1987, for instance, was followed by anguished complaints from Imran about Australian umpiring in 1988–9; in New Zealand, immediately after that visit to Australia, the team under his direction was involved in the most deplorable exhibition of attempted intimidation of umpires that I have seen anywhere in the world.

As one of the best all-rounders in the history of the game he has always been well-equipped to lead by example and his inherited qualities as a leader have given him a natural authority over teams he has captained. This has led to notable triumphs over major Test-playing nations and usually they have involved important contributions with ball, bat or both, by Imran himself. He has been, for longer than most, a truly great cricketer. This serves to make his public pronouncements more closely observed than those of less distinguished practitioners and it has to be said that the throwing of stones in his own glass house is not unknown.

No one could have done more than Imran to avert defeat in the first Test of this series of 1982 (7 wickets for 52 and top scorer for Pakistan in the game) and he made the right tactical moves at the right time in the victory at Lord's when David Gower took over from the injured Willis to captain England for the first time.

Sri Lanka to India
1982
Tour captain: B. Warnapura

Madras: *Match drawn*

This one-off match, the first official Test between the two neighbours, was played on the nearest Indian Test ground to the tourists' country and gave Warnapura his final taste of captaincy. Barely a month later he was banned, along with four other members of his touring party, for contracting to play in a South Africa tour. Duleep Mendis, one of Sri Lanka's finest batsmen, achieved the distinction of scoring 105 in each innings of the Test in which 1,441 runs were scored for the loss of 33 wickets.

Australia to Pakistan
1982

Tour captain: K. J. Hughes

Karachi: *Pakistan won by 9 wickets*
Faisalabad: *Pakistan won by an innings and 3 runs*
Lahore: *Pakistan won by 9 wickets*

This was another tour which gave Kim Hughes little cause for rejoicing. Apart from defeat in all three Tests, he had to contend with crowd disturbances which were the norm in Karachi and which twice forced the tourists to leave the field until it had been cleared. Hughes' quicker bowlers could make nothing of the bland pitches and his spinners – Yardley, Bright, Sleep and (occasionally) Border – were never as penetrative as Imran Khan's slow bowlers. The result was that Pakistan were never bowled out in any of their six innings. It was Australia's worst performance in a rubber since their 4–0 defeat in South Africa 13 years earlier, and it was no surprise when Greg Chappell resumed his captaincy of Australia in the next home series.

England to Australia
1982–3

Tour captain: R. G. D. Willis

Perth: *Match drawn*
Brisbane: *Australia won by 7 wickets*
Adelaide: *Australia won by 8 wickets*
Melbourne: *England won by 3 runs*
Sydney: *Match drawn*

Because of the ban on those players who had been to South Africa, a team well below full-strength went to Australia under the captaincy of Robert George Dylan Willis. It was an obvious choice in some ways, a strange one in others.

Willis was a highly respected figure in the England dressing-room, having been in Test cricket since the 1970–1 tour to Australia when he was flown out as a replacement. Thus, his experience was vast and it was felt that he would be a sound, steadying influence on a party which included a number of players with only limited experience at international level. On the other hand, he was now 33 years of age and was, above all else, a specialist fast bowler of no great subtlety who relied on raw pace (plus bounce) to get his wickets. He was, therefore, really in need of a captain to nurse him carefully and to hoard his bowling energies to be used in bursts for maximum effect. It was difficult to see how he could be expected to do this for himself while pondering upon other aspects of captaincy and rapidly changing tactical situations.

Willis had at all times great support from his players, was never short of helpful advice, and in return showed 100 per cent loyalty to the tourists. He was personally close to Botham, in particular, and supported him steadfastly in Botham's flickering feud with the media. This had been manifest since 1981 when, after his own magnificent performance at Headingley, Willis had chosen to be critical of the critics in a TV interview – scarcely the time or the occasion for churlishness. His appointment for this (and subsequent) series threatened to create further player–media problems because in spite of the cricket correspondents' liking and respect for Willis as an individual and a big-hearted bowler there now arose aspects of his captaincy which were open to criticism. It has to be said that while he was at all times courteous and helpful to me as BBC Cricket Correspondent, there were times when (and I hated to do it) critical comment had to be made.

He had his problems on this tour because (a) Chappell, as ever, was a determined and aggressive opponent; (b) the batting, particularly the opening pair, was never able to give England a solid start; and (c) Botham, who had had four brilliant years and whose all-round talents were now desperately needed, had an extremely modest tour by the standards he had set.

Nevertheless, he had one heroic moment when, in Melbourne, Botham took the vital last wicket to bring England victory by just three runs when the last-wicket pair, Border (62 not out) and Thomson (21), had put on 70 runs. It gave Botham 1,000 runs and 100 wickets against Australia in just 22 matches but as the fielding captain in a situation where a last-wicket pair scored 70 runs, Willis caused a few English hearts to flutter on that occasion.

The party, who were also involved in a triangular contest of one-day internationals and failed to reach the finals, went on to New Zealand for three more one-day internationals and lost them all. David Gower was now being tipped as the next England captain.

India to Pakistan
1983
Tour captain: S. M. Gavaskar

Lahore: *Match drawn*
Karachi: *Pakistan won by an innings and 86 runs*
Faisalabad: *Pakistan won by 10 wickets*
Hyderabad: *Pakistan won by an innings and 119 runs*
Lahore: *Match drawn*
Karachi: *Match drawn*

Gavaskar's party ran into Imran Khan's batsmen in their very finest form with massive scoring from Javed Miandad, Zaheer Abbas and Mudassar Nazar, which his own men could not match. The Indians had little to console them, apart from Kapil Dev's bowling (8 for 85) in the final Test and the record established by that delightful little man Gundappa Viswanath, in the same game. For a country whose Test cricketers had for many years appeared and disappeared with bewildering rapidity, he played his 86th consecutive match. Gavaskar's brother-in-law, he had for many years been the joker of the Indian side, a man whose whimsical humour could raise the spirits of the most despondent party. In earlier years he had amused his captain, Pataudi, with his 'speeches' in Maharati – a language he could scarcely speak at all, even though it was his brother-in-law's native tongue. My personal memories of him, off the field, include a flight from Bombay to Hyderabad (India) during which the overhead luggage compartments kept flying open and depositing their contents on passengers' heads. After three such incidents, 'Vishy' opened his kit bag from under his seat, took out a batting helmet and wore it for the remainder of the trip.

India to West Indies
1983
Tour captain: Kapil Dev

Jamaica: *West Indies won by 4 wickets*
Trinidad: *Match drawn*
Guyana: *Match drawn*
Barbados: *West Indies won by 10 wickets*
Antigua: *Match drawn*

Three consecutive defeats by big margins and a lost rubber in Pakistan was too much for the Indian Board of Control to stomach. Bombay had had control and the result had been a humiliation at the hands of their next-door neighbours; back swung the pendulum to north India and Kapil Dev, the country's answer to Ian Botham (but with the handsome profile of a matinee idol), was the new captain. One complaint I had heard from Indian officials was that Gavaskar was not expert at handling his bowling . . . that his policy was to build up huge scores and make himself secure from defeat before his thoughts turned to possible victory. If that had been true, Gavaskar would not have been alone in his thinking as a captain of India and in any case he was the man who, more than any other batsman in the side, would have to do most of the building. But it was really a gross underestimation of Gavaskar's cricket brain and tactical ability.

Now came Kapil Dev, the best fast bowler India had produced by a very wide margin, whose batting had been improving steadily since his first Test five years previously. He had taken 100 Test wickets by the time he was barely 21 and the Board looked to him to lead from the front with ball *and* bat. His greatest triumph was to come in four months' time when he led India to victory over the West Indies in a World Cup one-day international final (bowling them out for 140 at Lord's on 25 June) which was regarded as India's greatest day in cricket history and Kapil Dev became a national hero. For the moment he was up against Lloyd's immensely powerful team which was a settled and confident unit, enjoying the luxury of being able to 'blood' new players one at a time – men like Winston Davis and Gus Logie – without the overall strength being affected.

Gavaskar made only one big score in the Tests and a succession of failures meant that Kapil Dev could never rely on a solid start. In his 50th Test (the second of this series), however, Kapil Dev completed 2,000 runs and 200 wickets and one touch of chivalry in this game should be noted. With the match destined to be drawn, Richards, skippering West Indies in Lloyd's absence from the field, took it into the final half hour so that Kapil Dev could complete an unbeaten century in what had been a notable Test for him.

Sri Lanka to New Zealand

1983

Tour captain: D. S. De Silva

Christchurch: *New Zealand won by an innings and 25 runs*
Wellington: *New Zealand won by 6 wickets*

Because of the ban on 14 of their established players, Sri Lanka were able to field a mere nucleus of experience alongside eight new caps in these two Tests in which they were manifestly far from being international class. They were led by Somachandra de Silva, an excellent leg-spinner and useful middle-order batsman who had considerable experience of league and Minor Counties cricket in England. They found it difficult to bowl out the New Zealanders cheaply and even more difficult to withstand the fast, and medium-fast, attack of Hadlee, Chatfield, Cairns and Snedden.

Australia to Sri Lanka
1983
Tour captain: G. S. Chappell

Kandy: *Australia won by an innings and 38 runs*

The major Test-playing countries were rallying round to provide top-class experience for the newest member of the International Cricket Conference and Greg Chappell's Aussies scored a massive 514 for 4 declared on the new ground in the ancient capital of the island. The Asgiriya Stadium – which I had visited in 1982 when it was newly excavated and being landscaped – thus became the world's 54th Test ground, and one of the most attractive in its mountain setting.

New Zealand to England
1983
Tour captain: G. P. Howarth

The Oval: *England won by 189 runs*
Headingley: *New Zealand won by 5 wickets*
Lord's: *England won by 127 runs*
Trent Bridge: *England won by 165 runs*

Scarcely had the tumult and shouting died after India's World Cup victory than there was new rejoicing in the furthest flung outpost of Commonwealth when New Zealand registered their first win in a Test in England. Headingley was the setting for the historic moment which gave the tourists their first win overseas for nearly 14 years. What delighted Geoff Howarth and his men as much as anything was that it was achieved without a single wicket from Richard Hadlee, upon whom New Zealand's attack had depended heavily for so long. It prompted me to ask Howarth, some years later, where New Zealand cricket would head when Richard finally reached retirement. He replied:

Of course there will be life after Hadlee. He is a very fine bowler, the like of which may never be seen again. But so was Trueman a fine bowler; so was Lillee. There will always be someone who comes along to do a job, even if not to do it as spectacularly as Richard. New Zealand might not be as effective for a few years when he has gone but they will find their own level. Hadlee has set the targets and young players will emerge to aim at them.

Howarth, having lived through momentous and changing days in world cricket, has some highly pertinent views on the altered face of Test cricket:

Umpires have always made mistakes, some fewer than others. Frank Chester must have made mistakes, along with Syd Buller, Charlie Elliot and other great adjudicators in other countries. Umpires today *must* be as good as, if not better than, those of the past despite – perhaps *because of* – the increased pressure they have from TV replays and from media scrutiny generally. I like to think there is a big difference between umpiring in England and in most other countries and so there should be since almost all those who 'stand' in England are ex-players and those who are not have only reached the top through standards of excellence at a slightly lower level. For international matches I think a panel of the *best*, rather than simply *neutral* umpires would help.

It is, sadly but undeniably, true that standards of behaviour on the field have declined. The responsibility for this starts with the players themselves, then the captain, then the managers and finally the Boards of Control. All can play a part in restoring the dignity and good manners of the game.

Pakistan to India
1983
Tour captain: Zaheer Abbas

Bangalore: *Match drawn*
Jullundur: *Match drawn*
Nagpur: *Match drawn*

The Indian Board took the opportunity to spread the gospel of Test cricket a little wider. Jullundur became the world's 55th venue and Nagpur staged its first Test for 14 years. With Imran Khan unavailable, Zaheer Abbas led Pakistan in a rubber which was the third between these countries to fail to produce a clear result but it had its moments bordering upon farce.

In Bangalore, with no result other than a draw even remotely possible, Zaheer led his men from the field then had to lead them back again when a disagreement over the number of overs which had to be bowled on the final day had been sorted out. In an atmosphere of confused irritability, Gavaskar was able to take his score from 87 to complete his 28th Test hundred before stumps were finally drawn. In Jullundur Zaheer was asked, and refused, to play on the scheduled rest day when the previous day's play had been washed out. And in Nagpur, when Amarnath withdrew because of illness just before the start of play, none of the three remaining players in India's squad of 14 was deemed to be a suitable replacement so that Sandeep Patil had to be flown, in a chartered plane from Bombay, to bat on the second day.

West Indies to India
1983
Tour captain: C. H. Lloyd

Kanpur: *West Indies won by an innings and 83 runs*
Delhi: *Match drawn*
Ahmedabad: *West Indies won by 138 runs*
Bombay: *Match drawn*
Calcutta: *West Indies won by an innings and 46 runs*
Madras: *Match drawn*

This series, following on the visit by Pakistan, gave India's cricket fans a three-and-a-half month season of nine Tests but there was little pleasure in it for them because at the end of December they had not won a single match. As the World Cup-holders, the Indian team were hero-worshipped throughout the whole country; there had been a national holiday declared after their win at Lord's, dancing in the streets, triumphant processions through Delhi and Bombay. Now Indian cricket came down to earth with a vengeance.

Clive Lloyd, who had regarded his team's performance in that final as 'so appalling' that he wanted to resign – and, indeed, had to be persuaded to carry on – knew all about the reception the Indians had received on their return and was determined to exact full retribution. Using permutations of his fast bowlers – Marshall, Holding, Davis, Roberts, Daniel and Baptiste – he always had a 'fresh' pace attack of men who were able to extract at least *some* life from the flat Indian wickets.

When Holding and Marshall, with a little help from Roberts, bowled out India for 90 in their second innings in Calcutta the heroes were transformed into villains in the eyes of an 80,000 crowd. Jeering multitudes threw fruit, stones and bottles, broke windows in the team coach and injured two of its occupants. Lloyd and his men returned home in triumph, while India licked their wounds. In the course of the series, Gavaskar had overtaken Boycott's record of 8,114 Test runs and Ahmedabad had become the 56th Test ground.

Pakistan to Australia
1983–4
Tour captain: Zaheer Abbas/Imran Khan

Perth: *Australia won by an innings and 9 runs*
Brisbane: *Match drawn*
Adelaide: *Match drawn*
Melbourne: *Match drawn*
Sydney: *Australia won by 10 wickets*

These were more than usually turbulent times in Pakistan cricket. The country was at this time under the military rule of General Mohammed Zia-ul-Haq and as this was not generally recognised around the world as a democratically elected government, the general was anxious to see the country appear to be represented by good sporting ambassadors. The poor showing in the World Cup was a great disappointment in itself; that the Cup had been won by India was seen as a serious blow to prestige, so it was regarded as doubly important that a better performance should be achieved in Australia. That basis was not, perhaps, an ideal one on which to select a tour party and its leader . . .

Imran Khan, who was later to write, 'The history of Pakistan is one of nepotism, inefficiency, corruption and constant bickering,' was unfit, because of injury, to bowl at the time the party was being chosen and so the selectors decided against him as captain.

Imran, an admirer and a protégé of A. H. Kardar, was far from happy about military interference in cricketing matters and was outspoken in his views: 'After Kardar's retirement, Pakistan cricket was thrown to the wolves, the cricket bureaucrats whose progeny still rule the game.'

The selectors' decision against Imran as captain was overruled by Air Marshal Nur Khan, President of the B C C P, so bureaucracy in this instance was interfering in a *pro*-Imran stance. The selectors now resigned en masse. There were legal problems involving Sarfraz Nawaz who was regarded as being a one-man awkward squad and without him, and Imran, to bowl Australia piled up 436 for 9 in the first Test which was enough to achieve an innings victory.

Zaheer Abbas led Pakistan in this and the next two Tests. In the second Test, torrential rain saved his side from what looked likely to be a second defeat by an innings. And in the third it was the batting of Mohsin Khan, Javed Miandad and Qasim Omar which came to their rescue when Australia again scored prolifically.

The Air Marshal, back in Pakistan, resigned and was replaced as President of the Board by Lt General Ghulam Safdar Butt, so cricket was still in the hands of military administrators. Imran was restored to the captaincy for the two final Tests but still could not bowl; one game was drawn when Imran made 83 and 72 not out, and the other lost. Australia, too, had certain problems with Hughes as captain being given something of a rough ride by his three senior players, Greg Chappell, Lillee and Marsh. They announced their retirement at the end of the series and the Aussies faced a re-building situation with their three most experienced Test players gone. It may be purely a personal view, but I always think of those three fine players as a Three Musketeers-like trio and there can be little doubt that the gentler-natured Kim Hughes thought of them in that way – though perhaps not in such an admiring context! Lillee had taken 355 wickets, Marsh had made 355 dismissals and Chappell had held 122 catches apart from his batting which averaged over 50. Nevertheless, with or without personal problems, Australia had won the series without losing a Test and Pakistan had even more difficulties to overcome.

England to New Zealand and Pakistan
1983–4
Tour captain: R. G. D. Willis (D. I. Gower)

Wellington: *Match drawn*
Christchurch: *New Zealand won by an innings and 132 runs*
Auckland: *Match drawn*

Karachi: *Pakistan won by 3 wickets*
Faisalabad: *Match drawn*
Lahore: *Match drawn*

This was a disappointing and demoralising tour in every way. It marked a further deterioration in the relations between the players and the media, though not specifically the cricketing Press. After the total humiliation in Christchurch, which saw New Zealand enforce the follow-on for the first time in 53 matches with England, allegations against certain England players of drug-taking, drunkenness and woman-ising brought a squad of news reporters flooding into New Zealand. In some cases, they followed the tour party to Pakistan and a tour which had started pleasantly (with a warming-up visit to Fiji, brilliant batting by Botham and Randall in Wellington) virtually disintegrated in a welter of recrimination and bad feeling. Both series were lost – a 'first' for both home countries – and Bob Willis ended his captaincy of England on a depressing note. Within a few months, his career as a Test player also came to an end and it was little short of tragic that a bowler who had given such wholehearted service to his country's cricket should quit in such circumstances.

This is not the place to discuss in detail the newspaper allegations of misconduct by the England team abroad but it has to be said that after losing the second Test in New Zealand they staged a party of such a nature that one would have thought they had just won a series, and the World Cup, in rapid succession instead of being bowled out for 82 and 93 to lose in six sessions of play. It was the most deplorable performance I have ever seen from an England team but the players did not accept that their batting or bowling was open to criticism.

Australia to West Indies
1984

Tour captain: K. J. Hughes

Guyana: *Match drawn*
Trinidad: *Match drawn*
Barbados: *West Indies won by 10 wickets*
Antigua: *West Indies won by an innings and 36 runs*
Jamaica: *West Indies won by 10 wickets*

Kim Hughes took his party to the West Indies with mixed feelings. While he obviously missed the skill and experience of Chappell, Marsh and Lillee in the Tests, he was at least free from their criticism but there were still men in his ranks who needed a firm hand. Geoff Lawson, for instance, showed ostentatious 'dissent' in the first Test when an lbw appeal was turned down and the management fined him for the offence. Rain and bad light curtailed the first two Tests but in Barbados, after scoring 429 in their first innings, Australia were dismissed for 97 in their second. The next two matches were lost just as emphatically and in fact West Indies did not lose a single second-innings wicket through-out the series.

Hughes had an unenviable task in coaxing more resolute batting from a relatively inexperienced line-up where broken fingers were regularly featured in the casualty reports. When Rodney Hogg was allowed to bowl a sequence of 12 bouncers in Jamaica without any interference from the umpires, Lloyd and his men smiled gently. Good bowler Hogg might be, fiery-tempered he might sometimes show himself, but a Holding, a Marshall or a Garner he was not. West Indies were now beginning to look quite unbeatable and Lloyd's policy of continuous, ultra-fast bowling, though unsatisfactory to aesthetic tastes, could not be faulted in Caribbean eyes.

New Zealand to Sri Lanka
1984
Tour captain: G. P. Howarth

Kandy: *New Zealand won by 165 runs*
Colombo (Sinhalese SC): *Match drawn*
Colombo (Colombo CC): *New Zealand won by an innings and 61 runs*

Sri Lanka's inaugural Test against England in 1982 had been played at the Saravanamuttu Stadium, Colombo. Now two further Tests were played on different grounds in the same city. Without an experienced opener to partner John Wright, skipper Howarth took on the job himself, a move which was successful in the first Test but not in the other two.

West Indies to England
1984
Tour captain: C. H. Lloyd

Edgbaston: *West Indies won by an innings and 180 runs*
Lord's: *West Indies won by 9 wickets*
Headingley: *West Indies won by 8 wickets*
Old Trafford: *West Indies won by an innings and 64 runs*
The Oval: *West Indies won by 172 runs*

Even without five players who had been banned for playing in South Africa, the awesome tide of West Indian power swept England aside with almost contemptuous ease. Holding, Garner and Marshall, backed up by Baptiste and Davis, were well enough known to all the English batsmen but in Tests they were able to raise their fast bowling to an even more devastating level than in county cricket. Even though Lamb showed they could be handled, with three centuries, and Broad and Fowler resisted well at times, the batting as a whole never succeeded in concert and the result was the most humiliating defeat England had ever suffered in a home series.

Having captained England impressively when Willis was ill during the winter tour in Pakistan, David Gower was the home captain on the receiving end of the West Indian blast in a summer where Test batsmen spent most of the time ducking and weaving in the interests of self-preservation. Cries for the application of Law 42 to prevent physical intimidation in the form of persistent fast, short-pitched deliveries went unheeded. Lloyd replied to critics of his policy by insisting that restriction to one such delivery per over removed the bowler's element of surprise which was undoubtedly true. England were unable to reply in kind with Willis, now 35, on the brink of retirement and Botham having lost both his edge and his out-swinger; England were unable to respond either with reciprocal force or with scientific precision.

In the first Test, Warwickshire batsman Andy Lloyd played only half an hour on his debut before he was struck on the head by a ball from Marshall and took no further part in the season. At Old Trafford, Paul Terry of Hampshire, in his second Test, had a forearm broken by Davis and returned at the end of the innings to try to bat one-handed, with his left arm in a sling. There was no shortage of courage shown in the series but courage was not enough and a disturbing element of a different kind was now reported from the England dressing-room. One relative newcomer to the camp asked, thoughtfully, at the end of the day's play for a discussion on the next day's tactics in the field – what would be the general policy, what would be the line to bowl, and to what sort of fields? He was told, abruptly, 'Never mind that – let's get to the pub.' The West Indians had created a situation where the England old guard were now not merely demoralised, but seemingly disinterested.

Sri Lanka to England
1984
Tour captain: L. R. D. Mendis

Lord's: *Match drawn*

With some relief, England saw the back of the West Indians and turned their attention to Sri Lanka, here for a one-off Test. With a gesture which can only be described as misguidedly patronising, Sri Lanka were put in to bat with members of the England side forecasting an end to the game before close of play on Saturday – the third day. The tourists responded with their highest score in their brief Test history and declared at 491 for 7. They delighted the Lord's crowd with some exceedingly stylish batting, playing through the line of the ball in a way which had seemingly gone out of fashion in this country.

Their captain, Duleep Mendis, scored a splendid 111, which included three sixes and came off only 112 balls and there were two other Sri Lankan centuries in the match – Wettimuny 190 and Silva 102 not out. England had now gone 12 Tests without a win and the newest Test-playing country had provided a salutary lesson at the end of a chastening summer.

India to Pakistan
1984
Tour captain: S. M. Gavaskar

Lahore: *Match drawn*
Faisalabad: *Match drawn*

Gavaskar was back in charge for this two-match tour and solid batting by both sides was the order of the day. Seven centuries (one of them, by Qasim Omar, a double hundred) were scored and only twice was a side bowled out completely.

New Zealand to Pakistan
1984
Tour captain: J. V. Coney

Lahore: *Pakistan won by 6 wickets*
Hyderabad: *Pakistan won by 7 wickets*
Karachi: *Match drawn*

New Zealand's new captain was Jeremy Vernon Coney, known as 'The Mantis' from his tall, slim and slightly-stooped figure, a man with interesting views on tour captaincy. His first experience of the job gave him a chance to put theories into practice:

You have a group of people who wouldn't necessarily get together for long periods, now living for three or four months in conditions which are not easy . . . tours like India and Pakistan where you are going to visit places of a type you are not used to going to.

The players are sometimes going to have to cook for themselves, not be able to have a social drink together, to go out to a theatre or to relax in that sort of way . . . things that at home they are normally able to do as part of their everyday routine. You then face a captain's problem of trying to find a way of ensuring that his men are going to perform to the best of their ability when they are out on the field. A captain, therefore, has to be creative in his ideas when he and his touring party are *off* the field.

Coney, an imaginative and highly intelligent man, came up against umpiring problems straightaway in Pakistan. He confesses:

It was the all-pervasive feeling of frustration which got to me. The feeling that we weren't really being allowed to play as well as we might. I don't mind losing – I don't like it, mind you, but I can accept it and I think most Test players can – but when you get, day after day, a situation where you feel things are not quite going your way, that creates other problems for you as a captain because that sort of thing spreads like wildfire through a team. It demands the utmost discipline from a captain, then from senior players. You simply cannot have men coming back into the dressing-room, throwing their bats and saying, 'Oh, I was done again,' and 'I wasn't anywhere near the ball.' That sort of stuff has got to be stopped immediately. But the frustrations undoubtedly were there. The effort that we had put into preparing for that tour was rigorous and so the sense of frustration increased.

Paradoxically, Coney regards that tour as one of the most enjoyable he ever undertook because despite his on-the-field frustrations he was with a pleasant group of tourists who devised a whole range of ways of finding pleasure in a new environment: . . . 'the places we saw, the contests we organised, the things we did together, the opportunity to understand each other at a different level and in different cir-cumstances.'

More views from the engaging Jeremy Coney in due course. For the moment, he returned from his first tour as captain with a record of two defeats in three Tests, a lot of happy personal memories but a fairly critical opinion of playing conditions in Pakistan. He had registered a complaint about umpiring standards and a two-man commission appointed by the B C C P reached the conclusion that there *had* been mistakes, mostly favouring the home side.

West Indies to Australia
1984–5
Tour captain: C. H. Lloyd

Perth: *West Indies won by an innings and 112 runs*
Brisbane: *West Indies won by 8 wickets*
Adelaide: *West Indies won by 191 runs*
Melbourne: *Match drawn*
Sydney: *Australia won by an innings and 55 runs*

The West Indies bandwagon rolled on, following a never-ending circuit of the globe. During the English summer the players, with only minimal exceptions, were employed by counties; for the remainder of the time they patrolled the Test grounds of the world, with a short break to fit in their own domestic Shell competition. It was the ambition of every other captain somehow to beat the West Indies; most of them knew how it could be done but very rarely could they find the necessary conditions, or apparatus, to accomplish it. Somehow you had to contrive a way of getting on top in the early stages of the game. Then, the theory was, morale would buckle and resistance crumple. Ah! But just how did one get on top of this juggernaut of a team, battering all opposition inexorably into submission?

West Indies were susceptible to the moving ball – either in the air or off the pitch – or so the story went. Not many bowlers were able to swing it in West Indian conditions and there was little to help the spinners in the Caribbean, not even in Trinidad these days. Richard Ellison had shown at The Oval in 1984 that their batsmen were fallible if the away-swinger was working and the following winter the Australians found their answer in Sydney where the pitch was increasingly receptive to spin bowling. Murray Bennett and 'Dutch' Holland bowled them to an innings defeat – but by that time Clive Lloyd's tourists had the rubber in the bag with three Test victories and one draw. The captain who had changed the whole face of Test cricket now decided, at the age of 40, to retire with a record of 110 matches in all, a batting average of 46.67 and 19 hundreds. Lloyd had been captain in 74 Tests (averaging 51.30 with the bat) of which 36 were won, 12 lost and 26 drawn. Vivian Richards was his logical successor.

England to India
1984–5

Tour captain: D. I. Gower

Bombay: *India won by 9 wickets*
Delhi: *England won by 8 wickets*
Calcutta: *Match drawn*
Madras: *England won by 9 wickets*
Kanpur: *Match drawn*

David Gower had been judged a success when in Pakistan in early 1984 he had to take over the reins from Bob Willis and there was a considerable lobby for his appointment as captain against the touring West Indies during the English summer of 1984. When the appointment was made and a disastrous series ensued it was in no way attributed to faulty captaincy. Gower was generally considered to have been unfortunate in running up against such a majestic opposition with his own forces depleted by the suspensions still applying to the 1982 South African 'rebels'.

His appointment to lead the winter tour to India was, therefore, a popular one and when Botham announced that he was unavailable for selection this was seen as an indirect help to Gower since the all-rounder's strong and rumbustious personality was thought likely to be too much for Gower to handle through a long and difficult tour. He had the severe misfortune to lead his party into Delhi immediately before the assassination of Mrs Gandhi, which threw the whole country into bloody turmoil. England retreated to Sri Lanka until civil unrest had been cleared up and then returned to India to win the series by two Tests to one. As often happens in these cases, the problems drew the party closer together and the tour was regarded as a happy one, England recovering well from the opening defeat in Bombay. After 54 Test innings, dating back to 1978, Mike Gatting at last scored his first Test hundred and gave himself the confidence which had been inexplicably missing for so long. The tourists were unhappy about much of the umpiring but sensible captaincy by Gower and the tactful management of Tony Brown prevented any major disruption of the tour. Indeed, the problems were now largely in the province of the home captain, Gavaskar, whose longstanding simmering feud with Kapil Dev was now very much a public matter. Kapil was openly critical of Gavaskar's cautious approach to declarations; Gavaskar was equally blunt about Kapil's cavalier approach to batting on occasions.

Gower had a modest tour as far as his own batting standards were concerned but with no 'revelations', no war with the media, no confrontations with umpires (a suggestion, here and there, of dissatisfaction but no open revolt) and a winning series, his leadership was undoubtedly a success.

Australia to England
1985
Tour captain: A. R. Border

Headingley: *England won by 5 wickets*
Lord's: *Australia won by 5 wickets*
Trent Bridge: *Match drawn*
Old Trafford: *Match drawn*
Edgbaston: *England won by an innings and 118 runs*
The Oval: *England won by an innings and 94 runs*

Australia, who had been harder hit than any other country by players' involvement in Kerry Packer's 'Circus' six years earlier, now lost four potential tourists who had been banned for playing on unauthorised visits to South Africa. Allan Border, with seven years' experience of Test cricket, was the new captain and if ever a man led by example it was Border on this trip. He scored 1,355 runs in all and at times seemed to stand alone against the opposition, not only in the Tests but in many of the county games as well. His bowling was thin, with the outstanding exception of Craig McDermott who performed heroically with little or no support.

It was difficult to form any accurate judgement of Border as a captain except to take the view, unequivocally, that his inspiring lead deserved a better response. He generally followed a policy of going into the Tests with four bowlers and thus created difficulties for himself when three so often lacked penetration. Border played a superb innings of 196 (followed by 41 not out) at Lord's which swung the game and was given out at Trent Bridge in circumstances which suggested a shabby piece of sharp-practice by England's close fieldsmen. The game was marked, too, by some childish behaviour by Botham which went totally unchecked by his captain and raised doubts once more about Gower's strength of character.

Nevertheless, the Ashes were won back in a series which was never dull and often reached great heights, no more so for Gower than at Edgbaston, where he put Australia in to bat and won by an innings, scored a quite superb 215 and set an outstanding personal example in the field. This is Gower's Test:

ENGLAND v. AUSTRALIA

Edgbaston, 1985

AUSTRALIA

First Innings			Second Innings	
Wood c Edmonds b Botham	19		(2) c Robinson b Ellison	10
Hilditch c Downton b Edmonds	39		(1) c Ellison b Botham	10
Wessels c Downton b Ellison	83		c Downton b Ellison	10
Border c Edmonds b Ellison	45		(5) b Ellison	2
Ritchie c Botham b Ellison	8		(6) c Lamb b Emburey	20
Phillips c Robinson b Ellison	15		(7) c Gower b Edmonds	59
O'Donnell c Downton b Taylor	1		(8) b Botham	11
Lawson run out	53		(9) c Gower b Edmonds	3
McDermott c Gower b Ellison	35		(10) c Edmonds b Botham	8
Thomson not out	28		(11) not out	4
Holland c Edmonds b Ellison	0		(4) lbw b Ellison	0
Extras (lb4 wl nb4)	9		Extras (b1 lb3 nbl)	5
Total	335		Total	142

Bowling: Botham 27–1–108–1; Taylor 26–5–78–1; Ellison 31.5–9–77–6; Edmonds 20–4–47–1; Emburey 9–2–21–0

Bowling: Botham 14.1–2–52–3; Taylor 13–4–27–0; Ellison 9–3–27–4; Edmonds 15–9–13–2; Emburey 13–5–19–1

ENGLAND

First Innings

Gooch c Phillips b Thomson	19
Robinson b Lawson	148
Gower c Border b Lawson	215
Gatting not out	100
Lamb c Wood b McDermott	46
Botham c Thomson b McDermott	18
Downton not out	0
Ellison ⎫	
Emburey ⎬ did not bat	
Edmonds ⎪	
Taylor ⎭	
Extras (b7 lb20 nb22)	49
Total (5 wkts declared)	595

Bowling: Lawson 37–1–135–2; McDermott 31–2–155–2; Thomson 19–1–101–1; Holland 25–4–95–0; O'Donnell 16–3–69–0; Border 6–1–13–0

Pakistan to New Zealand

1985

Tour captain: Javed Miandad

Wellington: *Match drawn*
Auckland: *New Zealand won by an innings and 99 runs*
Dunedin: *New Zealand won by 2 wickets*

With Imran Khan guesting in Australia and Zaheer Abbas not ready to tour when the trip began, Pakistan handed the captaincy once more to

Javed Miandad, perhaps not the most tactful of moves since he had been involved in a number of the controversial decisions in the home series with New Zealand which had led to Jeremy Coney's official complaint. His side was a little short of experience but was fortunate in the choice of manager, Yawar Saeed, whose sense of humour in handling Press conferences proved very useful indeed. A number of hairline decisions went New Zealand's way but there was no official complaint from the Pakistan camp and the series ended 2–0 in New Zealand's favour. With Coney introspectively unhappy about his own captaincy in Pakistan, Howarth had been recalled for this series.

New Zealand to West Indies
1985
Tour captain: G. P. Howarth

Trinidad: *Match drawn*
Guyana: *Match drawn*
Barbados: *West Indies won by 10 wickets*
Jamaica: *West Indies won by 10 wickets*

This tour was not one of Geoff Howarth's happier experiences even though his team registered two honourable draws. His 19-year-old opening batsman, Ken Rutherford, was shattered by bagging a pair in his first Test and Howarth had to move up the order at a time when – wrestling with the problem of whether to wear spectacles or contact lenses – he would have been happier at number 5 or 6. He came in for a certain amount of criticism in the first Test for resting Hadlee too early in the second innings and then dropping a slip catch in a situation where his side were seen as being in a position to win. It was not the best point at which to end a Test career which had seen New Zealand Test cricket take impressive steps forward. Howarth had played a major role in that progress.

India to Sri Lanka
1985
Tour captain: Kapil Dev

Colombo (Sinhalese SC): *Match drawn*
Colombo (Saravanamuttu Stadium): *Sri Lanka won by 149 runs*
Kandy: *Match drawn*

Less than 12 months earlier, Kapil Dev had been dropped by the Indian selectors for his public row with the captain, Gavaskar. Now he was very much back in favour and took over the captaincy in Sri Lanka where the home side achieved a notable success by winning the second Test and drawing the other two. It was a historic moment in Sri Lanka's brief history and Kapil, with a fairly experienced and competent party (though without Gavaskar), was once again under fire at home, particularly in Bombay! The home win, in the second of the two Tests in Colombo, came from a solid batting performance in the first innings, a well-gauged declaration in the second and some excellent bowling by the quicker pair of Sri Lankan bowlers, de Mel and Ratnayake. It was a shattering blow to Indian pride.

Sri Lanka to Pakistan
1985
Tour captain: L. R. D. Mendis

Faisalabad: *Match drawn*
Sialkot: *Pakistan won by 8 wickets*
Karachi: *Pakistan won by 10 wickets*

It did nothing for Indian pride when Sri Lanka went to Pakistan immediately after their success at home and were well beaten in two Tests after their honourable draw in Faisalabad where they totalled 479. Mendis, however, had a miserable tour with the bat and his side generally were unable to cope with either the fast bowling of Imran Khan (playing under Javed Miandad's captaincy) and the increasingly impressive Wasim Akram, or the spin of Tauseef Ahmed and Abdul Qadir.

New Zealand to Australia
1985
Tour captain: J. V. Coney

Brisbane: *New Zealand won by an innings and 41 runs*
Sydney: *Australia won by 4 wickets*
Perth: *New Zealand won by 6 wickets*

New Zealand cricket really came of age in this series and if Pakistan had caused Coney doubts about his ability to captain a Test side, they were gone when he returned home from Australia.

The opening win in Brisbane was the highpoint of Coney's cricketing life in competitive terms although his wide-ranging interests enabled him to find pleasure and satisfaction in many other aspects of his Test career. But there is a very special rivalry between the two Southern Hemisphere countries and as a visitor to both of them while this series was taking place I observed it with detached (and sometimes amused) interest. When Australia were struggling to avoid defeat in Brisbane, for instance, no one I could find was willing to discuss the match. In fact, it was difficult to find anyone in Sydney (where I watched its progress on TV) to acknowledge that a Test Match was in fact taking place. In New Zealand during the Perth Test I was not surprised to note that the atmosphere was one of unbridled delight.

Hadlee's 9 for 52 and 6 for 71 feat in the first Test was a great bowler's response to Australian critical suggestion before the series that he was past his best and he held the catch which deprived him of an all-ten performance. Coney, nevertheless, saw the Test in a more rounded way:

We held our catches for Hadlee and we prevented singles being taken when it mattered . . . all the little things that some people don't perhaps follow in depth went well . . . all those little things worked for us. I thought New Zealand performed at a level which was extremely good in terms of team effort. While there were – there always will be – outstanding individual contributions, cricket is a team game rather than an individual encounter and I felt that on this particular occasion this group of men played extremely high-quality cricket. I enjoyed being part of that.

AUSTRALIA v. NEW ZEALAND

Brisbane, 1985

AUSTRALIA

First Innings		Second Innings	
Wessels lbw b Hadlee	70	(2) c Brown b Chatfield	3
Hilditch c Chatfield b Hadlee	0	(1) c Chatfield b Hadlee	12
Boon c Coney b Hadlee	31	c Smith b Chatfield	1
Border c Edgar b Hadlee	1	not out	152
Ritchie c M. Crowe b Hadlee	8	c Coney b Snedden	20
Phillips b Hadlee	34	b Hadlee	3
G. Matthews b Hadlee	2	c Coney b Hadlee	115
Lawson c Hadlee b Brown	8	(9) c Brown b Chatfield	7
McDermott c Coney b Hadlee	9	(8) c and b Hadlee	5
Gilbert not out	0	c Chatfield b Hadlee	10
Holland c Brown b Hadlee	0	b Hadlee	0
Extras (b9 lb5 nb2)	16	*Extras* (lb3 nb3)	6
Total	179	Total	333

Bowling: Hadlee 23.4–4–52–9; Chatfield 18–6–29–0; Snedden 11–1–45–0; M. Crowe 5–0–14–0; Brown 12–5–17–1; Coney 7–5–8–0

Bowling: Hadlee 28.5–9–71–6; Chatfield 32–9–75–3; Snedden 19–3–66–1; M. Crowe 9–2–19–0; Brown 25–5–96–0; Coney 3–1–3–0

NEW ZEALAND

First Innings

Edgar c Phillips b Gilbert	17
Wright lbw b Matthews	46
Reid c Border b Gilbert	108
M. Crowe b Matthews	188
Coney c Phillips b Lawson	22
J. Crowe c Holland b Matthews	35
Brown not out	36
Hadlee c Phillips b McDermott	54
Smith not out	2
Snedden } did not bat	
Chatfield	
Extras (b2 lb11 nb32)	45
Total (7 wkts declared)	553

Bowling: Lawson 36.5–8–96–1; McDermott 31–3–119–1; Gilbert 39–9–102–2; Matthews 31–5–110–3; Holland 22–3–106–0; Wessels 1–0–7–0; Border 0.1–0–0–0

India to Australia
1985–6
Tour captain: Kapil Dev

Adelaide: *Match drawn*
Melbourne: *Match drawn*
Sydney: *Match drawn*

India were the third party to that Australian summer's triangular series with Kapil Dev somehow retaining the captaincy despite the reverse in Sri Lanka and Gavaskar opening the batting with 166 not out in Adelaide, 172 on a spinner's pitch in Sydney – and a couple of single-figure scores in Melbourne. Kapil gave a great lead in the first Test with 8 for 106 but had to rely heavily on his slow bowlers in the other two games. India had very much the better of the argument in all three drawn Tests and Kapil's prestige was substantially re-established.

Australia to New Zealand
1986
Tour captain: A. R. Border

Wellington: *Match drawn*
Christchurch: *Match drawn*
Auckland: *New Zealand won by 8 wickets*

With an Australian team now playing in South Africa during the Southern Hemisphere summer which was arguably as strong, or very nearly so, as the one the selectors were able to field in official Test cricket, the Aussies once again found themselves in a transitional stage. Border's team's bowling was neither strong enough nor varied enough and the batting was patchy although the captain played well, as ever, particularly in Christchurch where he scored 140 and 114 not out. He was having a long and hard apprenticeship as captain, finding himself in charge of sides only marginally stronger than those Simpson had had to lead when called out of retirement.

England to West Indies
1986
Tour captain: D. I. Gower

Jamaica: *West Indies won by 10 wickets*
Trinidad: *West Indies won by 7 wickets*
Barbados: *West Indies won by an innings and 30 runs*
Trinidad: *West Indies won by 10 wickets*
Antigua: *West Indies won by 240 runs*

A whitewash in the home series of 1984 was followed by this in the West Indies 18 months later and it was Gower's misfortune to be England's captain on both occasions. This time he had additional problems to those presented in the purely cricketing sense by the formidable home side, still not firing on all cylinders under Richards and finding the engine spluttering from time to time against other opposition, but still far too capable for an England side which seemed half-beaten before it started.

The peripheral difficulties were centred on Botham, at this time the most colourful and controversial personality in world cricket. His affairs were managed by a man called Tim Hudson whose avowed intention it was to make his client not only the wealthiest cricketer in the world but a Hollywood film star as well! Botham irritably shrugged off all suggestions that the style of management was not in his best interests and insisted that he believed 100 per cent in Hudson. Thus, irrespective of success or failure, his career strode (sometimes strolled) forward in a megawatt glare of publicity of all kinds. It was scarcely surprising, therefore, that Gower's party had the company not only of bona fide cricket correspondents but also of news reporters, feature writers and

TV camera crews not interested in any way in the cricket but with a distinctly unwholesome preoccupation with what the team – and in particular I. T. Botham – did in their off-duty moments.

It would have been entirely possible to sympathise with Gower and his men in this goldfish-bowl existence had not the captain adopted, it seemed, a somewhat cavalier attitude to the microscopic scrutiny of the supplementary media party. And when the results of the Tests became progressively worse the *cricketing* Press who, as ever, started out with a supportive attitude to England's players, were forced to look with a critical eye at purely cricketing matters. While more conscientious members of the party were taking net practice, Gower was pictured taking a cruise on a pleasure boat, or sunbathing on a Barbados beach. Despite all the efforts of the manager, Tony Brown, to hold back the tide of unfavourable publicity, a large body of England supporters, combining holiday with Test-viewing, saw a party which was being humiliated on the field once again yet failing to present any sort of serious image as a highly paid professional group of international cricketers.

The adjective most generally applied to Gower's style of leadership is 'laid back' which can be interpreted in a number of ways from quietly controlled to sloppy, slipshod and slap happy.

Pakistan to Sri Lanka
1986
Tour captain: Imran Khan

Kandy: *Pakistan won by an innings and 20 runs*
Colombo (Colombo CC): *Sri Lanka won by 8 wickets*
Colombo (Saravanamuttu Stadium): *Match drawn*

While England were struggling in the West Indies, Imran Khan's Pakistan team were shocked by a defeat in Colombo in which the tourists' batting twice failed completely against medium-pace bowling. It was a strong Pakistan team so Sri Lanka's win was no fluke and the deciding match was drawn after the home side had made themselves secure from defeat.

India to England
1986
Tour captain: Kapil Dev

Lord's: *India won by 5 wickets*
Headingley: *India won by 279 runs*
Edgbaston: *Match drawn*

England returned from the West Indies all too clearly under the impression that their summer at home was going to be a good deal easier. The term, of course, is relative: 'easier' does not necessarily mean 'easy', and so it proved with two series defeats for the home side, now skippered by Mike Gatting.

Kapil Dev's Indians – with peace at least temporarily restored between himself and Gavaskar – led a party which looked strong in batting with two faces new to English eyes, the cheerfully uninhibited Srikkanth to open and the precociously talented Azharuddin in the middle order. It was the bowling, however, which took England by surprise. Modestly gifted on paper, the attack performed heroically under some skilled guidance from Kapil who showed that in this sphere at least he was a more aggressive captain in the field than Gavaskar. There was ammunition, too, for the weapons of those who had for long pointed out that a regiment of overseas professionals coming here each summer were gaining invaluable experience of English conditions and English players' vulnerability. Madan Lal, for instance, who seemed to improve with age, had played much league cricket here apart from his previous tours, as had Chetan Sharma and Shastri. England were bowled out for 102 and 128 at Headingley in conditions which should have been much more familiar to their batsmen and they topped 300 only once (at Edgbaston) due largely to Gatting's fighting 183 not out.

New Zealand to England
1986
Tour captain: J. V. Coney

Lord's: *Match drawn*
Trent Bridge: *New Zealand won by 8 wickets*
The Oval: *Match drawn*

Coney brought his New Zealanders in the second half of the summer, feeling that he had a reasonable chance of winning the series and equally determined to enjoy every aspect of the tour in his own way. In his own words:

I regard England as an old New Zealand. Everywhere you go there's a depth of history about it. If you are interested in that sort of thing, then the mind goes back to William the Conqueror, or whoever. This is where it actually happened. That's special, I think. You hear about these things in your fourth or fifth-form days, in a semi-comatose state, and suddenly it's there, in front of you.

His team took the rubber by virtue of their win at Trent Bridge made possible, in arithmetical terms, by a maiden century from John Bracewell, batting at number 8. But Coney will have none of that:

I am not interested in that sort of thing. I regret the way the media has leapt on board the personality cult. I don't care who does well in a day's play. I am interested in *the team* doing well and whether it is Richard Hadlee or John Bracewell who shines doesn't concern me in the slightest.

And a final word from an engaging character who lived and played through times when so many of the game's standards were being eroded:

I think behaviour on the field has deteriorated, at least a little. We have trial by television, we have entered the age of the Thespian. If you think a decision is a bad one you can make your feelings quite clear in all sorts of ways, not only to the spectators in the ground but to those at home. I regret the passing of some of the traditions. When I started in 1973 we always went through to the opposition dressing-room and had a beer with them. It doesn't always happen now. It did not reduce the competitiveness of it all, or sap it in any way.

Does he think the personality cult has cheapened the game?

I do, because it appeals to the ego. All the trappings of individual success seduce you; you become hoist on your own petard and take on a character which is not you. It is very easy, in fact, to think that you are able to do *anything*. You start behaving differently and become a different person.

What about umpiring standards and players' reluctance to accept decisions?

As a principle, I think the majority of players would like to see a panel of the best neutral umpires. The situation which gives rise to this debate is very largely due to the pressure put on umpires by trial by television. That has appalled me in Australia and when I saw it here [in New Zealand] with the big screens erected in the ground for instant replays I thought the game had finally lost its sanity. Perhaps it was inevitable . . . the old march of commercialism, I'm afraid. Unless someone is prepared to stand up to that sort of thing and say,

'No. We won't have it here,' it will inevitably lead to numbers on players' backs, then names on their backs. That's the next step, isn't it? In the meantime, respect for umpiring decisions will continue to decline – and the standards of the game with it.

Australia to India
1986
Tour captain: A. R. Border

Madras: *Match tied*
Delhi: *Match drawn*
Bombay: *Match drawn*

Border found himself in the nerve-racking position of fielding captain in a game which ended in a tie. In the heat and humidity of Madras he kept his head admirably in the trickiest of situations and returned unbeaten from a series which was, in part, rain-affected and played in its entirety on good batting pitches. He took with him probably the best – certainly the most experienced – side Australia could field at that time to play Kapil Dev's men so rich in batting talent and getting better all the time.

West Indies to Pakistan
1986
Tour captain: I. V. A Richards

Faisalabad: *Pakistan won by 186 runs*
Lahore: *West Indies won by an innings and 10 runs*
Karachi: *Match drawn*

After losing the first Test when Abdul Qadir (6 for 16) bowled out the tourists for 53 in their second innings, Richards fielded two slow bowlers in Lahore: Harper bowled just one over in the match and Butts was not called upon at all! Walsh, Gray and Marshall did all that was necessary on a sub-standard pitch and a West Indies total of 218 was enough to give them victory by an innings. Umpires from India were used in the second and third Tests . . . but there were still complaints!

Sri Lanka to India
1986–7
Tour captain: L. R. D. Mendis

Kanpur: *Match drawn*
Nagpur: *India won by an innings and 106 runs*
Cuttack: *India won by an innings and 67 runs*

Mendis was still skipper of a Sri Lankan side which had shown clear signs of improvement over the past two years but on this trip his own form as a batsman deserted him completely. Kapil Dev's spinners won the second and third Tests for him.

England to Australia
1986–7
Tour captain: M. W. Gatting

Brisbane: *England won by 7 wickets*
Perth: *Match drawn*
Adelaide: *Match drawn*
Melbourne: *England won by an innings and 14 runs*
Sydney: *Australia won by an innings and 55 runs*

The debacle in the West Indies, followed by home defeats at the hands of India and New Zealand, had prompted a clamour for the appointment of a cricket manager. Some critics suggested he should have complete responsibility for selection of teams and overall control of tour parties, as well as the England team at home. This had been advanced as the best way of improving a poor record in recent years and in mid-season an approach was made by the T C C B to Ray Illingworth whose name had been regularly mentioned in the Press as the best-qualified candidate. The 'offer' was couched in such derisory terms that Illingworth had no option but to decline, despite the fact that the idea of England management, in principle, appealed to him strongly. Such were the terms suggested to him that the inescapable conclusion had to be that the Board *did not want him* to accept.

Later that summer, after other candidates had been considered, the appointment went to Mickey Stewart, the cricket manager of Surrey, and thus the tour party to Australia was led by Gatting as captain, Stewart as cricket manager and Peter Lush, the Board's marketing executive with great experience of the public relations field, as tour manager. It was a spectacularly successful trip with a four-cornered competition involving England, Australia, West Indies and Pakistan, the Benson and Hedges Challenge (limited overs games), won as well as the Test series which retained the Ashes.

Gatting's appointment for the previous summer's series, and now the winter tour, was generally popular. He had displayed great courage after sustaining a dreadful facial injury in the West Indies. He flew home for an operation, then returned to face the fast-bowling attack once more. As Gower's vice-captain he had been well clear of the allegations levelled at some other senior members of that party claiming lack of application and conscientiousness. He was reported to have rebuked Botham for his 'wrong attitude' on at least one occasion in the West Indies.

In military terms, Gatting would be the sergeant-major who had taken over the company when its officers had been wiped out. His was definitely a promotion from the ranks and no conscious effort was required on his part to be 'one of the boys'. He was an experienced tourist, having made his first one in 1977–8, had been captain of his county since 1983, was a sound and gutsy batsman, a good close fieldsman and could be useful as an occasional, stand-breaking type of medium-pace seam bowler. He was used to handling his own spin-bowling attack (having the country's best pair in Edmonds and Embu-rey) as well as the contemporary emphasis on pace. It is in no way an attempt to damn the man with faint praise if one says that there was no credible alternative to him at that time.

Gatting had no natural, God-given gift of leadership. He had learned, and was still learning, from experience. The respect he received from his players came from his own determination as an unflinching batsman, a fielder who would stand as close as he ever asked anyone else to do, and for appreciation that he was a professional's professional. He was no matinee idol in the eyes of the media, was far from being a lucid or glib communicator, and altogether he presented a composite picture of a sound and reliable leader, rather than one of flair and imagination. Most English supporters heaved a sigh of relief at his success in Australia. The basis of a solid, and rather more successful, future for English cricket seemed to have been established. The tour was completed, in contrast to that of the previous winter, without revelations, scandal, controversy or tantrums.

Pakistan to India
1987
Tour captain: Imran Khan

Madras: *Match drawn*
Calcutta: *Match drawn*
Jaipur: *Match drawn*
Ahmedabad: *Match drawn*
Bombay: *Pakistan won by 16 runs*

This series brought two of the world's greatest all-rounders into opposition as captains. Both Imran Khan and Kapil Dev were more successful on this occasion as batsmen than with the ball and in the only Test which brought a result, Imran's slow left-armer (Iqbal Qasim) and off-spinner (Tauseef Ahmed) were marginally more successful than Kapil's two left-armers (Shastri and Maninder Singh) and off-break bowler, Yadav. Because of the sterile nature of four drawn Tests, neither captain found himself able to assert tactical domination.

New Zealand to Sri Lanka
1987
Tour captain: J. J. Crowe

Colombo (C C): *Match drawn*

Jeff Crowe, elder brother of Martin, took New Zealand to Sri Lanka for a solitary, high-scoring game in which 803 runs were scored for the loss of only 14 wickets. Crowe, more experienced than his highly talented brother, had played in Australian Sheffield Shield cricket and scored 120 not out in this one-off match. A sound batsman and excellent slip-catcher, he was a thoughtful if undemonstrative cricketer who, as Coney had done, seemed to lack confidence in his own ability as a captain, at least in the early stages of his career at this level. This affected his own performance as a batsman, as was clear later that year in Australia.

West Indies to New Zealand
1987

Tour captain: I. V. A. Richards

Wellington: *Match drawn*
Auckland: *West Indies won by 10 wickets*
Christchurch: *New Zealand won by 5 wickets*

There had been much speculation around the world on whether the West Indians would be able to maintain their reputation for near-invincibility under Vivian Richards that they had shown with Clive Lloyd as captain. Lloyd had been an extremely good batsman; Richards was outstandingly the best in the world at that time. Lloyd, through his long service, had seen all his players develop during his own time as a Test regular and presented a father-figure image; Richards, too, had been a West Indies player while *his* side matured but presented a more abrasive image than Lloyd. While the one gave an impression of thoughtful, professional regard for the opposition, the other projected an image of contemptuous dismissal. While Lloyd ambled amiably to the crease, Richards positively strutted. It was going to be an interesting succession.

In this series Richards showed little inclination to consult his vice-captain, Holding, in the first Test and was more frequently to be seen having discussions with Greenidge; Holding took no part in the second and third Tests, returning home before the end of the tour. In the Christchurch match, the captain raised a few eyebrows by bowling Marshall right through a morning's play and into the afternoon – at which point the new ball became due! He could, of course, point to the fact that he had plenty of alternative fire-power in Garner, Gray and Walsh but to bowl the fastest man in the world into the ground before taking the new ball struck some observers as a little odd; the West Indies, in fact, lost the match. In at least one respect (in Wellington) Richards showed a tactical awareness in slowing down the game as New Zealand sought to get into a position to make a challenging declaration – he bowled himself at length in using one ball for 177 overs so that Wright and Martin Crowe, in a partnership of 241, were never able to score quickly enough. I examined the ball at the end of the innings. It resembled a bundle of rags and one could understand John Wright's rueful confession that it was 'impossible to get it off the square'.

Pakistan to England
1987

Tour captain: Imran Khan

Old Trafford: *Match drawn*
Lord's: *Match drawn*
Headingley: *Pakistan won by an innings and 18 runs*
Edgbaston: *Match drawn*
The Oval: *Match drawn*

After an opening Test in which his tourists were severely mauled but saved by rain from a worse fate, Imran Khan experienced another rain-soaked match at Lord's where a Test never even began to take shape. His moment came, however, at Headingley in the form of a massive win in which he played a notable part personally with 10 wickets in the match for 77 runs. Imran by now had a tight organisational grip on his men and played the last three matches with a tigerish, almost Chappell-like aggression. From his power-base established by the batting of Javed Miandad, Salim Malik and Mudassar Nazar, he was able to deploy his fast bowling resources (himself, Wasim Akram and Mohsin Kamal) so effectively that his spinners were rarely called upon to do much bowling at all until the final Test on the excellent pitch at The Oval.

With so much play lost during the series, however, there was time and newspaper space for 'comment' features of a critical nature and the slowing down of the games by Pakistan in particular gave some writers the subject material they needed. One of the worst instances was provided by Javed Miandad, acting-captain while Imran was off the field, but the tour captain was quick to object to the strictures while his manager, Haseeb Ahsan, was a man who seemed to revel in his frequent opportunities to be quoted in controversial contexts. Imran was particularly incensed at what he interpreted as accusations of cheating and he reacted sharply to a statement by the recently appointed England team manager, Mickey Stewart, calling for 'stricter control over what constitutes a genuine injury'. The atmosphere in which the Tests were played, therefore, was generally acrimonious and during the frequent intervals while the rain fell – as well as the official Press Conferences at the end of the day – small knots of reporters, captains and managers were often to be seen huddled together on the production line of the following day's controversies.

There can be no doubt that the voluble Haseeb Ahsan went over the top in some of his widely-publicised complaints, notably when the tourists sought (unsuccessfully) to have David Constant and Ken Palmer removed from the panel of Test umpires, a move (and failure) which was to have repercussions the following winter.

It all served to sour a series victory which, in the end, was achieved on merit. At Headingley, the captain exposed the weakness of English batting on a seam bowler's pitch and in atmospheric conditions suitable for swing bowling – the very stuff of English cricket. More delays, some natural and some contrived, and the altercations which resulted, tended to obscure the breathtaking final stages of the Edgbaston match which either side could have won in the final 20 overs. And when, at The Oval, the pitch gave both sides an opportunity to show their respective standards of excellence, Pakistan had very much the better of a drawn game which they might well have won but for the batting of England's captain, Mike Gatting.

Imran had won the cricket war hands down but the result of the battle of words was not so clear-cut. Gatting, for all his splendid lead as a batsman, came under critical fire for an occasion at Edgbaston when, after a stoppage for bad light, the umpires (Meyer and White-head) stood ostentatiously alone in the middle waiting for an extremely delayed re-appearance by the England fieldsmen. The explanation, when it was finally given, was lame and unconvincing. England's suspicions that *English* umpires were now giving Pakistan the benefit of doubts after the touring management's overtures was sadly but manifestly clear. When respect for judicial fairness and impartiality was called into question in this country, even if only by hint and innuendo, the game was coming to a sorry pass.

England to Pakistan
1987
Tour captain: M. W. Gatting

Lahore: *Pakistan won by an innings and 87 runs*
Faisalabad: *Match drawn*
Karachi: *Match drawn*

Following the fourth World Cup, played in India and Pakistan (where there was widespread disappointment when it was Australia, the winners, and England who contested the final rather than either of the two host countries), England played a three-match series in Pakistan which saw the game at international level sink to depths which, even after some of the unsavoury events of recent years, had been impossible to visualise. On a December lunchtime in England, television viewers gazed in disbelief at the spectacle of an England captain waving an admonitory finger at a Pakistan umpire as they engaged in heated and acrimonious debate at close range. Through the use of 'gun' microphones, the TV team was actually able to send home some of the angry exchanges. As *Wisden*, more in sorrow than anger, commented: 'The nation was then held spellbound by the spectacle of two grown men standing on their dignity without an inch of moral ground to support them.' The captain was Mike Gatting and the umpire was Shakoor Rana.

That England had suffered great frustration in the first Test and the second up to that point is quite clearly undeniable. The Press Corps with the England party, while aghast at what happened, went to great lengths to stress the pressure upon the team and its captain. It is equally important to remember that for 30 years touring teams had been playing Tests in Pakistan (and other M C C and Commonwealth sides before that). All had experienced erratic and eccentric umpiring but had managed to retain their respect, if not for the officials themselves, for the Laws and for the game. All previous touring parties had spent varying lengths of time living in accommodation which varied from the not-very-good to downright squalid with cooking and catering standards which were, to western eyes, primitive; they had had to contend with long days of travel in dusty and uncomfortable trains and with chaotic arrangements.

Gatting and his men were the very first party to find an hotel of acceptable standards in every city they visited; food and accommodation had improved dramatically and internal travel was now by air – quicker, if not always on schedule. Their conditions of employment, therefore, were very much better than any previous tourists had known. Yet when the chairman of the T C C B flew out to adopt a peacemaking role, one of his first moves was to award a £1,000 bonus to the players to *compensate for their privations*. Those who had made earlier tours had all the sympathy in the world with the modern players on their frustrations at the hands of umpires but, given the already high levels of pay for touring, found it difficult to understand the need for a bonus and equally hard to condone open and heated altercation between a captain and an umpire.

Gatting could certainly be applauded for having the interests of his team at heart, for 'looking after his boys' rather than indulging in some purely self-centred crusade, but that TV picture, nevertheless, was one which shocked a large number of cricket-lovers at home. In an autobiography, published shortly afterwards, the captain made a spirited and impressive defence of his stand which earned him *more* sympathisers (while incurring the displeasure of the T C C B on contractual grounds) but in the last analysis the view of the editor of *Wisden* had to be seen as the right one:

I doubt if there is a cricketer anywhere who has not been upset by an umpire's decision, especially when – as can happen in club and village matches – that umpire has affiliations with 'the other side'. But without the unchallenged acceptance of the principle that the umpire's word is final, what chance does the game have? Professional sportsmen set the standards of behaviour for those who play the game at all levels, just as those in authority have a responsibility to ensure that they do.

Those who said 'Amen to that' now watched, with fascinated horror, the ever-widening ripples on a particularly murky pond.

England to Australia and New Zealand
1988
Tour captain: M. W. Gatting

Sydney: *Match drawn*

Christchurch: *Match drawn*
Auckland: *Match drawn*
Wellington: *Match drawn*

After playing a drawn match in Australia as part of the bicentenary celebrations, England played three more in New Zealand and this time made few friends during their visit. Churlishness and boorishness on the field were now becoming an ingredient of one Test after another and on the occasion of the match in Sydney to celebrate the arrival of the first immigrants to Australia, Chris Broad knocked down the stumps with his bat after being bowled for 139. He was fined for the gesture; and another fine followed in New Zealand, this time for Graham Dilley, for audibly voicing his displeasure when an appeal was turned down in the first Test. Because of ever-improving efficiency of microphones his words were heard plainly by televiewers in Britain but a friend in the crowd that day in Christchurch wrote to me to say no microphone was necessary for the spectators in Lancaster Park. She heard the expression on the back row of the main stand! It was obviously impossible for Gatting, as captain, to prevent spur-of-the-moment verbal reaction from one of his bowlers but the time had come, surely, for a team meeting at which the management of a tour side should issue final warnings in the matter of bad cricketing manners? At home, the T C C B were sufficiently concerned to instruct the England selectors to consider a player's conduct as well as his form when picking the Test side. Meanwhile, the New Zealand public showed their disapproval of this disturbing trend by declining to support the series. International cricket was digging its own grave.

Sri Lanka to Australia
1988
Tour captain: R. S. Madugalle

Perth: *Australia won by an innings and 108 runs*

Although the tourists were no match for Border's side, the continuing
ability of the small island to find new faces, new names from such a
minute catchment area was highly impressive. The new captain was
Ranjan Madugalle who had shown great talent as a schoolboy and had
been top scorer in Sri Lanka's inaugural Test. Captaincy, at least in this
Test, appeared to affect him as it had Mendis and he totalled only 13
in his two innings.

Pakistan to West Indies
1988
Tour captain: Imran Khan

Guyana: *Pakistan won by 9 wickets*
Trinidad: *Match drawn*
Barbados: *West Indies won by 2 wickets*

Imran Khan's party arrived in the Caribbean to find West Indian captains, umpires and senior players involved in furious *internal* squabbles
and allegations of cheating! The disputes ranged from the petty to the
patriotic (when the Leeward Islands' manager accused a Trinidadian
umpire of calling the new giant of fast bowling, Ambrose, for throwing
in order to keep him out of the Test side so that Gray, a Trinidadian,
would get that place).

Imran had, in fact, planned to retire after the Pakistan tour to England
and the World Cup on the sub-continent, hoping to go out on the
highest of high notes. Pakistan were now the second-best team in the
world, easily recognisable as such, in Tests and the thought of a head-
on confrontation with the best team in the world appealed to Imran's
competitive nature. His phone rang incessantly; around 100 letters a day
were delivered to his home, pleading with him to abandon retirement for
one last tilt at the West Indies; and when General Zia himself appealed
to Imran's patriotic instincts – 'the country needs you' – he took up
the challenge.

Imran applied himself to the series with great diligence, took 7 for 80 in Georgetown and led Pakistan to a notable victory. Greenidge skippered the West Indies in the absence of Richards who returned, however, to draw the second and win the third Test. With the pace of Marshall, Walsh, Benjamin, Ambrose and Patterson ranged against him, Imran nevertheless inspired his team to a squared rubber in which they batted bravely, no one more so than Javed Miandad who averaged 56.4. The win in Guyana must rank as one of the most outstanding in Imran's long list of successes as a Test captain.

WEST INDIES v. PAKISTAN

Guyana, 1988

WEST INDIES

First Innings		Second Innings	
Haynes c Yousuf b Imran	1	b Ijaz Faqih	5
Simmons b Ijaz Faqih	16	b Qadir	11
Richardson c Shoaib b Imran	75	c Yousuf b Qadir	16
Greenidge c Malik b Akram	17	b Imran	43
Logie lbw b Qadir	80	c Yousuf b Imran	24
Hooper c Akram b Imran	33	c Malik b Qadir	30
Dujon lbw b Imran	15	c Imran b Shoaib	11
Benjamin lbw b Imran	2	c Miandad b Shoaib	0
Walsh b Imran	7	c Yousuf b Imran	14
Ambrose not out	25	not out	1
Patterson b Imran	10	b Imran	0
Extras (b2 lb3 w2 nb6)	13	*Extras* (b4 lb8 nb5)	13
Total	292	Total	172

Bowling: Imran 22.4–2–80–7; Akram 14–5–41–1; Faqih 14–0–60–1; Qadir 24–2–91–1; Mudassar 5–2–9–0; Malik 1–0–6–0

Bowling: Imran 14.4–0–41–4; Akram 6–1–7–0; Faqih 15–4–38–1; Qadir 25–5–66–3

PAKISTAN

First Innings		Second Innings	
Mudassar Nazar b Ambrose	29	lbw b Patterson	0
Ramiz Raja c Haynes b Patterson	5	not out	18
Shoaib Mohammad c Greenidge b Walsh	46	not out	13
Javed Miandad b Patterson	114		
Salim Malik c Greenidge b Patterson	27		
Ijaz Ahmed c Haynes b Ambrose	31		
Imran Khan c Simmons b Benjamin	24		
Salim Yousuf lbw b Walsh	62		
Ijaz Faqih b Hooper	5		
Abdul Qadir b Walsh	19		
Wasim Akram not out	2		
Extras (b21 lb8 w4 nb 38)	71	*Extras* (nb1)	1
Total	435	Total (for 1 wkt)	32

Bowling: Patterson 24–1–82–3; Ambrose 28–5–108–2; Walsh 27–4–80–3; Benjamin 31–3–99–1; Hooper 12–0–32–1

Bowling: Patterson 2–0–19–1; Ambrose 1.3–0–13–0

West Indies to England
1988

Tour captain: I. V. A. Richards

Trent Bridge: *Match drawn*
Lord's: *West Indies won by 134 runs*
Old Trafford: *West Indies won by an innings and 156 runs*
Headingley: *West Indies won by 10 wickets*
The Oval: *West Indies won by 8 wickets*

If Richards was not quite able to emulate Lloyd's feat in winning all five Tests in England, he looked with the greatest satisfaction on four wins and a drawn game at Trent Bridge where rain and bad light curtailed the hours available for play. With the power of Patterson, Marshall, Ambrose, Walsh and Benjamin at his disposal and England seemingly resigned and indifferent to their fate, Richards' captaincy proceeded largely on automatic pilot lines – a change of bowling now and again but with pace usually giving way to pace. The West Indies captain knew he had it in the bag before he started.

With the exception of the winter 1986–7 in Australia, England's cricket in recent years has had a languid look about it and while only the most besotted optimist could have anticipated success against the West Indies, a fair number of followers at least *hoped* for a more determined and professional approach. Gatting fell from grace in remarkable fashion when the most squalid of the tabloid newspapers announced that he had entertained a young lady who was not his wife in his hotel room on the Sunday evening (rest day) of the Trent Bridge Test. For this alleged indiscretion the selectors felt it right, in pursuance of their brief from the T C C B to take behaviour into account as well as form, to relieve Gatting of the captaincy.

It was impossible not to sympathise with Gatting who was deposed for an incident entirely unconnected with cricket and which occurred in off-duty time. It was brought to the public gaze by one of the grubbier enterprises of a section of the Press which for some years now had been 'covering' cricket in a way that did no favours to the game and which disgraced journalism. Yet the selectors, in the light of the unfavourable publicity resulting from the 'revelation' and following the dictates of the T C C B, had little or no alternative. What really opened the selectors to criticism was the decision to appoint as captain John Emburey who, despite his experience at Test level, really had to be seen as struggling to retain his place as a *player*. He lasted for two Tests and then the mantle fell onto the shoulders of Chris Cowdrey, who reigned for but one. When Gooch became captain for the final Test, and the single one with Sri Lanka, the England performance at last took on some slight semblance of purposefulness. In all truth, one had to strain a little to detect it but close scrutiny of small details made it possible. Had Cowdrey not had to stand down because of injury a small piece of cricketing history might have been changed. He could well have been captain in India the following winter, in which case the tour would probably have gone ahead. (As it was, the Indian Government objected to Gooch as captain because of his record of having played in South Africa.) Cowdrey, when fit again, was disappointed at not being called up for the match with Sri Lanka, thus opening the way for his selection to tour India, and misguidedly blamed Peter May, the chairman of selectors. May, in fact, wished to persevere with Cowdrey but was 'talked out of it' by his three colleagues (selectors traditionally do not vote, per se, but seek to reach agreement by rational discussion). It had been another depressing summer.

Sri Lanka to England
1988
Tour captain: R. S. Madugalle

Lord's: *England won by 7 wickets*

Madugalle again led Sri Lanka who were unable to reproduce their batting form of 1984.

Australia to Pakistan
1988
Tour captain: A. R. Border

Karachi: *Pakistan won by an innings and 188 runs*
Faisalabad: *Match drawn*
Lahore: *Match drawn*

In the light of Pakistan's performance in the West Indies five months earlier, Border had no illusions about the task confronting his party but Imran had now retired (again) and Javed Miandad had not the same inspirational powers as a captain. Border knew him well enough as a tough and 'difficult' opponent and appreciated Javed's ability to lead by personal example. Even so, he was not prepared for the Pakistan skipper's 211 in Karachi against a modest Australian attack and he did not anticipate the collapse of his batting, twice, in that first Test against bowling which was modestly opened by Mudassar Nazar and Aamer Malik. It was a terrible blow and although Border, with his own batting and extensive use of his spinners in Lahore, got into a position to win the final Test and square the series, he could not quite pull it off.

New Zealand to India
1988
Tour captain: J. G. Wright

Bangalore: *India won by 172 runs*
Bombay: *New Zealand won by 136 runs*
Hyderabad: *India won by 10 wickets*

John Wright had been waiting patiently in the wings for several years before the call came to lead his country. One of the most pleasant and likeable men in the game, he was a popular captain of a young and relatively inexperienced side in which Greatbatch achieved notable success in India but few of the other newish batsmen did.

The party suffered more than the usual share of 'stomach trouble' and Hadlee, while taking as many wickets as the other front-line bowlers together, was one of the more seriously affected. Nevertheless, in a cheerful letter I received from the captain, John Wright spoke warmly of the togetherness of the party, especially in adversity. Once again it was possible to see the advantages for touring teams from the smaller countries with a modest number of media men who are integrated into the party and can usually be helpful in their support.

West Indies to Australia
1988–9
Tour captain: I. V. A. Richards

Brisbane: *West Indies won by 9 wickets*
Perth: *West Indies won by 169 runs*
Melbourne: *West Indies won by 285 runs*
Sydney: *Australia won by 7 wickets*
Adelaide: *Match drawn*

Richards' tourists had the series comprehensively won after the first three Tests and although the two final games brought an Australian win and an honourable draw which were seen as the start of a renaissance, the West Indies were in no doubt whatsoever about who had put up the more impressive performance. It was an acrimonious series with the visitors loud in their condemnation of umpiring standards. Such was their truculence and acerbity on the field that the Umpires' Association set out a list of formal complaints about the tourists' behaviour and submitted it to the Board of Control, naming four players in particular, one of whom was the West Indian captain. Standards now seemed to be slumping still further with almost every tour.

Pakistan to New Zealand
1989
Tour captain: Imran Khan

Dunedin: *Match abandoned without a ball bowled* (rain)
Wellington: *Match drawn*
Auckland: *Match drawn*

Imran, who had recently been extremely free with his advice on all manner of subjects in the *Daily Telegraph*, was once again persuaded on to the field of play with Pakistan in the World Series in Australia and began by voicing disapproval of some of the selections which had already been made for the tour party. On arrival in Australia, he echoed some of the West Indian complaints about umpiring and then launched an attack on the World Series limited-overs competition which was now a regular part of the Australian summer. It would, he said, 'kill' Test cricket eventually and there was certainly a measure of agreement with that view in many quarters, perhaps back home in Pakistan where attendance at Test cricket had been dwindling for some time while bigger crowds were seen at the one-day internationals.

In New Zealand, things took a turn for the worse. The manager, Intikhab Alam, was critical of umpiring decisions to local newspapermen and in broadcasts to Pakistan, claiming that some decisions were due to incompetence, *others to bias*. On 7 March, after the tour was over, Imran wrote in the *Daily Telegraph*: 'In the third Test in Auckland our team became despondent and believed, no matter what, they were not going to win. Every time we appealed the New Zealand Press and team accused us of trying to cheat their batsmen out.'

I watched that Test and I saw as many as *nine* Pakistan fieldsmen careering in a tight circle round the umpires, arms in the air, capering and shouting. I saw Imran, far away at wide mid-on, join in an appeal for a bat-pad catch at short leg. I saw New Zealand's senior umpire, Steve Woodward, approach the Pakistan captain in what I later learned was an appeal to Imran to curb the excesses of his players and I watched Imran shrug his shoulders and walk away. It was the most blatant and excessive attempt to intimidate umpires into giving decisions I have ever seen anywhere in the world.

Imran (again in the *Daily Telegraph*) complained: 'Abdul [Qadir] is a bubbly, emotional person who thrives on tension and appealing is part of his nature. What annoys me is that someone like Robin Jackman was indulged by the English Press as a great competitor, appealing and gesturing every time the ball looked anywhere close to hitting the wicket. Abdul is the same but when he appeals he is called a cheat.'

It is undeniably true that Jackman was an extremely *loud* appealer and he used a certain amount of theatrical back-up to his shouts. He was not alone in that. I don't think it is true for one moment to say that he 'appealed and gesticulated every time the ball looked anywhere close to hitting the wicket.' And it is absolutely and completely not the case that his appeals were supported by nine Surrey (or England) fieldsmen cavorting close to any umpire with arms above their heads.

Imran 'strongly recommended' that when the I C C met on the issue of neutral umpiring all Test captains should be present to argue the case for an international panel. One would hope that if the I C C ever took that course the arguments would have a more consistent base than Imran's.

India to West Indies
1989
Tour captain: D. B. Vengsarkar

Guyana: *Match drawn*
Barbados: *West Indies won by 8 wickets*
Trinidad: *West Indies won by 217 runs*
Jamaica: *West Indies won by 7 wickets*

The balance of power having once again switched from Delhi to Bombay, India were now skippered by Dilip Vengsarkar, the stylish middle-order batsman who had led his country in the home series against New Zealand. Although he had 14 years of Test cricket behind him, Vengsarkar sadly proved himself no leader of men abroad though he was not helped by the forces provided for him by the selectors. The party was thin in the extreme as far as bowling was concerned and only one batsman (Sanjay Manjrekar) averaged more than 30 in Tests, while the fielding was far from international standard both in catching and retrieving. Relieved of the cares of captaincy, Kapil Dev bowled well, but he could not do it all alone and that shrewdest objective observer of Indian cricket, D. J. Rutnagar, trenchantly commented in the *Daily Telegraph:* 'Except for a rejuvenated Kapil Dev . . . the Indian bowling would not have served a good club side. Poor though the bowling was, more could have been made of it by Vengsarkar. Nobody suffered more from his ineptitude than the young leg-spinner, Narendra Hirwani, who started the tour with a record of 36 wickets from four Test matches and will go home a disillusioned man.' India's cricket was now in disarray and continued so through 1989.

Australia to England
1989
Tour captain: A. R. Border

Headingley: *Australia won by 210 runs*
Lord's: *Australia won by 6 wickets*
Edgbaston: *Match drawn*
Old Trafford: *Australia won by 9 wickets*
Trent Bridge: *Australia won by an innings and 180 runs*
The Oval: *Match drawn*

The Allan Border seen in England in the golden summer of 1989 was a very different captain from the one who had led Australia here in 1985. His batting was as valuable to his side as ever but he now appeared as a decisive, shrewd, calculating and knowledgeable leader. His experience as an Essex player had been used to assess the strengths and weaknesses of England-qualified players, just as Terry Alderman's spells with Kent and Gloucs had given him equally valuable insight, while Dean Jones had had a season in league cricket to accustom himself to the slower pace and lower bounce of English pitches. Ranged alongside these assets was the experience and cricket brain of the tour manager, Bobby Simpson. While the Australians' relative success in the two final Tests of their summer against the West Indies was undoubtedly viewed as more significant by the Aussies than anyone else, it had certainly given them a new belief in their own ability. On their arrival the tourists – on any sane judgement of recent results around the world – ranked as bottom of the six-nation league table (Sri Lanka excluded) with England just one rung further up the ladder. Man for man, there did not seem a great deal of difference in the respective strengths of the two sides with England, perhaps, looking to have a slight edge.

How wrong such a judgement turned out to be. Border (and Simpson) had a match plan for every game, bearing in mind the state of the pitches, which were uniformly easy paced throughout a sunny season. They had a bowling plan for every England batsman and a field to complement it. But above all, the essential difference between the sides lay in (a) leadership and (b) attitude. Border was dynamic where Gower was, as ever, 'laid back'. The Australians were alert, interested, involved, while England seemed for much of the time to be mechanically going through the motions. Two major exceptions proved to be Robin Smith, South African-born but showing a lead (which others, sadly, seemed incapable of following) in pride in playing for England, and 'Jack' Russell, a splendid wicket-keeper who also showed courage, flair and application with the bat after an early setback at Headingley.

While England's performance had clearly been going steadily downhill for some time, one had to look a little deeper for an explanation of an utterly disastrous summer. In March the T C C B had changed the structure of selection, appointing a sub-committee of four to pick England's captain who would then join Ted Dexter (chairman) and Mickey Stewart (cricket manager) as a sort of sub-sub-committee in charge of picking the England squad. The T C C B's Cricket Committee was made up of Dexter, Ossie Wheatley (former Cambridge University, Warwicks and Glamorgan bowler), A. C. Smith (former Warwicks captain, Oxford University Blue and now chief executive of the Board), and Mickey Stewart.

Dexter at this time was reported as favouring the appointment of Gower as England captain and he bore the brunt of considerable criticism throughout the summer in consequence. Only in December was it revealed that he and Stewart had wanted the restoration of Mike Gatting but this had been vetoed by Wheatley – using a prerogative which had not been made public. It was not even known to the full membership of the T C C B and only came to light at a Press Conference following the T C C B's winter meeting on 6 and 7 December.

The summer debacle could not be blamed entirely on Gower, of course; a captain is largely helpless if his side does not perform competently. But it was the way in which England seemed entirely without match plans in the field which dismayed the more responsible critics – the way in which games seemed to be allowed to drift, out of control. The captain cut short at least one end-of-play Press Conference during the series and did not turn up at all for others, leaving Stewart to try to defend the seemingly indefensible. In his previous reign as captain, Gower had offended some cricket correspondents by an attitude which smacked of patronising arrogance. He had been seen to attend Press Conferences with an air which seemed to say, 'I am a very fine fellow indeed and quite the most intelligent chap in this room.' Journalists who resented this attitude as misguided and inaccurate were not slow to recall it when Gower ducked his responsibilities by missing Press Conferences.

The captain, in consequence, had a very bad Press during the summer, not always from the cricket correspondents but with great regularity from the headline writers of at least three tabloids who had developed to a high degree the art of crude but succinct vulgarity. That some of this was over the top is undeniable, just as it had been when directed at Gatting two years earlier; it was certainly unwanted by those who had watched, and read about, their cricket in an era of greater dignity. But Gower never seemed to ask himself if, perhaps, he had not contributed at least in part to his own downfall. He preferred to fall back on the Botham formula, now the vogue in the England dressing-room, of blaming 'The Press' for his discomfort. It was not a very intelligent view to take at all.

And what of Dexter, whose appointment had been regarded in some sections of the media as marking the beginning of a brave new world of England cricket? In August, A. C. Smith was quoted as saying 'the chairman had been surprised at technical faults he had seen amongst England's players – batsmen and bowlers.' What, one wondered, could have been so surprising to the chairman of the Selection Committee? Technical faults of the most basic kind – such as batsmen playing *across* the line and bowlers apparently incapable of bowling one side of the wicket – had been painfully obvious for several years. Why had it suddenly come as a surprise to Mr Dexter after his years as a television pundit and newspaper critic? At the end of the season he startled even those who had known him for some amiably eccentric theories in his days as a player and captain by announcing that he was 'not aware of any errors he had made during the season'. There was something almost Biblical in that protestation.

The shambles on England's part must not be allowed to detract from the merit of the Australian tourists and their captain. Three months before the trip Ian Chappell had written in the *Sydney Sun-Herald*: 'In the past two series against England (one away and one at home) the Australian team have tended to be a bit too friendly to the opposition on the field. The English players have thrived on this, winning both series comfortably. I'd like to see the Australians develop a bit of hate for the opposition during the playing hours. Now would be a good time to start the process.'

Border clearly took the advice to heart and played the series hard. Taylor, Jones and Waugh gave him the platform of runs he needed to dictate the course of one Test after another; Alderman mowed down the wickets by the simple virtue of bowling line and length with minimal (but enough) movement in the air and off the pitch to defeat batsmen with faulty technique. Those were the 'star' names but there was at all times immense support from every member of the party in practical terms and in attitude on the field. From the England dressing-room came complaints about 'sledging' out in the middle but since there was no overt clash to set a bad example to younger spectators and tele-viewers, no discourtesy to umpires, no bumper war, this could only be seen as strengthening the legend of the whingeing Pom. The Aussies won because they played better cricket, attacking cricket, winning cricket, at all times and in every department of the game. Border may have taken some time to reach the full flowering of his captaincy but in this series there could not be the slightest doubt about it. The fourth Test at Old Trafford, the one in which he won the Ashes, is Allan Border's match:

ENGLAND v. AUSTRALIA

Old Trafford, 1989

ENGLAND

First Innings		Second Innings	
Gooch b Lawson	11	c Alderman b Lawson	13
Curtis b Lawson	22	c Boon b Alderman	0
Robinson lbw b Lawson	0	lbw b Lawson	12
Smith c Hohns b Hughes	143	c Healy b Alderman	1
Gower lbw b Hohns	35	c Marsh b Lawson	15
Botham b Hohns	0	lbw b Lawson	4
Russell lbw b Lawson	1	not out	128
Emburey lbw b Hohns	5	b Alderman	64
Foster c Border b Lawson	39	b Alderman	6
Fraser lbw b Lawson	2	c Marsh b Hohns	3
Cook not out	0	c Healy b Hughes	5
Extras (lb 2)	2	Extras (lb6 w2 nb5)	13
Total	260	Total	264

Bowling: Alderman 25–13–49–0; Lawson 33–11–72–6; Hughes 17–6–55–1; Hohns 22–7–59–3; Waugh 6–1–23–0

Bowling: Lawson 31–8–81–3; Alderman 27–7–66–5; Hohns 26–15–37–1; Hughes 14.4–2–45–1; Border 8–2–12–0; Waugh 4–0–17–0

AUSTRALIA

First Innings		Second Innings	
Taylor st Russell b Emburey	85	(2) not out	37
Marsh c Russell b Botham	47	(1) c Robinson b Emburey	31
Boon b Fraser	12	not out	10
Border c Russell b Foster	80		
Jones b Botham	69		
Waugh c Curtis b Fraser	92		
Healy lbw b Foster	0		
Hohns c Gower b Cook	17		
Hughes b Cook	3		
Lawson b Fraser	17		
Alderman not out	6		
Extras (b5 lb7 w1 nb6)	19	Extras (nb3)	3
Total	447	Total (for 1 wkt)	81

Bowling: Foster 34–12–74–2; Fraser 36.5–4–95–3; Emburey 45–9–118–1; Cook 28–6–85–2; Botham 24–6–63–2

Bowling: Foster 5–2–5–0; Fraser 10–0–28–0; Emburey 13–3–30–1; Cook 4.5–0–18–0

India to Pakistan
1989

Tour captain: K. Srikkanth

Karachi: *Match drawn*
Faisalabad: *Match drawn*
Lahore: *Match drawn*
Sialkot: *Match drawn*

India's internal problems continued during the summer, with disputes between many senior players and the Board of Control over an unauthorised exhibition match in Canada and then the demands of the players for a substantially increased fee for their tour of Pakistan. Brinkmanship continued on both sides until the very last minute but agreement was reached in time for Krishnamachari Srikkanth to take over as captain in a series of high-scoring draws.

Two umpires from England, John Holder and John Hampshire, provided neutral adjudication; Javed Miandad became the first Pakistan player to reach 100 Tests (and scored a century to celebrate) and young Manjrekar confirmed the batting success he had shown in the West Indies earlier in the year. Srikkanth followed in Gavaskar's footsteps as an opening batsman-skipper and while he found his own form slumping seriously he at least returned home without being defeated. My first glimpse of Srikkanth, in Bombay and Pune in 1981, gave little indication of durable qualities – either long-term or in the immediate future – in the slim young man with a battered, bound and obviously much-loved piece of willow. He looked very much as though he had been called up from a local recreation ground at the eleventh hour to play but he startled everyone by hooking Bob Willis – a quicker bowler than anything around in India – joyously to the long-leg boundary and then repeating the shot off Ian Botham. It was Indian batting of a type few people had seen, except occasionally from Sandeep Patil. It couldn't last, we mused . . . either the innings or the career. But here he was, eight years later, more mature in style and temperament but still willing to flourish the bat at an early stage of an innings.

To complete a busy and eventful year, Arjuna Ranatunga led Sri Lanka in Australia after John Wright's New Zealanders had played a single Test there.

Index